how to decorate

how to decorate

hamlyn

An Hachette Livre UK Company
www.hachettelivre.co.uk

First published in Great Britain in 2006 by
Hamlyn, a division of Octopus Publishing Group Ltd
2–4 Heron Quays, London E14 4JP

www.octopusbooks.co.uk
www.octopusbooksusa.com

First published in this format in 2008

Distributed in the U.S. and Canada by Octopus Books USA:
c/o Hachette Book Group USA
237 Park Avenue
New York NY 10017

ISBN: 978-0-600-61789-1

A CIP catalogue record for this book is available from the
British Library

Printed and bound in China

10 9 8 7 6 5 4 3 2 1

Contents

Introduction

Whether you have a whole new home or just one room that requires redesigning and updating, consider what needs doing in terms of practical repair and decoration. You'll need to think, too, about design style, colours, patterns and textures; ideas for floors, walls and fabrics; and about everything from essential furniture to those all-important finishing touches. But where do you start?

Bright ideas and basic skills

Decorating can be a daunting task, but once you've completed the boring yet necessary preparatory work such as filling cracks, stripping or sanding, it can also be great fun. It's exciting and satisfying to see your design scheme come to life as you choose a style of décor you'd like to live with, paint or paper walls, lay your chosen tiles and flooring and employ colour and pattern in your home – designing, decorating and furnishing it to suit your lifestyle and personality.

Today's ranges of paint, wallpaper, fabric, tiles and flooring options are immense, and many of the materials and equipment that go into making and maintaining a comfortable and attractive home are more widely accessible and easier to use than ever before. But how do you choose the right colours, patterns and finishes for the effects you want to create? Is there a special technique for papering around a doorway? Do you paint the walls or the ceiling first? How do you calculate how many tiles to buy? What colour works best with another? How can you create the illusion of spaciousness? How do you make your own curtains? How can you give your bedroom a contemporary look, or a classic look?

Focusing on bright ideas and basic skills, this comprehensive book provides the solutions to these and many more decorating and design issues. You'll

Many do-it-yourself stores offer a paint-mixing service, which adds hundreds more possible shades to the already huge selection of ready-mixed paint colours.

find it a useful source of practical advice and inspiration, which you can read at leisure or follow project by project. There are step-by-step instructions for repairing and preparing surfaces prior to decorating; for painting, papering and tiling; for sanding and laying floors; and for making various soft furnishings from bed linen to cushions. It includes information on the tools you'll need for specific projects, suggestions for choosing materials and guidance on estimating quantities, plus plenty of ideas on decorating styles, on colour as well as on treatments for floors and walls. Lastly, the chapters on the main rooms in any home – kitchen, living room, bathroom, bedrooms and children's rooms – give you detailed advice and imaginative suggestions on how to tackle each of these rooms.

Plan ahead

Planning goes hand in hand with interior design and decorating. If you can live in your home for a while before imposing any major changes, you will gain a better understanding of what is required. Plan the space and furniture arrangements so that the rooms relate to their proposed purpose and function, and so that people will be able to move around comfortably. Take the time to discover where you need hardwearing and easy-to-clean surfaces, where you can opt for more fragile, delicate materials and where thick, sound-absorbing textures might make an appreciable difference. Seeing how the light levels in different rooms change with the seasons can help you assess which rooms would benefit from visually warming up in winter or cooling down in summer, or from shiny, light-reflecting surfaces.

Use this book to help you think about the style and ambience you would like to create. There are so many possibilities, but in a smaller property it is better to aim for continuity and use one style throughout. You may find it helpful to make up a mood board (see page 106), especially if you have existing items to incorporate in your design scheme.

Decorating involves more than just painting or papering. You have to consider elements like space, light and texture, too, so live with a room for a while before you decide how to style it.

The colours, materials and accessories you choose for each room you decorate are what define your personal style and give your home character.

If you do decide to do a lot of decorating, floor-laying and other do-it-yourself jobs, always plan things efficiently. Make sure that you have sufficient materials to complete the project (this includes the right tools, adhesives and sealants, for example, as well as paint or fabric) and, especially, allow enough time. Trying to finish painting a ceiling at midnight, or papering an awkward wall with a heavily patterned design after a busy day at work is a recipe for disaster. Working in good light, at a pace that suits you, will give a much more satisfactory, professional-looking result.

Above all, however, enjoy decorating and restyling your home. Discover the satisfaction to be had from planning your decorating project, seeing it through and delighting in the look of your newly decorated room(s). The sooner you start, the sooner you'll be finished – so get decorating!

Paint
basics

Painting tool kit

The way you apply paint is largely a matter of personal choice. Brushes in a variety of sizes are essential, and paint rollers or paint pads are also useful. You will also need a few vital specialist items in your painting tool kit.

Paintbrushes

For a good finish, choose brushes made with genuine bristle or good-quality synthetic fibres – as a rule, the more expensive brushes really do give the best results. Cheaper brushes are ideal, however, for outside work, such as applying preservative to wooden fencing or painting masonry.

Good-quality brushes that are well cared for (see box, opposite) improve with use. Loose bristles are shed and the tips become nicely rounded. Start a new brush on primer and undercoat, then use it for fine finishing as it ages.

Useful brush sizes include 12 mm, 18 mm and 25 mm (½ in, ¾ in and 1 in) brushes for painting edges and windows, and 10 cm, 12.5 cm, 15 cm and 20 cm (4 in, 5 in, 6 in and 8 in) brushes for painting walls. A radiator brush has an extra-long metal handle that allows you to paint behind radiators.

Rollers

An alternative to brushes, rollers are an easy and quicker way to apply paint to large, flat areas without leaving defined brushstrokes. Available in various widths and fabrics, they are best suited to applying water-based paints, which can be easily washed off the roller. When using solid emulsion paint, lift the roller direct from the container, but use a paint tray with liquid paint. Use a roller extension handle or tape the roller to a broom handle to paint ceilings or high walls. The different types of roller sleeve include:

Foam Easy to clean, but doesn't give the finest finish, and will tear if used on rough surfaces.

Mohair A hard roller with a very close pile, which gives a fine finish to smooth surfaces. It is not suitable for textured surfaces.

Sheepskin Expensive, but hardwearing and good for use on rough surfaces.

Shaggy pile Its deep, floppy pile makes it suitable for textured surfaces or for applying textured paint.

Radiator roller A small, deep-pile roller with a very long handle for reaching behind radiators and getting to other awkward spots.

Texturing roller A specialized roller for use with textured paint to produce a rag-rolled or other textured effect.

Paint roller with sheepskin sleeve

Radiator brush

Assorted-sized paintbrushes

Radiator roller

Paint pads

Light and easy to use, paint pads come in squares or rectangles and consist of fine mohair pile stuck to a layer of foam, bonded to a metal or plastic handle. Sizes range from 25 mm to 20 cm (1 to 8 in); some have a hollow handle to take an extension handle for painting ceilings or other out-of-reach areas without using stepladders. Paint pads are suitable for smooth or textured surfaces, but not rough finishes. A pad does give a very fine finish when gloss-painting flush doors.

Clean pads immediately after use. Note that proprietary cleaners can attack the adhesive holding the mohair to the foam.

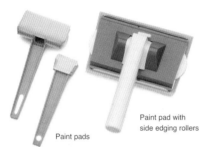

Paint pads

Paint pad with
side edging rollers

Other painting tools

If you are using liquid paint, it's useful to have a paint kettle into which to decant some. This makes carrying paint – especially up ladders – much easier, since not all paint tins have built-in handles. Paint kettles are also useful because, should the paint become contaminated in any way, then only the paint in the kettle is affected.

Other useful accessories include:

- Triangular or combination shavehooks, flexible scrapers and a Skarsten scraper for removing old paint
- Masking tape for protecting surfaces not intended to be painted
- Metal or plastic paint shield to restrict paint to the area being painted
- Tack cloth to pick up dust
- Protective sheets, old newspapers and clean, soft, lint-free rags
- Paint stirrers
- Brush cleaner suited to the type of paint

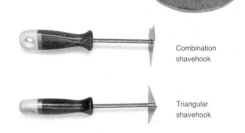

Paint kettle

Combination
shavehook

Triangular
shavehook

Cleaning and caring for paintbrushes

Remove excess paint from brushes, then clean those that have been used with water-based paint in warm, soapy water, and rinse well. Clean brushes covered in solvent-based paint using white spirit or a proprietary brush cleaner, then with hot soapy water, and again rinse well.

To clean roller sleeves and paint pads, remove the excess paint on old newspaper, then clean as for brushes, using water or white spirit as appropriate. Allow to dry.

After cleaning, shake vigorously to remove excess water. Then, while still damp, slip an elastic band over the brush tip to hold the bristles firmly together. As long as the elastic band is not too tight, it will ensure that the bristles keep in good shape, with no stray whiskers. Hang the brush up to dry, bristles facing downwards. When completely dry, place the brush in a sealed polythene bag to keep free from dust, and store so that the bristles remain flat.

Choosing paint

Paint is usually the most economical choice for decorating. There is a vast range of paints, formulated to meet all the many different requirements of the home decorator. The difficulty comes in deciding which colour and finish you want from the thousands available.

Types of paint

Traditionally, painting bare wood or metal involves a three-step application of primer, one or two coats of undercoat and a top coat, with a light sanding down between coats. Walls and ceilings are much simpler, however, requiring only one to three coats of emulsion paint, although a primer on bare plaster or an undercoat before a change from a darker to a lighter shade may be necessary first. Developments in paint technology mean that many modern paints now combine two or more of these steps, making life much easier. Paints have also become cleaner to use and more environmentally friendly. There are more water-based versions of paints than ever before, and some paints are even described as 'organic'. Free of solvents or other harmful chemicals, these paints are biodegradable and allow walls to breathe. Your choice of paint will depend to a large extent on the type and condition of the surface you are painting and on your personal preference.

Paints can generally be divided into one of two categories – water- or solvent-based paint. The label on the paint tin will tell you which is which. It will also list its recommended uses and, most importantly, covering power. Generally speaking, you can apply solvent-based paint over existing water-based paint provided it is sound, but you cannot use a water-based paint over a solvent-based one.

Water-based paint Quick drying and without a strong solvent smell, water-based paints include emulsion, distemper and water-based gloss and eggshell. The brushes and equipment may be cleaned with warm soapy water.

Solvent-based paint Solvent-based paint, which includes oil- and alkyd-based paint, is made from a mixture of oils and resins. It is a slower-drying paint and has a harder finish. Examples include traditional eggshell and gloss paint, and enamel. You can thin solvent-based paint that has thickened with white spirit, unless the manufacturer's instructions dictate otherwise. The brushes and equipment need cleaning with a solvent such as white spirit or turpentine.

Primer

Primer seals a surface to prevent subsequent layers of paint sinking in and disappearing. There are primers created specifically for bare wood, metal and bare plaster, while universal primers are designed to suit all three surfaces. Other types of primer among the many available include aluminium primer, used for specific surfaces that need a high level of protection, and stabilizing primer, which is needed to seal the powdery or flaky surface of walls painted with old paints like limewash or distemper (see opposite).

Where possible, it is a good idea to work with the same brand of primer, undercoat and top coat, since they are formulated to work together.

Undercoat

Undercoat obliterates the previous colour and gives body to the next coating. Note that some gloss paints are self-undercoating and will say so on the label.

Personalizing a room by using a number of different colours is fun, but avoid colours that clash – you will quickly tire of the combination.

Emulsion

Emulsion is mostly used for walls and ceilings, although some modern high-performance emulsions can also be used on wood and metal. Because it is water-based, emulsion is quick-drying, easy to use (and to rinse out of brushes) and reasonably odourless. It comes in traditional liquid form and a non-drip jelly-like form, while emulsions designed for ceilings tend to be solid or semi-solid and come in a tray, ready for use with a roller. Emulsion that is too thick can be thinned with a little water.

The modern range of emulsions includes metallic effects and paints with subtle textures like suede, which are ideal for feature walls, but the widest choice of colours is found in vinyl matt and vinyl silk emulsions. Vinyl matt emulsions have an attractive, sometimes chalky look, which shows up scuffs and finger marks; vinyl silk emulsions have a light-reflective quality that will magnify any surface imperfections, but are wipeable. Emulsions known as vinyl satin or soft sheen are designed for use in kitchens and bathrooms. They often contain fungicide to deter mould growth and stand up better to washing down and condensation. There are also extra-tough, scrubbable paints in bright colours that are designed for children's rooms.

At the other end of the scale, there are several ranges of non-vinyl emulsions that produce the soft, almost chalky finish of old period paints. These are particularly good for old houses, but their painted surfaces are more difficult to clean.

One-coat emulsion paint has extra covering power and will save you time, but perhaps not money, and the choice of colours is not always as great.

Emulsion paint specially formulated for kitchens is moisture- and stain-resistant. It is designed to withstand steamy hot atmospheres and be easily wiped clean if splattered with food.

Traditional paints

The original precursors to emulsion, traditional paints tend to be water-based and are particularly suitable for use in historic houses. Such paints include limewash, which is made from slaked lime, and distemper. Made with natural resins, ordinary distemper has a flat, powdery or chalky finish, which allows the plaster beneath to breathe. Generally speaking, distemper cannot be washed, although some strengthened versions are wipeable.

Textured paint

This special paint contains fine aggregate, which gives it a thicker, rougher texture. It can be used on walls and ceilings to hide surface imperfections such as small cracks or joins in plasterboard. Apply the paint thickly with a textured roller or use an ordinary roller and, before the paint starts to dry, use a rubber-bristled stippling brush to produce a variety of different effects. It is a permanent form of decoration and difficult to remove.

Gloss and eggshell paint

These provide a more durable surface than emulsion and are mostly used on wood and metal. Traditionally solvent-based, these paints are now also available in water-based versions, some of which are quick-drying.

Paint is an inexpensive way to transform a room, but do choose the appropriate finish of paint. For example, shinier finishes are more likely to show up any surface imperfections.

The infinite range of colours available can make choosing paint difficult. Try and use inexpensive tester pots first to envisage how a colour will look in a certain room.

Keying surfaces

Keying a surface means that you create a finish to which a further coat of paint, plaster or varnish will adhere. To key a surface, you may need to rub down with wire wool or glasspaper, or simply wash with sugar soap solution. Refer to the manufacturer's instructions for the new finish.

Specific-use paints

There are a number of paints designed for specific surfaces. Radiator enamel, for example, is formulated to maintain its whiteness where ordinary solvent-based paint would crack and yellow with the heat of a radiator. Other heat-resistant paints suitable for pipes and hearths are available in a limited range of colours.

There are also various special paints designed to spruce up domestic kitchen appliances like dishwashers and refrigerators, to cover melamine and acrylic surfaces like kitchen units and to overpaint existing wall tiles. Use these according to the manufacturer's instructions – you may need to use a primer and/or key the surface to be painted.

Rust-resistant paint is an enamel-formulated paint, which inhibits the penetration of rust. No primer or undercoat is needed. It is available in a smooth or indented 'hammered' finish.

Liquid gloss (usually solvent-based), when properly applied, will produce a high-sheen, perfectly smooth and very hard surface, but is more prone to drips and runs; the jelly-like non-drip version (both solvent- and water-based) gives nearly as good a finish. Alternatives to gloss are flat matt, often chosen for an authentic period look for wood, and various mid- to low-shine finishes, typically called eggshell, satin or silk. These have a less 'hard' look than gloss and, although not as hardwearing, can be washed down to remove sticky finger marks.

When painting bare wood, you will need to use a primer first. If painting over another colour, a self-undercoating paint should cover the old colour without the need for a separate undercoat. As with emulsions, there are one-coat gloss and eggshell paints designed to save time by condensing the traditional three-stage application.

Floor paints

Floor paints provide a protective finish for wood, concrete and tiled floors, and are designed to withstand heavy wear and tear. Applied by brush or roller, they can be solvent- or water-based. The latter are a good alternative to using coloured stains (see opposite) on wooden floorboards – they give a more solid effect and are particularly effective at giving a new lease of life to unattractive floorboards or where some boards have at some point been replaced and the different age of the woods shows (see page 76).

Paint your floorboards to disguise unattractive and differently aged boards. Use purpose-made floor paint for a hardwearing finish designed to withstand the movement of furniture and people.

The specialist paints now readily available allow you to completely modernize junk shop finds like this previously dark-stained hall table and make a feature wall using pearlized or metallic paints.

Decorative-effects paint

You'll find a huge range of paints and glazes in craft shops and do-it-yourself stores for achieving special effects such as sponging, rag-rolling, bagging and stencilling (see pages 28–33). Pearlized and metallic paints are another alternative for decorating primed wood, walls and metal.

Woodstains and varnishes

All articles made of wood need treating with a preservative or finish to preserve and protect the surface. The quality of the surface of the bare wood will affect your choice of finish. Painting, for example, would hide any slight surface defects, whereas any blemish in the wood is immediately accentuated when a clear finish is applied. It is therefore important that all woodwork is clean and smooth before decorating work begins.

All finishes alter the colour of wood to some extent. Woods like mahogany and walnut, for example, turn much darker even when a completely clear finish is applied. You can get a rough idea of the colour the wood will take when treated with a clear finish by dampening a small area with ordinary water. If this colour is too light for your needs, you can stain the wood before finishing.

Stains

Woodstains can be used to alter the natural appearance of wood. They are available in natural wood colours and other colours designed to harmonize with decorative schemes but that still let the grain show through. You can stain wood only to a darker colour; for a lighter shade you must apply bleach or a limewash. Do test the stain on an offcut or on an area that is normally out of sight to check that you like the effect, as it is notoriously difficult to remove stain, even immediately after it has been applied. If the wood has an open grain, but you want a smooth finish, apply grain filler to fill the pores, rubbing it across the grain. If you need to use a wood filler for cracks or holes in the wood, be aware that fillers do not take up the colour of stain as well as the wood.

Varnish stains colour and finish the wood in a single operation. Bear in mind that each extra coat of varnish stain will darken the colour of the wood and, unless brushed on very evenly, the colour will vary with the thickness of the film. When wood is stained with a penetrating dye, the colour will not vary – no matter how many coats of clear finish you later apply.

Varnishes

Available in water- and solvent-based versions, varnish provides a clear and very durable gloss, satin or matt finish. Polyurethane is a varnish with a plastic finish.

Oil finishes

Oil finishes, such as teak oil and Danish oil, are easier to apply than polyurethane and other varnishes. On new wood, you will need to apply two coats, either with a brush or a mildly abrasive pad, cleaning off excess oil with a cloth. Teak oil and Danish oil both leave the wood with a soft, lustrous finish that is truly resistant to liquids. You can also add stains to them.

Waxing

This is popular for treating newly stripped pine. Some waxes colour the wood a little – improving the bleached-out effect of pine that has been stripped, and giving the surface an 'antiqued' look. To preserve the natural look, make sure that the wax is colourless.

Always rub the wood down first with fine-grade steel wool. If you apply the wax with a soft cloth, it will produce a natural satin finish. For a higher gloss, allow the new wax to dry completely and then buff it vigorously with a soft duster or clean, soft shoe brush.

How much paint do I need?

Before you start decorating, you need to work out how much paint to buy. This will depend on the surface to be painted and how many coats of paint it will require. This will be affected by the porosity of the surface as well as its overall texture and possibly its colour.

Buying paint

Household paints are generally sold in 500 ml, 1 litre, 2½ litre and 5 litre tin sizes. A few paints, such as white emulsion and paints for exterior walls, come in larger sizes. Smaller quantities – for example, 250 ml, 100 ml and 50 ml – are available in some brands. Always buy sufficient paint and check the batch number on each tin to ensure that they come from the same mixing, as colour can vary subtly but noticeably between batches.

Calculating quantities

To cover a smooth, sealed surface, be guided by the coverage indicated on the tin. As a general guide, 1 litre of paint covers an area as follows:

General-purpose primer	10–12 sq m (12–14 sq yd)
Undercoat	15 sq m (18 sq yd)
Gloss/eggshell paint	15 sq m (18 sq yd)
One-coat gloss	10 sq m (12 sq yd)
Emulsion paint	10–14 sq m (12–17 sq yd)
One-coat emulsion	8 sq m (10 sq yd)

How much paint?

To work out the total area of wall to be painted, measure all around the room (or just one long wall and one short wall and double the calculation if the room is a simple rectangle with no recesses) and multiply by the height. This will give you a figure in square metres or yards. Subtract 1.8 sq m (2 sq yd) for each door, then measure the width and height of the windows (ignore any small ones) and subtract their area, too. Remember to multiply by the number of coats the walls will need (see opposite).

To work out the quantity of paint required for standard windows with several panes, simply multiply the width of the overall frame by the depth, and treat it as a solid area. For large picture windows, make the same calculation, but deduct 50 per cent. For metal windows, deduct 25 per cent. For flush doors, multiply

Use a paint tray and roller rather than a paintbrush to cover large areas like walls and ceilings more quickly. Don't overload the roller or you will splash paint as you work.

the height of the door by the width and add a further 10 per cent for the edges. For a panelled door, add 25 per cent. Once you know the total surface area to be covered, you can work out how much paint to buy by dividing this figure by the one given for coverage (spread rate) on your tin of paint (see box, opposite).

How many coats of paint?

The number of coats of paint you apply depends on the existing colour (if any), the type of surface you are working on (its porosity and condition) and the quality of the paint you are using. Bear in mind that you will need more paint to cover a dark colour than if you are painting a light surface with a similar or darker colour. Also, highly textured and very porous surfaces like newly plastered walls may be very 'thirsty', so double the quantity suggested on the paint tin label (or, for the latter, heavily dilute the first coat of emulsion or use specially formulated 'new-plaster emulsion').

It is always better to apply two, or even three, thin coats of paint rather than a single thick one of topcoat, which could result in a patchy-looking finish.

If, despite your calculations, you find yourself running out of paint, stop at a convenient corner, angle or other natural feature while you still have paint left. Try not to start a new tin of paint in the middle of a wall or ceiling in case of colour variation.

When calculating how much paint to buy, bear in mind the porosity of the surface being covered. New plaster, for example, takes up a lot of paint, so dilute the first coat.

To overpaint an existing colour with a lighter one, it is more economical to coat it with inexpensive white emulsion first rather than apply several coats of your final colour.

Preparing to paint

Preparing the surface to be painted is paramount for good-looking and long-lasting paintwork. Preparation may involve simple cleaning, stripping away layers of old paint or repair work such as filling cracks to ensure that the surface is sound and ready to paint.

If you are able to empty the room completely of furniture before decorating, it makes the job much easier. Protect the floor with sheeting unless it will ultimately be carpeted over.

Cleaning

When preparing painted surfaces for redecoration – whether walls, ceilings, woodwork or floors – you don't need to remove the old paintwork if it is in good condition. Simply wash the surface with a strong sugar soap solution or another degreasing agent to break any glaze and remove grease to which the new coat will not adhere. Then rub over the surface with a flexible sanding pad to improve the key (see page 14), and dust it down before applying the new paint.

Stains on walls or ceilings, due for example to water damage, will sometimes bleed through new decoration if not treated beforehand. Seal the stained area with an aluminium primer-sealer or with a proprietary aerosol stain block.

Unpainted metal should need only cleaning and priming (radiators often come ready-primed). Follow with an undercoat.

Stripping

If the existing paintwork has been badly applied or consists of so many layers that it causes windows and doors to stick, then you should remove the paint. Surfaces that have been poorly painted, or overpainted several times, can take on a treacle-like appearance, robbing architraves and mouldings of their fine detail. Plaster ceiling roses look particularly unattractive when they have been painted too often.

The main choices for stripping are using either chemicals or heat. However, dry scraping may be possible using a Skarsten scraper for convex surfaces, such as banister handrails. Use a shavehook on finer mouldings. Make sure that you protect your eyes and hands, and wear a simple face mask.

If the paint is old, buy a simple detector kit from a hardware (houseware) store to check whether it contains lead. If it does, chemical stripping is the best way to remove the paint because the alternatives could result in lead poisoning. You could inhale lead particles if you sand or scrape lead-based paint, and heating lead paint produces toxic fumes.

Think carefully before stripping back wood in order to stain and varnish it. You'll need to do a great deal of sanding to remove all the primer from the pores of the wood; if any remains, the stain will look patchy.

Rub down previously painted metal with emery paper. Remove rust with a wire brush and use a filler to fill chips and dents. Apply a coat of metal primer and follow with an undercoat.

Chemical stripping

Chemical stripping can be expensive if large areas are involved. The secret is to be patient while the chemical works – otherwise you may have to apply more coats to get down to the bare wood or metal.

Chemical strippers are traditionally solvent-based, although safer and environmentally friendly solvent-free strippers are becoming available. If working with the former, protect any exposed skin and your eyes, as some products could cause minor burns or localized irritation to the skin. In addition, avoid breathing in the vapours and keep the stripper away from vulnerable items.

Chemical strippers generally come as a liquid or gel, which you apply with a brush and scrape away when the paint bubbles and breaks up. Alternatively, there is a paste that you trowel on and allow to set before lifting it away with the point of the trowel. This works well on mouldings, since it lifts paint out of hollows. You must always neutralize a chemical stripper immediately after use using water or white spirit according to the manufacturer's instructions.

Instead of using chemical stripper yourself, you could take large, relatively portable items like doors, window shutters and unglazed sashes to specialists for stripping. This involves immersing the item in a paint-stripping solution. However, there is a risk of the wood discolouring, and the joints in woodwork may open up as any old glue or filler dissolves.

Heat stripping

Most paint softens quickly when you apply heat with a blowtorch or hot-air gun, wrinkling and bubbling up so that you can scrape it away fairly easily, but take great care not to overdo it, since the paint may ignite. Don't use newspaper on the floor to catch the hot, flaking paint because of the risk of fire, and always have a bucket of water to hand in case of emergencies. Hold the scraping tool so that the stripped paint cannot fall on to your hand and burn you. Cotton gloves provide adequate protection.

A blowtorch A blowtorch burns liquid gas either from a small container attached to the torch head or from a larger cylinder connected to the torch by a tube. The naked flame can be extremely hot, so keep it moving all the time to avoid scorching the wood or cracking glass if you are stripping a window frame.

A hot-air gun This tool resembles a powerful hair dryer, blowing a jet of air through a very hot electric element. Having no flame, it is safer than a blowtorch, but is still sufficiently hot to char wood and crack glass, if not used carefully. It usually comes with different nozzles, allowing you to adjust the airflow.

Using a heat stripper

1 Hold a hot-air gun or blowtorch in one hand about 15–20 cm (6–8 in) from the paintwork and a scraper in the other and keep the tools moving together. Use a shavehook for scraping mouldings. Try not to dig into the wood or scorch it – scorch marks can bleed through new paint. If you are burning paint off window frames, keep the heat away from the glass or it will crack.

2 After you have removed the paint, rub the wood down with medium-grade glasspaper following the direction of the grain and paying particular attention to any mouldings.

Stripping radiators

If you have any radiators in your home whose paint surface is in need of attention, it's a good idea to strip the existing paint from them before repainting them, since they lose their heat efficiency if covered with too many layers of paint. To do this, use a sanding attachment for a power drill.

Stripping around door handles

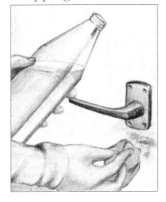

You will achieve a neater finish if you remove door handles and any other door furniture before stripping paint from a door. If for some reason a metal door handle cannot be removed, use a thin piece of plywood to shield it from the direct heat of a hot-air gun or blowtorch. If you are using a chemical stripper, it may not affect the metal, but test it first on a small area that cannot be readily seen – such as the inside surface of the door handle.

Making repairs

Once you have stripped and cleaned the walls and ceiling, you need to examine them for any defects, such as cracks and gaps in the plaster. Most such problems should have become evident during the preparation stages; some others, however, may not initially be obvious. The most common of these is 'blown' plaster, which occurs when patches of plaster lift away from the underlying wall. When rapped with your knuckle, blown plaster has a distinctive hollow sound. Ideally, you should hack out this defective plaster and patch with fresh material.

Although replastering an entire room is a major job, and requires considerable skill and professional expertise, it is relatively easy to undertake minor repairs yourself.

Gaps between woodwork and walls

You commonly find cracks in the plaster where a wall abuts door and window frames, and gaps between walls and skirting boards (baseboards). They are usually caused by the movement of the woodwork with temperature and humidity changes. Clear any loose material out of these cracks or gaps with the point of a small trowel, then fill the gap with a gun-applied acrylic frame sealant or expanding foam filler. These grip better than cellulose filler and tolerate some movement. Frame sealant needs to touch both surfaces so as to seal the gap – if the gap is particularly wide or deep, bridge it with a strip of wood or polystyrene first. Expanding foam filler sinks right in and expands to fill the gap – trim off the excess when set.

Cracks between walls and ceilings

These weak spots rarely stay sealed, whatever material you use, because any slight movement of the building will reopen the cracks. An expanding foam filler is the easiest material to use, but the best solution to a very noticeable gap that keeps reappearing is to hide it with decorative coving, covering the angle where the two surfaces meet. Available in different styles, sizes and materials (such as polyurethane, gypsum or plaster), coving is available ready-coloured or you can paint it.

Cracks and holes in walls

Fill small cracks with a cellulose filler and large cracks with a plaster repair filler (see illustrations, opposite). If you are not using a ready-mixed product, make sure that you use clean water to mix the plaster and clean the mixing bucket after each mix, as any residues of set plaster will reduce the setting time of subsequent mixes and may weaken them.

If the cracks are particularly wide or deep, fill them in stages. Each layer should be no more than about 1 cm ($\frac{1}{2}$ in) deep. Score the surface of each layer to provide a key for the next layer, which you apply when the previous layer is set but not completely dry. The filling material is likely to absorb more paint or wallpaper paste than the original plaster, so prime it with one or two coats of universal primer or emulsion before starting to redecorate.

If you have to fill a large cavity in a wall, packing it with filler is wasteful and the filler may crack unless you apply it in a laborious series of layers. Instead, where possible, pack the hole with broken brick or stone and push cement in to fill the gaps and firm it all up – small bags of ready-mixed mortar are convenient for these minor jobs. Once you have packed the hole to within 5 cm (2 in) of the wall surface, you can apply an all-in-one do-it-yourself plaster. (Developed for do-it-yourself use, this plaster requires no undercoat plaster and can be applied up to about 5 cm (2 in) thick, directly on to brickwork or similar walls.)

For plastering large areas, it is a good idea to nail temporary guide battens to the wall. These enable you to bring all the plastered surface to the same level. When the plaster has set, remove the battens and fill the grooves level with the rest of the job.

Filling a crack

1 Start by carefully raking out any loose material from the crack, using the corner of a flexible filling knife or a narrow wallpaper scraper.

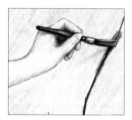

2 Using a small paintbrush or plant mister, wet the crack with water. This stops the plaster from drying out the filler too quickly, causing it to crack or fall out.

3 Now fill the crack by drawing your filling knife loaded with filler across it, at right angles to the crack. Repeat until the crack has disappeared, leaving the filler slightly proud of the surrounding plaster.

4 Leave the filler to set hard (a deep crack may need a second application), then sand it back flush with the surrounding plaster using medium-grade glasspaper.

Patching plasterboard

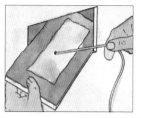

1 Cut a piece of plasterboard just larger than the hole. Tie string to a nail and feed it through a hole in the centre. Dab the edges with plaster.

2 Insert the new piece through the hole and pull the string tight while you fill the recess in front with plaster. When the plaster is set, cut the string and fill the hole.

3 To repair a corner, pin a batten on one side flush with the corner and fill the opposite side with plaster. When set, move the batten and repeat on the other edge.

How to paint

Never rush a painting job – you must wait for one coat of paint to dry completely before applying another. Emulsion paint dries quickly, so you don't have to wait too long between coats, but oil-based paint requires a little more patience. Refer to the label on the paint tin for the manufacturer's instructions regarding drying and recoating time.

Handy hints

- Make sure that the paint tin is free of loose dust and dirt before opening the lid. If the label instructs you to stir the paint, use a length of wood to do so.
- Never use a brush with a rusty ferrule, as this will discolour the paint.
- Store paint in a cool, dry place free from exposure to frost.
- Paint the lid of the tin so that you can see the colour at a glance when you need to do a little touching up.
- Before you use a new brush, or one that has been stored for any length of time, manipulate the bristles by rubbing them briskly in the palm of your hand in order to loosen and remove any dust and broken bristles.
- Dip no more than one-third of the paintbrush bristles in the paint and wipe off the excess (string or thin wire tied across the top of the paint tin or kettle is useful for this purpose).

How to paint interior walls

Choose your decorating tools according to the finish you require. For a smooth surface, use a brush, a foam or mohair roller or a paint pad; for a deeper texture, or to cover a rough surface, use a brush or a shaggy pile roller (see page 10). Whatever painting tool you use for the main area of the walls, you will need a small paintbrush for the edges.

1 If painting with a brush, choose the widest brush you can comfortably hold. Begin at the top of a wall and run bands of paint downwards in vertical strips, leaving a slight gap between the bands. Then brush across the wall to blend the bands of paint, finishing with light, vertical strokes of the paintbrush.

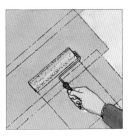

2 Rollers and pads are easiest to use with shallow rectangular trays. Most have a built-in shelf or, for pads, a rolling edge, against which you can squeeze off the excess paint. To use a roller, work it in all directions, taking care to merge the joins and fill in any gaps, and finish off with light strokes in a single direction. It is best to work over a small area at a time. Don't roll too quickly or the paint will fly off the roller. Allow the roller to shed all its paint before reloading it. Don't paint too thick a coating; instead, apply two (or more) thin coats as you would with a brush.

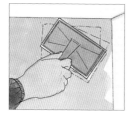

3 Use a paint pad in much the same way as a roller, applying paint in a criss-cross pattern. A pad applies only a very thin coat of emulsion, so you will have to repeat this process to give two or even three coats – especially if you have a base colour to hide. Paint pads are especially useful for running along wall edges.

How to paint woodwork

If using gloss or eggshell paint, first seal bare wood with a wood primer. When dry, rub down lightly with fine glasspaper, dust off with a lint-free rag and apply a layer of undercoat (to give body to the final coat), unless you are using a paint that combines undercoat and topcoat. Dispense with the primer if covering a sound painted surface. If painting over a different, especially a darker, colour, use a self-undercoating paint or as many coats of undercoat as necessary.

Apply the paint in parallel strips a short distance apart following the grain of the wood. Then, without reloading the brush, draw the bristles across the grain to spread the paint over the uncoated area. Finish off with light strokes following the grain again to ensure

When painting woodwork, always follow the grain of the wood. Choose a good-quality paintbrush that won't leave hairs in the paintwork and don't overload the brush with paint.

Masking paintwork

Masking around glass window or door panes saves a lot of time and effort later. Run strips of masking tape around the edges of the glass where they meet the woodwork. Leave a narrow margin to allow a thin line of paint to overlap the glass and form a seal. Using a small brush, and holding it like a pencil, apply paint in the direction of the grain. Peel away the tape as soon as the paint is touch dry.

even coverage and a smooth finish. Always brush out towards an edge to prevent the paint forming an unsightly ridge.

Paint care

Fill small, screw-top jars with any leftover paint. If all air is excluded, the paint will keep indefinitely and can be used later for touching up. Label the jars carefully, indicating paint type and where you've used it. If you leave leftover paint in the bottom of its original container, it will soon evaporate.

Paint that has been stored for some time can be affected in two ways. If there is a brown liquid floating on top, just stir it thoroughly back into the rest of the paint. If a skin has formed on the surface, cut around this with a knife and discard once you have scraped away and returned to the tin any paint on its underside. Strain the paint before reuse, either with a paint strainer or by passing it through a clean nylon stocking. Fix the stocking loosely over the tin with an elastic band and push the nylon down into the paint, then dip your brush into the uncontaminated paint. If an emulsion tin has become rusty, transfer the unaffected paint to a clean container.

Interior painting

Ideally, you should decorate in a well-ventilated area and during daylight hours to take advantage of the natural light. If you paint under artificial lighting, you may overlook gaps in the coverage. For best results, paint an interior in a strict order, from the highest to the lowest point in the room.

From start to finish

To paint any room, always start with the ceiling, since some paint will inevitably drip or be splattered on to the walls.

Handy hints

• Although you can paint a ceiling from a stepladder, it involves a lot of tiring leg work, since you have to climb up and down to move the steps. It is much simpler to make a platform using stepladders or trestles and a scaffold board (see page 39).

• When painting walls and ceilings, allow yourself enough time to complete the work. You can do one wall at a time, but you must paint the whole ceiling in one go.

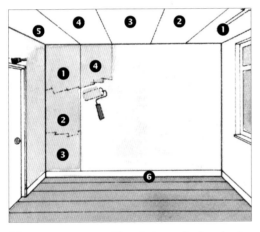

1 In an average room with a window and a door, begin painting the ceiling at the window end and work across the ceiling covering the surface in parallel bands approximately a metre or a yard wide until you reach the door end (see numbers **1–5** on the illustration above). Work an area that is comfortable to reach from your standing point, whether you are on a makeshift platform or a stepladder. If there is a ceiling rose or light fitting in the middle of the ceiling, paint neatly around this with a small paintbrush and then continue painting in parallel bands.

2 The next step, if necessary, is to apply primer and undercoat to all the woodwork – frames, door and skirting boards (baseboards) – in the room (see page 23) and allow it to dry completely, preferably overnight.

3 Next, paint the walls or any other large surfaces in the room. Start in the top left-hand corner of one wall and work with a brush, roller or paint pad, covering an area of about a square metre or yard at a time. Work your way down the wall from the ceiling to the floor in vertical bands (see numbers **1–4** on the illustration, left). Continue to paint the rest of the first wall and then the remaining walls in this order. Complete one wall in full before you begin the next. To paint around a window, paint around the frame with a small brush and then fill in the surrounding wall space with a larger brush, roller or paint pad.

4 Once this is done, give the door and window frames a topcoat. Then paint the door of the room and add any covering to the floor last. Paint the coving and skirting boards (baseboards) after the ceiling and walls are completely finished.

Painting interior doors

Remove as many fittings from the door as possible, since handles, escutcheon plates and hooks are difficult to paint around. Put old newspaper under the door to protect the floor and to prevent picking up dust on your brush. Select your painting tools according to the surface of the door. Use a 75 mm (3 in) wide brush for a flush door or flat panels of a panelled door, and smaller brushes (50 mm/2 in and 25 mm/1 in) for decorative mouldings and door edges, and for cutting in. With all doors, paint the edge opposite the hinges last so that you have something to hold on to.

Handy hints

• Smearing a little petroleum jelly over the door hinges and other fittings will protect them from being touched with paint.

• Keep checking your paintwork for runs (see page 34) so that you can brush them out before the paint dries.

Flush doors

Mentally divide up the surface area into small sections (see illustration, below), and try to work quickly to avoid tide marks or visible joins.

Panelled doors

For a panelled door, the sequence for painting is a little more complicated (see illustration, below) and you'll need two or three different-sized paintbrushes.

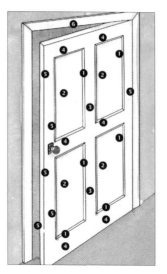

1 Begin at the top left-hand corner (or top right-hand corner if you are left-handed), covering to about half the width of the door (**1**). First, work using vertical brushstrokes, then brush across these with light horizontal strokes.

2 Complete the other sections (**2–6**) in the same way. It is important to work the brushstrokes consistently so that the finish of the door will be even.

3 Use a small brush to complete the edges of the door (**7**), then paint the frame of the door last (**8**).

1 First, paint the mouldings around the panels (**1**) and then the panels themselves (**2**). Start with the upper panels and work from top to bottom. Begin each panel at the top and work downwards, painting vertical brushstrokes followed by light horizontal ones.

2 Next, paint the section that runs down the middle of the door and divides the panels (**3**). Continue by coating the horizontal rails, starting at the top and working down (**4**).

3 Complete the outer strips and then all the edges (**5**).

4 Lastly, paint the whole door frame (**6**).

Painting interior windows

Remove any window catches or handles if possible before painting windows. This makes it easier to paint and gives a better finish. To make a temporary window catch, fix a small nail to the underside of the bottom rail, attaching it to an old wire coathanger and hooking this into a screw hole in the window frame.

Don't be tempted to use too wide a paintbrush and do use a paint shield as you work to protect the panes, or mask the glass with tape (see page 23). Remove any dry paint from the glass carefully later, using a scalpel, razor blade or glass scraper.

(see page 23)

Handy hint

When painting windows, aim to paint them as early in the day as possible so that they may be dry enough to close by nightfall. If you close the windows before the paint is completely dry they are liable to stick and cause problems.

Sash windows

To paint a sash window (see illustration, below), push the rear sash down and the front one up so that at least 20 cm (8 in) of the lower rear sash is exposed.

1 Paint the bottom rail of the rear sash and as much of the exposed upright sections as possible.

2 Pull the rear sash up so that it's almost shut and paint the rest.

3 With the front sash slightly open, paint its frame.

4 When both sashes are dry, paint the surround, shut the window and paint the exposed part of the runners, but not the cords. Paint the sill last.

Casement windows

With a casement window (see illustration, below), fix the window slightly ajar.

1 First, paint the rebates (**1**) and then the horizontal and vertical crossrails (**2**).

2 Paint the horizontal top and bottom sides and edges (**3**), then the vertical sides and edges (**4**).

3 When the window is dry, paint the frame (**5**), including the edges.

4 Leave the sill (**6**) to the end, to avoid smudging; if the stay needs painting, do it last of all so that you can use it until the very end.

that your brush does not pick up dirt or fluff from below the skirting (baseboard) by moving a sheet of card or an offcut of wood along the floor as a shield as you paint.

Painting stairwells

A stairwell is one of the most difficult areas to decorate, but it is quite possible to paint this part of the home yourself, even if you are inexperienced.

The first thing you need is some form of scaffolding. The most reliable solution is to hire a staircase platform, which is designed to fit neatly on to stairs by means of adjustable legs. However, if you are not worried by heights, then you can construct your own platform using stepladders and a scaffold board (see page 39). Make frequent checks that the scaffold board is centrally placed and has not slipped out of position, particularly as you climb on and off it.

By using a roller or a paint pad with an extension pole, you can greatly increase your reach and apply paint overhead on the ceiling and high up on the stairwell walls.

Painting picture rails and covings

Before painting picture rails, make sure that they are free from dust, dirt and grease, particularly along their top surface. It is usual to work in a similar type of paint as for the walls, which is likely to be emulsion, although you may want a contrasting colour to pick out the detail of the picture rail. Using a small paintbrush, paint along the run of the rail, shielding the wall in the same way as for painting skirting boards (baseboards).

With covings it is also usual to use the same type of paint as for the walls. The paint can either match the walls or the ceiling or be in a contrasting colour, which will help to emphasize any detailing. Use a paint shield or masking tape for a neat finish.

Painting stairwells can be tricky and requires using some form of scaffolding or platform on which to stand and a roller or paint pad fixed to an extension pole.

Painting skirting boards

When the rest of the room is freshly painted, a discoloured skirting board (baseboard) will mar the overall effect. Painting the skirting (baseboard) is a quick job that is best left until after the walls are completed. Because skirtings (baseboards) are low down and narrow, work with a small brush and use a hardwearing paint that will withstand knocks. Wipe down the skirting (baseboard) with a damp cloth to remove any dust and vacuum along its bottom edge to remove any dirt or fluff in the carpet that may stick to the wet paint. Lay down newspaper to protect the floor. To protect the wall, use a piece of stiff card or a slim offcut of wood and hold it to shield the wall while you brush. If the wall has been dry for some time, then you can use low-tack masking tape – but remember to peel away the tape before the gloss or eggshell paint hardens. Work the brush following the direction of the skirting (baseboard), making horizontal strokes and working your way in one direction around the room. When you come to painting close to the floor, ensure

Handy hint

Any decorating job will be quicker if you can remove all the furniture from the room and cover the floor completely with polythene sheeting or a dust sheet.

Paint effects

Paint effects such as colourwashing, sponging or rag-rolling create depth and visual texture, and can lend interest to a bland expanse of wall. Such techniques all involve painting a base coat over a surface, then applying a glaze and manipulating it using a variety of 'tools' for a decorative effect.

Successful paint effects

Whichever paint effect you choose, the wall or ceiling to be decorated must always be properly prepared. No paint finish will disguise bad workmanship like unfilled cracks or dirty walls, so be prepared to spend some time on surface preparation. The next step is to apply a base coat or two of matt or silk emulsion to the surface to be decorated and allow to dry.

The secret of successful paint effects is to employ subtle complementary tones rather than strong contrasts and to test all the different techniques and colour combinations on odd sheets of lining paper, pieces of wood or hardboard before applying to the wall. In this way you can see beforehand the finished look and decide whether it's what you want. You may find you need to reduce the amount of pressure on the tool you are using or perhaps thin the glaze – with practice you will soon build the skills required to achieve the results you want.

Handy hints
• Keep a clean cloth to hand to remove any excess paint, drips or mistakes.

• Wait for the glaze to dry thoroughly before correcting errors or making improvements.

• If possible, complete a whole wall before finishing a painting session so that there are no visible joins in obvious places.

Materials and equipment

The following tools and materials are used for creating a wide range of broken colour effects. Other tools for patterning a glaze can be things you already have around the house such as rags, combs, sponges and even scrunched-up newspaper and plastic bags. Some specialist brushes are expensive, so look for synthetic substitutes, which can be of excellent quality. Ideally, it is best to reserve brushes either for paintwork or for varnishing, and not to mix them between the two jobs. Clean brushes scrupulously, taking care not to leave any paint or varnish near the handle end of the brush.

Acrylic paint Available in tubes in an extensive range of colours, it is water-soluble and useful for tinting emulsion paint. It becomes waterproof when dry and dries very quickly, making it convenient to use.

Flat fitch This hog's hair brush is useful for applying glazes in small or difficult areas.

Flogger A horsehair brush made with very long, coarse bristles, this is used to tap, or 'flog', a wet glaze to give a finely flecked finish.

Glaze A see-through film of colour used for creating special paint effects, available in acrylic and solvent-based versions. Acrylic glazes are easier to use, have fewer fumes and are less likely to yellow with age.

Jamb duster This is usually used to remove dust before painting a surface. It is also useful as a softening and blending brush instead of a dusting brush.

Mottler A brush made from hair, available in a range of different sizes. It is used primarily for dragging (a paint effect that gives the appearance of fabric) or to simulate woodgrain.

Polyurethane varnish A solvent-based varnish available in different finishes, it is easy to apply and provides good surface protection.

Softening brush Use just the tip of the brush to blend solvent-based glazes gently after they have been applied but are still wet.

Sponge A natural sea sponge is the best type for creating a sponged paint effect.

Universal stainer A chemical dye that dissolves in white spirit. Use it to tint emulsion and solvent-based paints and glazes.

White spirit Also called turpentine substitute. Use it to dilute solvent-based paints and varnish, and to distress solvent-based paints and glazes when they are still wet.

Painting stripes on a plain wall introduces pattern and colour to the room – simply use masking tape to define the stripes and a plumbline or spirit level to ensure straight lines.

Painting stripes

A simple way to give a plain painted surface an interesting pattern is to use masking tape to create bold stripes. First, paint the walls the colour of the lighter stripe. Decide how wide the stripes are to be (they could be uniform or alternately wide and narrow) and, when the base coat is dry, smooth a length of masking tape along one edge of the proposed stripe and a second length down the other. Press the tape down firmly with the back of a teaspoon to prevent paint seeping underneath. Apply the second stripe colour with a brush, or sponge or cloth if you wish to create a subtle ragged stripe effect. When the paint is dry, peel off the tape slowly and carefully.

Choose low-tack masking tape, specially designed for delicate painted surfaces, and remove it carefully as soon as the paint is dry. Using curved masking tape will allow you to paint uniform wavy lines neatly instead of straight ones, if preferred.

Using glazes

Paint effects are best created using a glaze, traditionally known as scumble. Although you can use thinned ordinary paint instead, a glaze is preferable because it remains workable for a long time. Since it doesn't dry quickly, you can wipe off any mistakes and start again if you are not happy with the results. You can either buy ready-made glaze or 'effects' paint in a range of translucent and pearlescent colours, or create your own glaze by mixing emulsion or eggshell paint and/or a tint or pigment with a colourless acrylic or oil glaze according to the manufacturer's instructions.

When using a glaze, the trick is to work in small sections and always keep the wet edge 'open' so that there are no obvious joins between sections. Ideally,

work with someone else so that one person can apply the glaze and the other follow quickly behind, creating the special effect.

When you have completed your paint effect and it is fully dry, apply a coat of clear, matt polyurethane varnish or a water-based acrylic varnish over the top for a hard, protective finish.

How to apply a glaze

1 Apply the tinted glaze in random strokes over the eggshell base colour. Be sure to cover the walls evenly.

2 To create a dragging effect, apply the glaze, then line up a spirit level vertically on the wall and indent slightly to give a guidemark for vertical strokes.

3 With a clean brush (about 75 mm/3 in wide), drag straight down the wet glaze so that vertical strokes are left behind.

Colourwashing

Choose the same colour paint as the base coat or a colour close in tone but slightly darker and mix up a wash of emulsion and water, in equal parts. Gradually increase the water to make a thin colour that will not run down the wall in heavy droplets, but will allow the base colour to show through when it is applied on top. Alternatively, use a thinned glaze or 'effects' paint as a wash over the whole surface for a more durable finish. Once you have tested your colourwash on a sample area, continue to apply the remaining colour using either a wide decorator's brush in sweeping criss-cross strokes or a car-polishing mitt or soft cloth to achieve a cloudy effect. When this coat is dry, apply a further coat in a toning colour if you like.

How to get the look

1 Apply the emulsion base coat and leave to dry. Use a large decorator's brush to apply the diluted top coat in random strokes.

2 Soften off any hard lines with a dry softening brush while the top coat is still damp.

Sponging

Sponging is one of the easiest decorative paint finishes to achieve and you can use two or more colours. Choose your first topcoat colour and make up a glaze. Dip a natural sea sponge into the glaze, taking care to wipe off any excess. Use it to sponge the wall using a dabbing, twisting movement to achieve an uneven, mottled effect. Cover the whole wall and allow to dry. If required, start at the beginning again and apply a second coat using another colour until the wall is evenly covered.

How to get the look

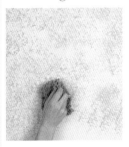

1 Apply the base emulsion and leave to dry. Dip a piece of natural sponge into emulsion and dab it across the surface.

2 When the first sponged layer is dry, take a new piece of clean sponge and dab on the second colour to soften the first.

Ragging

Similar in principle to sponging, ragging involves scrunching up a lint-free rag into a ball and using this to apply glaze in a contrasting shade to the base coat. Dip the rag into the glaze, remove the excess, then dab the rag straight on to the wall. Keep dipping the same side of the rag into the glaze and dabbing at the same angle with even pressure to achieve a uniform pattern. For a more random effect, frequently rearrange the paint-covered rag, dabbing with even pressure. Avoid overloading the rag with glaze.

Rag-rolling is a variation of ragging and its soft, mottled paint effect is excellent for disguising bumps or surface irregularities. It involves literally rolling a piece of rag scrunched into a sausage shape over a coat of wet glaze or paint. Either match the tone of the top colour with the background, or introduce a slightly darker tone on top.

How to get the look

1 Paint on the glaze in vertical strokes. Over large areas, join the strokes at varying levels across the wall to avoid an obvious join line.

2 While the glaze is still wet, blot the surface with a piece of hessian (burlap) to break up the glaze.

Bagging

Bagging relies on a scrunched-up plastic bag to achieve a traditional broken-paint finish. The result can be beautifully subtle, producing an effect similar to the look of crushed velvet. You can use a pale shade over a darker base coat or vice versa – experiment first with different colours.

How to get the look

1 Working on a small section at a time, use a wide brush to apply the topcoat of glaze or thinned paint in vertical strokes.

2 Now press an inside-out, scrunched-up thin plastic bag down on to the paint, immediately lifting it up and pressing down on the next spot in a dabbing motion, to produce a crinkled effect. Take care not to smudge the paint as you lift the plastic bag. Overlap the bagging slightly as you work along the wall to avoid the appearance of bands where one section finishes and another starts.

Stencils and stamps

Stencilling and stamping are fun and easy techniques that allow you to create some original designs, and the choice of stamps and precut stencil templates, available from craft and do-it-yourself stores, is enormous. You are not restricted to decorating walls – floors, furniture and soft furnishings can all be decorated, too.

Stencilling

If you are using a repeating pattern, for example if you are creating a design of linked motifs for a border around a room, you'll need to do some careful planning and measuring. Start stencilling from the centre of the wall and work outwards, until you come to a corner or a break. Find the correct position for a horizontal pattern with a spirit level, or use a plumbline to align a vertically repeating stencil correctly. If a design looks gappy, add extra motifs between existing ones.

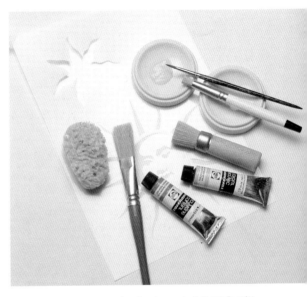

A precut stencil, a sponge, various brushes and artist's acrylic paint are the main requirements for stencilling, all of which are available from craft stores and some do-it-yourself stores.

Handy hints

• Test your design and colours on a piece of paper or hardboard before you start.

• Acetate stencils are ideal for uneven doors or walls. They mould to the surface and prevent paint seeping behind the stencil.

Applying colour

There are a number of different ways of applying colour to precut stencils, and many different effects can be achieved. Tones of colour can be built up in layers or colours can be blended into one another. Experiment to find the method of applying paint that best suits the work you are doing or that you prefer:

Stencil brush The stiff bristles hold only a small amount of paint and are designed to produce neat, sharp-edged stencilled designs. Take up a little paint on your brush, remove any excess and apply it with a light dabbing or stippling motion.

Sponge For covering large areas of stencil cut-outs, a small piece of sponge is quicker to use than a brush. A sponge is very economical and gives a distinctive mottled effect. Dampen the sponge slightly, take up a small amount of colour, remove any excess and apply with a light dabbing motion. Colours can be blended as you work, or left to dry between coats.

Foam roller A small foam roller is the most economical method of achieving a dense, even coverage for stencilling large motifs, especially on fabric.

Aerosol sprays Aerosols are not ideal for use with all stencils. Not only can the fumes be hazardous, but careful masking with newspaper is essential if you do not want to spray the surrounding area. Seepage of paint under the edges of the stencil can also be a problem, so apply the paint lightly from above. Sprays are wonderful, however, for working with large areas of flat colour and particularly good if you are working on fabric and floors.

Multi-colour stencils

If you are working in more than one colour, remember firstly to ensure that the first colour is completely dry before you embark on the next colour. Secondly, if you are working with more than one stencil, cut out small alignment marks on each before you start so that you can see exactly where to match up the pattern.

How to get the look

1 Mark the centre position of each motif using a ruler and pencil. Line up the centre of the stencil with a pencil mark and secure with low-tack masking tape at either side of the stencil. With a small amount of paint on the stencil brush, apply paint through the stencil in a stabbing motion.

2 Once the first colour is dry, realign the stencil and apply a second colour in the same manner as before.

Stamping

Printing patterns on to fabric, wallpaper or walls is an old art that has never quite been lost. You can still pick up inexpensive woodblocks in antique and second-hand shops and stalls, and many craft shops and mail order firms stock modern wood or rubber stamping blocks and inks.

There is also an ever-widening choice of stamps designed for use with either emulsion or acrylic paint directly on to walls or ceilings. They are cut in firm foam and are easy to work with. You can quickly create a pleasingly looser, less formal pattern on a wall than with wallpaper, or a larger stamp might provide an eye-catching motif above each door in a corridor. As with stencilling, you may need to use a spirit level or plumbline with a soft pencil to mark out your line.

How to get the look

1 Tip a little paint onto a plate and load the stamp by pressing it into the paint. If you have trouble achieving an even coverage of paint on the stamp, apply it with a small roller.

2 Apply the paint-loaded stamp firmly to the surface to be decorated. Remove it immediately, and take care not to drag the stamp or the motif will smudge.

Paint faults and problems

Good-quality modern paints rarely give any trouble. Flaws with the finished results are usually due to poor surface preparation or problems with the surface on which the paints are applied. Here are some common faults and remedies.

Runs

Also known as sagging or curtaining, runs occur on vertical surfaces and are the result of too much paint being applied with an overloaded brush, roller or paint pad. Use a wide-bladed scraper to scrape off the runs when they are dry. Then rub down the surface by hand or using a sanding attachment on a power drill until the runs are eliminated and the surface feels really smooth when you run your hand over it. Unfortunately, runs can be extremely obstinate, so a lot of laborious rubbing down may be required before you can repaint.

Flaking

When paint has no grip on the undersurface, the topcoat of paint lifts and flakes off in dry fragments. It may be that the surface was too smooth, as with old gloss paint, or too chalky. It's best to strip back badly flaking areas, then provide a key for the paint to adhere to and redecorate.

Blistering

When air or water is trapped beneath the paint, the paintwork begins to bubble up. It occurs on wood if the wood is damp or if resin is drawn out of the wood by heat. The only sure remedy is to strip back the paint, ensure that the surface has thoroughly dried out, then redecorate from scratch.

Staining

Staining is often encountered when emulsion paint is applied over a stained area and the stain begins to bleed through. To remedy, allow the emulsion to dry completely, then spray the affected area with a stain sealer, which will dry in a few minutes. You can then paint over the affected area again.

Wrinkling

Wrinkling in solvent-based paint is caused by a second coat of paint being applied before the solvent has evaporated out of the first layer. It can also result if a topcoat is applied too thickly. A wrinkled surface shows patches of shrivelled or puckering paint, which is rough to touch. The best remedy is to strip back the surface and redecorate, making sure that you allow each coat to harden and dry thoroughly before applying the next. Also avoid applying paint too thickly.

Matt patches

These can occur in paint on wood where a priming coat has been omitted. Subsequent coats then soak into the wood, which results in a loss of the gloss finish in these areas. Unfortunately, applying further coats of paint rarely solves the problem, and the only effective solution is to strip back the paint to the wood and prime first before repainting.

Grittiness

This happens when dirt is picked up on a paintbrush and transferred to the surface during painting. It is particularly common when painting outside close to masonry. If the paint is still wet, simply wipe away the grit with a lint-free rag and repaint the area with a clean brush. If the paint has dried, however, rub it back with glasspaper and then repaint. If the paint in the tin is contaminated with bits of dirt, you'll need to strain it (see page 23).

Crazing

Crazing is a pattern of tiny cracks, similar in appearance to crazy paving. It occurs either when incompatible paints are used together or when a layer of paint is applied over a previous coat that was not completely dry. The solution is to rub the cracked surface until it is quite smooth, either by hand or using a sanding attachment on a power drill. Repaint when really smooth.

Runs can be brushed out if the paint is still wet. Otherwise, let it harden, then sand back to a smooth surface and repaint.

Bleeding

This fault occurs on painted wood containing knots that have not been properly sealed. The warmth of sunlight encourages the resin to bleed out of the knots, which damages the paint film. To correct this, strip back the damaged area to bare wood, treat the knot(s) with a knotting solution, allow to dry, then prime and repaint the affected area.

Stains, like grease, bleed through newly applied emulsion. Cover them with oil-based paint or an aerosol stain block, then repaint.

Poor drying

This is usually the result of paint being applied over a dirty or greasy surface. Strip back the paint and thoroughly clean the underlying surface. Be sure to remove any traces of grease and particles of dirt or dust before repainting.

Show through

Colour showing through is most often the result of a lack of undercoat. Bear in mind that a topcoat is really just a protective layer and is not designed to completely obliterate what lies beneath. To remedy this problem, rub down the surface well and apply enough undercoat until the colour is completely hidden, then apply topcoat again.

Grittiness results from dirt being transferred via the paintbrush to the painted surface. Keep paint clean and wipe grit away before it dries.

Insects

Insects find their way into newly applied paint all too easily, particularly during the summer months. They can also be a problem if there are any plants growing near to the painted surface. If the paint is still wet, lift off the insects with the point of a penknife or something similar and carefully smooth out the paint to erase the imprint, using your paintbrush or a lint-free rag. If the paint is starting to dry, leave it well alone until the paint is hard, and then rub the insect free with your finger.

Insects settling in newly applied paint are almost inevitable if you are painting outside. Try and remove them before the paint dries.

Wallpaper basics

Wallpapering tool kit

No expensive or specialized tools are usually required for hanging wall and ceiling coverings. However, a pasting table makes it easier to apply paste to long lengths of wallpaper or other material. Make sure that the scissors or knife you use to cut the wallpaper to length are sharp.

Basic essentials

Depending on the job, you may need some specialist tools for applying wallcoverings, but the following is a checklist of the basic essentials:

Pasting table A sturdy, purpose-made pasting table is a wise investment. Easy to move, store and put up, it provides a stable surface of ideal dimensions and makes pasting very much simpler. Alternatively, you can use a flush door laid over trestles.

Bucket Use a clean plastic bucket for paste, with string tied across the top between the handle joints, across which you can rest your pasting brush when it is not in use. You will also need something with which to stir the paste.

Pasting brush Choose a brush at least 10 cm (4 in) wide, and keep it only for pasting.

Scissors You will need a pair of long-bladed decorating scissors, and a small pair for trimming.

Craft (utility) knife This knife is for use with a steel straight edge or cutting guide for trimming vinyls and heavy papers. However, scissors are best for trimming thin, wet paper.

Smoothing brush Also known as a paperhanger's brush, this has stiff but soft bristles and is used to brush trapped air out to the edge of paper and press the wallcovering into place. Always keep it clean and dry.

Sponge Essential for wiping away any surplus paste while it is still wet.

Seam roller Use this small wood or plastic roller to press down seams once the wallcovering is up. Avoid using it on embossed papers or you risk making obvious 'tramlines'.

Plumb bob and line This is used to produce true verticals. It is an essential piece of equipment for starting every wallpapering job. A builder's line will hang better than ordinary string.

Chalk line A string covered in chalk which, when held taut and then snapped against a surface, is useful for creating a temporary marking line of chalk.

Pencil Use an HB or softer lead for marking the paper clearly. Too sharp or hard a pencil can tear more delicate papers.

Decorating scissors

Smoothing, or paperhanger's, brush

Seam roller

Pasting brush

Natural sponge

Plastic bucket

Craft (utility) knife

Steel tape A standard tape is typically 3.5 m (12 ft) long, which should be adequate for measuring the height of normal walls. But longer measures, if required, are widely available.

Rule It is important to have a rule long enough to span the roll's width – normally about 53 cm (21 in). A retractable rule may tear the paper, so it is better to use a fixed rule.

Set square A large plastic square (or any improvised square) is useful for checking that your cuts are consistently at a 90-degree angle.

Sanding pad Keep one of these to hand for sanding away any scraps of old wallpaper or lining paper you may find on a stripped wall just as you are about to hang the new paper. Likewise, a sharp scraper is a useful standby.

Clean rags Choose rags made of lint-free cloth, such as old sheeting, for wiping the pasting table as the job progresses. Other material may leave fibres on the table.

Water trough When hanging ready-pasted wallcoverings, you need a water-resistant trough in which to soak the cut sections.

Stepladder You will need at least one stepladder in order to reach the tops of the walls or the ceiling. If you have two stepladders or trestles and a scaffold board, you can erect a platform to work on (see illustration, above right).

A continuous platform is needed for papering a ceiling – rest a plank on two stepladders or trestles at a height that gives about 7.5 cm (3 in) between your head and the ceiling.

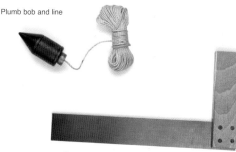

Plumb bob and line

Square

There are countless designs, colours and types of wallpaper to choose from, and some are easier to hang than others. Having the basic wallpapering equipment will make the job run more smoothly.

Choosing wallcoverings

The huge range of wallcoverings includes foil, plastic finishes, natural fibres and fabric as well as paper. The prices vary widely and some coverings are more durable and easier to hang than others. Choosing the right one for your needs can be a bit daunting unless you are familiar with the options available.

Lining paper

Lining paper is a plain, inexpensive paper designed to cover poor wall or ceiling surfaces before the application of a decorative covering of paint or an expensive wallcovering. (It is often the best way to hide thin cracks in ceilings, too.) Lining paper is hung vertically before painting or horizontally before covering with wallpaper.

Standard wallpaper

Standard wallpaper is available in a wide range of patterns and prices, including expensive hand-blocked and hand-printed wallpapers, which require more specialist handling. Standard papers are not washable or stain-resistant.

Flock wallpaper

A type of embossed paper, flock wallpaper comprises fibres of nylon, cotton, rayon or silk glued to a paper or vinyl backing, which create a raised pile with a velvety feel. Available mainly in traditional patterns, and usually in rich colours, the paper was originally developed to mimic velvet wall hangings. Flocks are expensive, and difficult to hang and to clean, although the washable vinyl versions are easier to handle.

Washable wallpaper

Easy to hang, this is ordinary wallpaper with a transparent plastic protective finish that makes it stain-resistant. It can be wiped or lightly sponged, but not saturated – too much water could weaken the wallpaper paste – and is particularly suitable for kitchens and bathrooms.

Vinyl wallcoverings

Comprising a layer of vinyl (applied as a spray, a liquid or a solid sheet) fused to a paper or fabric backing, these wallcoverings come unpasted or ready-pasted. Generally speaking, they are durable, tough and scrubbable and particularly suitable for bathrooms and kitchens. They must be hung with a paste containing a fungicide (which discourages mould), and it is important that seams do not overlap because vinyl will not stick to itself. Vinyls can be stripped quite easily.

The range of vinyls includes vinyl-coated papers, solid sheet vinyls, flock, metallic and textured vinyls.

Textured vinyls include heavy-duty 'contoured' vinyl, also called tiling-on-a-roll, which commonly features tile-effect patterns such as mosaic tiles, and blown vinyl. Blown vinyl, or 'expanded vinyl', has a relief pattern that gives a three-dimensional effect.

A vinyl wallcovering is the best choice for papering a bathroom because it is tougher than standard wallpaper and better able to withstand the moisture and hot atmosphere likely in bathrooms.

Pasted or unpasted?

Most papers are unpasted and require pasting before hanging (see page 49).

Ready-pasted wallpaper has a dried crystalline paste on the back, which is activated when the paper is immersed in water. It is easy to hang because there is no need for a brush and paste. However, you may still need to paste down any seams that start to lift.

Paste-the-wall coverings allow you to hang the paper straight from the roll and position and trim each drop as necessary.

Good for covering imperfect surfaces, it is available in a range of designs and colours, and can also be bought uncoloured for overpainting. Blown vinyl is washable, but the surface scuffs easily.

A textured wallcovering can add interest and subtle pattern to a room scheme and is useful for helping to disguise uneven walls. Some textured papers are designed to be painted over.

Relief and embossed papers

These papers have a raised surface and are particularly good for covering up poor plaster. Many are designed for overpainting, usually with emulsion or eggshell, but are tough enough to take an oil-based gloss paint. Some of the papers must be handled with care so as not to flatten the raised pattern. Once hung and painted, they can be extremely difficult to strip. The main types include the following:

Woodchip paper Chips of wood and sawdust within the paper give it a raised texture like oatmeal or porridge, with different grades from fine to coarse. It is inexpensive and ideal for covering less-than-perfect surfaces.

Anaglypta This is a trade name. The heavy-duty paper can look like finely modelled plaster. There are over 100 designs, some of which relate to specific period styles. It is made from wood pulp or cotton fibres, or a vinyl version is available. Generally, the more heavily embossed the paper, the more expensive it is.

Lincrusta Invented in the late 19th century, lincrusta is made from linseed oil and fillers. It is often modelled to resemble panelling and used on the lower part of the wall, then painted or stained to resemble wood. It is difficult to hang.

Foil wallcoverings

Foils comprise either aluminium foil or metallized plastic film fused to a backing of paper or scrim and overprinted with a pattern. The shiny finish helps to reflect light, which can enhance dark areas of a room, but will show up any poor wall surfaces. Foils are hardwearing, but they can be difficult to hang, and particular care must be taken around electrical fittings.

Natural fibres

These textured wallcoverings are made of natural fibres like raffia, sisal and hemp, which have been dyed and laminated to a backing material. They are suitable for walls in poor condition as long as they are exposed to very little moisture.

Fabric wallcoverings

Silk, linen and suede are examples of the modern luxury fabric wallcoverings available. Backed with paper or latex acrylic, they are sold either in wallpaper-sized rolls or by the yard or metre. Alternatively, unbacked fabric can be stretched in place over battens. Fabric wallcoverings require expert hanging and are expensive and difficult to clean.

Wallpaper examples

Hanging a wallcovering is a simple and quick way to decorate a wall or ceiling and the range of wallcoverings is enormous, encompassing a wide variety of materials, colours, patterns and textures. The swatches shown here are a tiny sample of the thousands available.

The pale gold verticals on this wallpaper look almost hand-painted against the roughly finished matt terracotta or red plaster base colour. Such subtle patternings offer a delicate shimmer to a wall, but stand one step further back and this paper gives a dense colour backdrop. These soft summer oranges and golds work well in a kitchen or conservatory, where they bring indoors a feeling of mellow sunshine and long balmy evenings.

A traditional Victorian chinoiserie pattern on hand-printed wallpaper is beautifully adapted for today's homes. Such painterly wallpapers make a bold statement and need not be used throughout a room. Instead, pick one to highlight a chimney breast, alcove or single wall.

Modern does not necessarily mean bright colours and stripped floorboards. It is possible to create sumptuous environments with a very fashionable flair. Take this willow-patterned wallpaper in elegant shades of pale honey, golden-cream and coral pink, and use it as the starting point from which to design a contemporary intimate living room or bedroom.

Rose patterns conjure up a country cottage feeling. This traditional wallpaper is a pretty example, appropriate for bedrooms, bathrooms or even an inviting family kitchen.

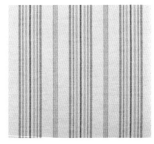

Natural shades of stone and ivory are accented with a subtle flash of pale gold. A traditional colour combination for wallcoverings is given a new lease of life in this raw, hand-painted effect. Choose it for a simple yet pleasing design solution in the living room or dining room, or for traditionally dark areas such as stairwells.

This unusual wallpaper design is reminiscent of Indonesian beach huts or rattan sun canopies in hot countries. The pale olive outline is a great colour to match paint to for the woodwork, or even a contrast-colour wall. This would be great in a light kitchen or a tranquil natural living room, teamed with chunky dark wooden furniture.

This delicate candy-striped wallpaper is reminiscent of seaside rock or swirled sugar sticks. It would be a good choice for a small flat, as larger stripes can enclose small rooms. Try this in the bedroom and contrast with solid blue voiles and delicate daisy-print cushion covers, or hang in the hallway for a light and bright entrance.

This tone-on-tone exaggerated stripe has a very elegant air, suitable for formal or informal settings. Such large-scale stripes work well in the bigger rooms or open areas within a house. For a dramatic look, use throughout the hallway, stairs and landing area.

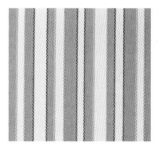

This ultra smart striped wallpaper suggests a formality suited to walls below the dado rail in classic-style hallways and dining rooms. However, it could look equally at home in a modern setting – used on a feature wall in a living room or bedroom and mixed with a range of tonal blues and creams.

Large-scale wallpaper does not have to be overbearing; it can be the making of a truly modern setting. Here, the flowing organic take on a natural pattern gives a new lease of life to walls. Neutral tones of buff and soft mink are enlivened by the addition of antique gold leaves. Combine with antique gold-dusted picture frames and simple block wood furniture.

A slightly iridescent wallpaper, this pattern plays with the subtle contrasts of matt and shiny surfaces. Like a mother-of-pearl shell, the look of this design varies from all angles and in different lights. A spectacular addition to any room, this paper would combine perfectly with soft blue satin quilts and pillows and glass-mirrored side tables in a bedroom.

How much paper do I need?

Strictly speaking, the term 'wallcovering' is more accurate, but, for convenience, the word 'paper' is used here as a generic term for all types of wall and ceiling coverings. The charts here will help you determine the number of rolls of paper required, but remember to take account of roll sizes and any pattern repeats.

Measuring up and calculating

To work out how many rolls of wallpaper you need, you can't just calculate the area to be covered because you need to work in complete vertical runs or 'drops' – joins halfway down a wall are not a good idea!

First, measure your drop, from the ceiling down to the dado or skirting (baseboard). The number of drops in a roll will depend on whether you have a pattern repeat to take into account. A standard roll is 10 m (33 ft) long. A paper with no repeat would provide four drops of up to about 2.4 m (8 ft) (you will need to allow an overlap top and bottom). Over that and you will get only three drops, although the leftovers will be useful

for areas over doors and below windows. Allowing for a pattern repeat will increase the wastage, but you should still get three drops unless the ceiling is very high. If papering only from dado rail to picture rail, you can expect to get five or six drops per roll.

To work out how many drops you need, simply measure all round the room. A standard roll is 53 cm (21 in) wide, so if your round-the-room measurement comes to 14 m (46 ft), that's 27 drops. At four drops per roll, you will need seven rolls; at three drops, you will need nine rolls. If in doubt, over-order, checking that you can return what you don't use.

Roll sizes

A standard roll is 10 m x 53 cm (33 ft x 21 in). The paper comes ready trimmed and is usually wrapped to keep it clean. The charts for calculating quantities (see below and opposite) are based on the standard roll size. However, some Continental European papers may be narrower than this, and American papers may be twice as wide. If selecting any of these papers, look in the manufacturer's sample book for guidance on coverage.

Repeats

Another variable to consider when calculating quantities of wallcoverings is the pattern repeat, since patterns need to be matched at every join. Sample books and the wrapping label will give the repeat

Calculating the number of rolls for walls

Measurement around room	8.5m (27ft10in)	9.75m (32ft)	11m (36ft)	12m (39ft4in)	13.4m (44ft)	14m (46ft)
Height from skirting (baseboard)						
2.13–2.29m (7ft–7ft6in)	4	4	5	5	6	6
2.30–2.44m (7ft6in–8ft)	4	4	5	5	6	6
2.45–2.59m (8ft–8ft6in)	4	5	5	6	6	7
2.60–2.74m (8ft6in–9ft)	4	5	5	6	6	7
2.75–2.90m (9ft–9ft6in)	4	5	6	6	7	7
2.91–3.05m (9ft6in–10ft)	5	5	6	7	7	8
3.06–3.20m (10ft–10ft6in)	5	5	6	7	8	8

measurement. The larger the pattern repeat, the greater amount of wastage you will need to allow for and the more rolls you will need. For a large, bold pattern, you may also need to allow for a dominant element to 'sit' well on the wall – awkward breaks such as headless animals, for example, are less noticeable at the bottom of the wall than at the top.

Patterned paper comes in the following types:
- Free-match papers have designs that do not require pattern matching, and so involve little wastage.
- Set-match, or straight-match, patterns have motifs that repeat in a straight line across the paper. Wastage will depend on the overall size of the pattern repeat, but it's not usually too much.
- Offset, or drop-match, patterns have a repeat in diagonal lines, and so each new length of paper has to be moved either up or down to allow for this. You can minimize wastage with drop-match patterns by cutting alternate lengths from two different rolls. A drop-match pattern is a good choice if your walls are not perfectly square.

In addition, some papers have a symbol on their wrapping label indicating 'reverse alternate lengths'. This means that you need to hang each length of paper the opposite way up relative to the previous one. Some free-match wallcoverings look best when reverse hung.

Batch numbers

Each roll of paper should be stamped with a production batch number. When selecting your rolls, check that all the batch numbers are the same. If they are not, this means that the rolls have been produced in different batch runs and there may be variations in colour and shading. For this reason, it's a good idea to buy more than you need. If you run out and have to buy one or two more rolls at a later date, they may

come from a different batch. If you do buy too many rolls, you can usually return any unopened ones. If you do have to finish off with rolls from a different batch, plan to use this paper in an alcove or recess, or somewhere in the room where any slight differences in colour or shade will not be immediately obvious.

Calculating the number of rolls for a ceiling

Measurement around room	Number of rolls required
9.75m (32ft)	2
10m (32ft10in)	2
11m (36ft)	2
11.5m (37ft9in)	2
12m (39ft4in)	2
12.8m (42ft)	3
13.4m (44ft)	3
14m (46ft)	3
14.5m (47ft7in)	3
16m (52ft6in)	4
16.5m (54ft2in)	4
17m (55ft9in)	4
17.5m (57ft5in)	4
18m (59ft)	5
19m (62ft4in)	5
19.5m (64ft)	5
20m (65ft9in)	5
20.5m (67ft3in)	6
21m (69ft)	6
22.5m (73ft10in)	7

16m (52ft6in)	17m (55ft9in)	18.5m (60ft8in)	19.5m (64ft)	20.75m (68ft)	22m (72ft2in)	23m (75ft5in)	
7	7	8	8	9	9	9	
7	8	8	9	9	10	10	
7	8	8	9	9	10	10	
8	8	9	9	10	11	11	
8	9	9	10	10	11	12	
9	9	10	10	11	12	12	
9	10	10	11	12	12	13	

Removing wallcoverings

If you are planning to redecorate a papered wall or ceiling – whether with emulsion or new wallpaper – it is often essential to remove the existing wallcovering first in order to achieve a smooth and professional-looking finish.

Removing different coverings

Work on one wall at a time and scrape off the covering from the bottom of the wall upwards, taking care not to dig into the plaster with the scraper. If you have to soak a covering before you can remove it, a steam wallpaper stripper will save you a lot of time and effort. Domestic models are available at a reasonable price or you could hire one for a day or weekend. Some steam strippers rely on boiling water as well as steam, so wear strong waterproof gloves and safety goggles for your own protection and keep children well away.

Once stripped, seal the walls with a watery solution of wallpaper adhesive and leave overnight. Wipe away dust with a damp sponge.

Standard wallpaper

To remove most standard wallpapers, you need to use a steam stripper or soak the paper with a mild mixture of warm water, liquid detergent and a little wallpaper paste – the paste will hold the water on the paper. Leave the soaked area for 20–30 minutes before starting to lift the covering with a flexible scraper.

1 Thoroughly wet the surface of the wallpaper, using a standard sponge or a water-filled plant mister.

2 Allow enough soaking time so that the old paste starts to dissolve before you try to remove the paper. Test a small area first. Then work your scraper underneath the paper and lift it away from the plaster. If you wait too long, however, the paper will dry out and the paste will re-adhere.

3 Water and electricity can be a fatal combination. As a precaution, turn off the main power when stripping around a light switch or power point and try to strip the paper without water.

4 Stubborn patches of paper and paste may require a second soaking.

Easy-strip and vinyl papers

Easy-strip wallcoverings and vinyl wallpapers have a thin, decorative top layer that you can easily pull away intact, leaving the backing layer stuck to the wall. The backing layer is not suitable as a base for painting, but may be satisfactory as a lining paper for a new wallcovering if it is thoroughly stuck down. If you do need to remove the backing paper, soak it with water and you should be able to strip it off relatively easily.

Simply loosen a corner of the vinyl at the foot of the wall, then pull the strip away, holding the vinyl out from the wall as you pull.

Embossed and washable papers

Embossed papers and washable wallcoverings, other than those with separate backing papers, can be difficult to remove. Roughing the surface with a coarse abrasive or a scraper like a Skarsten, to score the paper in a criss-cross fashion, will help steam or water to penetrate the paper and loosen the paste beneath. Allow plenty of soaking time before attempting to scrape the paper off.

Painted papers

You need to break down the surface of the paper with a coarse abrasive pad soaked in water before stripping. Don't use a wire brush – this may leave tiny metal strands embedded in the plaster of the wall, leading to rust spots later on. Soak the abraded wall with water and then strip away the paper.

Lincrusta

This type of covering is stuck in place using an extremely strong adhesive and is difficult to remove. Use hot water and a scraper to ease the sheets of lincrusta from the wall, taking care not to pull away the plaster with it. Soak and then remove any remaining adhesive that is still stuck to the wall.

Stripping ceilings

Most domestic steam strippers are perfectly safe to use because their water reservoirs contain only cold water – the steam is produced at the faceplate. (This isn't always the case, however, so make sure that you understand your stripper before you use it.) Press the steam stripper against the paper with one hand and hold a scraper in the other. As the steam penetrates the paper, it will start to lift away from the plaster. Use the scraper to encourage this process. Get as close as possible to the surface you are stripping, as holding the steam stripper at arm's length soon becomes tiring.

The technique is exactly the same for steam stripping walls.

Cork and expanded polystyrene tiles

At one time, cork and expanded polystyrene tiles were a popular covering for plaster in poor condition, so if you are intent on removing such tiles, be aware that the plaster underneath might be in need of attention. Use a flexible scraper to ease the tiles away from the wall or ceiling, one by one. When every scrap of cork or polystyrene has been removed, use a hot-air gun to soften the exposed adhesive before removing it with a flexible scraper or sharp shavehook. Take care not to damage the plaster and be careful to protect your eyes, hands and hair from hot adhesive, especially if you are working on a ceiling. If a slight residue of adhesive remains on the surface, remove it by rubbing very hard with a cloth dipped in a solvent thinner.

How to hang wallpaper

Hanging wallpaper is not a difficult job if you want to do it yourself, but it is essential that you apply it to a properly prepared surface, otherwise any imperfections in the wall surface will be obvious and your efforts will be wasted.

Order of work

If you are papering the ceiling, do this before you paper the walls. To paper the walls, start at the main window, working away from the light towards the longest unbroken wall. When you reach the corner of the room, go back and work from the other side of the window. If the room has a chimney breast or some other focal point, centre a length of paper on it and work outwards to the left and right, lapping around the edge of the chimney breast.

Before you start

All woodwork should be painted and dry, and walls and ceilings should be clean, dry and smooth. Give the walls and ceiling a final check for uneven filler or rough areas where any old wallcovering has been removed, and rub down with medium glasspaper where necessary.

If the ceiling or walls have been newly plastered, you will first have to 'size' them to prevent too much of the wallpaper paste being absorbed by the plaster and weakening the adhesion of the paper. An application of size also helps to slide your paper into place, by making the surface to be covered more slippery. Size may be bought as a paste or a powder, to be mixed with cold water. Spread newspaper around the bases of the walls to catch any splashes of size, then apply it to all the surfaces to be papered and leave it to dry – usually about an hour or two – before papering.

Collect all your tools together (see pages 38–39), set up your pasting table and place it under a window facing the light, so that you will be able to see where you have pasted. Make sure that the surface of the pasting table is dry and clean.

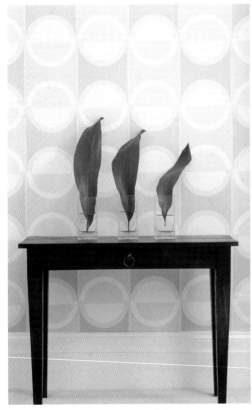

A boldly patterned wallpaper like this results in some necessary paper wastage, as it requires very careful matching at the seams so as not to detract from the overall effect.

Wallcovering adhesives

Different wallcoverings need different types and strengths of adhesive, so check on your covering's requirements before buying the paste and make sure that you buy enough. Using the wrong type of adhesive can result in the wallcovering failing to adhere, the surface discolouring or mould growing. As a general rule, the heavier the wallpaper, the stronger the adhesive you need.

All-purpose wallpaper paste contains a fungicide and can be bought either ready-mixed (usually in a handy tub) or as a powder to mix with water. The ready-mixed paste is convenient to use and a tub usually contains enough to do about five rolls of wallpaper, but it works out very expensive if you have a lot of wallpapering to do. You can also buy tubes of wallpaper paste for very small jobs such as borders or patches. These are often described as 'strong wallpaper paste'.

Handy hints

- Allow time for the paper to absorb the paste before hanging, and give the same 'soaking' time to every length.

- If using a paste-the-wall covering, apply the adhesive using a roller to an area slightly wider than the length being pasted. You can paste the next section without smearing paste on the paper.

- If you have to make a horizontal join, do not use a straight cut – tear the paper across the drop slightly unevenly and overlap for an almost invisible join.

- Paper often bubbles when first hung, but dries flat. Prick any remaining air bubbles with a pin and smooth out. Alternatively, try shrinking bubbles back into place by blowing the surface with a hair dryer.

- To remedy curling seams, ease open the seam, dab on a little paste with a cotton bud and smooth back with a seam roller.

- When hanging flock, protect it with a piece of lining paper.

Papering walls

1 Measure the drop and cut the first piece of paper to length, adding about 12 cm (5 in) to allow for trimming to fit.

2 Cut several more lengths, matching up the pattern exactly to the neighbouring piece each time. Number them in sequence on the reverse to avoid mistakes.

3 Take a window as your starting point, not a corner. From the edge of the frame, measure the width of the paper, less 1 cm (½ in), and mark on the wall. Suspend a plumbline from ceiling height to coincide with your mark. Draw the vertical in pencil or chalk.

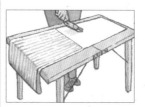

4 Lay the first length of paper face down on the pasting table, slightly overlapping the edge to avoid getting paste on the table. Weigh it down so that it does not roll up. Load the brush with paste, then apply paste evenly and liberally, working right to the edges. If the paper is longer than the table, let the pasted paper overhang while you paste the rest. Carefully fold the ends of the pasted paper back on itself to the middle, fold it again (take care not to flatten the folds) to make the length easy to move and leave to absorb the paste. This is important because the paper will continue to expand for some minutes. If it does not expand fully, you may get bubbles later on.

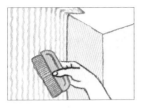

5 To hang, carry the first length of paper to the wall. Holding the top corners of the paper, start to unfold and press the top to the wall, sliding it to line up the edge with your vertical guideline. Smooth downwards and outwards using a smoothing or paperhanger's brush. Open the bottom fold and continue smoothing the paper down the wall. Lightly dab any bubbles flat.

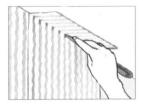

6 Use the edge of the closed scissors to press the paper firmly but gently into the top edge, under the cornicing or against the ceiling. Press very lightly to avoid tearing the damp paper, then peel back the paper and cut neatly along the crease. Smooth the paper back into place. Do the same at the bottom of the wall along the skirting (baseboard) and check for air bubbles. Scissors are preferable to a knife for trimming to avoid tearing, although on heavy papers like vinyls you can use a very sharp knife and steel straight edge. Place the straight edge just above the crease and cut.

7 Paste the next length in the same way and hang edge to edge (butt joined) with the previous piece – do not overlap. Match any pattern by sliding the paper up or down. Except on embossed paper, gently run a seam roller down the seam to stick the edges down firmly.

8 Continue hanging lengths, in the order described, and mark a new vertical guideline every time you turn a corner to ensure the pattern stays truly vertical. As you progress, clean up between each length. Wipe paste from picture rails, skirtings (baseboards) and window and door frames while it is still soft. Keep any trimmed pieces of paper for patching. Wipe the pasting table clean after each length. You will need to cut slightly shorter lengths above a radiator, unless you are able to move it. Leave about 15–20 cm (6–8 in) for tucking and smoothing.

Papering a ceiling is best tackled by two people – one to smooth down the paper and one to hold the pasted paper against the ceiling using a clean broom or purpose-made roller.

Papering ceilings

When papering a ceiling, you must be able to reach it safely and in reasonable comfort, so check how you will reach the highest point of the room. A short step-stool may be sufficient, otherwise make a platform you can stand on (see page 39), so that your head is about 7.5 cm (3 in) from the ceiling. Place the platform along the line of the first length of paper to be hung.

The best starting place is parallel with the window wall. This ensures that no shadows will be thrown should any paper overlap. The simplest way to mark the position for the first length is to mark the ceiling at each end with a pencil, the width of the paper away from the wall, then snap a chalk line between the two points to leave a line of chalk on the ceiling.

1 Measure the ceiling and cut the first piece of paper to length, adding 10 cm (4 in) to allow for trimming. Paste and fold the length of paper as described for papering walls (see page 49), and leave the paper to soak.

2 Lay the folded paper over a spare roll of paper, with the edge to be stuck first uppermost. Hold the roll in one hand, grip the top edge with the other hand, turn it paste-side up and apply it to the corner where you plan to start. Slide the paper to the chalk line and smooth it on to the ceiling. Move along the platform, releasing the folds as you go. Smooth the paper to the ceiling and get someone to hold the paper in place with a broom as you move along. Continue until the whole length is in position. Run over it with your smoothing or paperhanger's brush, making sure that the edges are well stuck down all along the length.

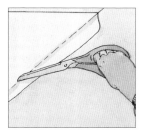

3 Press the paper into the end walls and crease it with your closed scissors as before.

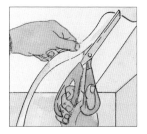

4 Trim 3 mm ($^1/8$ in) outside the crease so that the paper just turns on to the wall. Dab the paper back into place. Hang the second length, matching it to the edge of the first, then paper the rest of the ceiling in the same way.

Ready-pasted paper

Ready-pasted paper does not stretch, so there is less chance of it bubbling through expansion. Cut and hang the paper as above, but, instead of pasting, soak each rolled length in the water trough according to the manufacturer's instructions. Pull it out slowly, top edge first, allowing excess water to drain away.

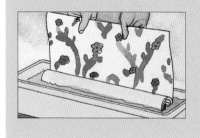

Pendant light fittings

1 To paper around a ceiling pendant, cut the paper to length, then mark on the back the position of the pendant. Allow for trimming.

2 Paste the paper and make a series of small cuts radiating out from the centre of the light position you have marked. Hang the paper normally. When you reach the light fitting, feed the pendant through the hole made by the cuts and press the paper into place around it.

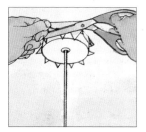

3 Crease each flap with the blunt edge of the closed scissors and carefully cut off the surplus paper 3 mm ($^1/8$ in) outside the crease marks. Press the paper into place and wipe the paste from the fitting.

Papering tricky areas

Papering flat areas of walls is straightforward. However, many rooms present potential problem areas such as alcoves, fixed radiator panels, light switches and fireplaces. Don't be daunted – simply follow the methods outlined below.

Window recesses

Follow the numbered sequence in the illustration above, allowing for small overlaps where indicated by the dotted line. Cut a special piece of paper for area **3** (testing its pattern match before pasting), with small overlaps to tuck behind **1** and **4**.

Around a door

1 Hang a full drop of paper as though the door were not there, then cut away the surplus to within 2–3 cm (1 in) of the frame.

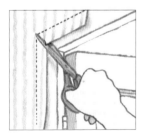

2 Make a diagonal cut at the frame corner and crease the overlap top and side into the frame using the closed scissors. Peel back, trim and smooth into place.

3 Now work from the other side of the door, and cut the length in the same way if the two pieces will meet above the frame. It is wise to drop a plumbline to the right-hand edge of this length so that you hang the piece vertically. If the two pieces will not meet, cut an infill piece to go above the door. If there is a pattern to match, cut and hang the infill before the next length is cut. If pattern matching is no problem, hang the next full length and then the infill piece afterwards.

Handy hints

- If you have never hung wallpaper before and are worried about matching patterns, choose a random pattern for your first attempt. A small all-over pattern is more forgiving of mistakes.

- Heavyweight embossed papers are not a good choice for ceilings; they may be too heavy to stick firmly and could come down on unsuspecting heads.

- A random pattern will help flatten out any angles in a room that you want to disguise.

- Bold geometric patterns can look as though they are sliding off any wall that is not perfectly straight.

Switches and sockets

1 First, switch off the power supply. Paste the paper down over the faceplate, then find the middle of the fitting and cut a cross in the paper, taking care not to scratch the plate. Trim back the paper, leaving about 1 cm ($\frac{1}{2}$ in).

2 Loosen the plate screws, ease the plate away from the wall, then tuck in the excess paper. Retighten the screws and wipe away the paste.

Metallic or foil wallcoverings must not be tucked behind switch plates, so if using these or if the face plate can't be unscrewed from the wall, simply press the cut paper lightly around the plate and mark it using scissors in the usual way. Pull each flap away and trim it to overlap by about 3 mm ($\frac{1}{8}$ in). Dab the pieces back into place and wipe the paste from the plate.

Fireplaces

If the fireplace is a feature of the room – and if it is on a chimney breast – it is best to hang a length of paper centrally on the chimney breast, and then paper out in each direction. Then, any slight discrepancy in pattern can be lost around the internal corners of the chimney breast.

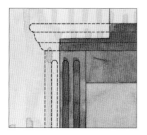

1 At the sides of the surround, cut the paper as if you were tackling a door frame (see illustration, above). You will also have to make cuts in the paper to let the mantelpiece come through. When measuring, allow extra paper to push into the mouldings.

2 Trim along the crease marks with scissors. With odd shapes, such as those made by a stone fireplace, make small cuts in the paper edge, mould it to the contours and crease it. Trim 3 mm (1/8 in) outside the creases so that the paper just turns on to the stone.

Radiators

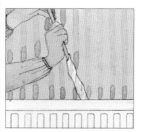

It may be possible to swing radiators away from the walls to allow you to paper behind. Try lifting the radiator. If it rises enough to clear the holding brackets, slightly loosen the pipe nuts either side and lean the radiator forward. If the radiator will not move, you will have to tuck the paper down behind it. Cut two slits corresponding to the holding brackets. Then use a radiator roller – or improvise with a length of wood wrapped in clean rag – to smooth the paper down into place behind the radiator. Don't worry about getting the joins exact, as the area is not easily visible.

You'll need some extra patience when papering awkward areas such as behind radiators and loft rooms with their sloping ceilings, but the effort is worthwhile, as this stunning paper demonstrates.

Tiling
basics

Tiling tool kit

Tiling is not difficult to master, but you will need some specific items in order to do it well. Whatever type of tile you are laying you will need some marking and cutting tools and the appropriate adhesive. For hard tiles like ceramic and quarry tiles you will also need grout and grouting tools.

Tools for marking

To lay floor tiles you need a chalk line (see page 66) to locate and mark the mid-point of the floor. For wall tiles you should nail temporary fixing guides to the wall to enable you to tile in straight lines. For these you'll need a pencil and tape measure, wooden battens, a hammer and some long masonry nails, and a spirit level and plumbline to check that the battens are truly horizontal and vertical.

Chinagraph pencil A chinagraph pencil is made of wax and used to temporarily mark ceramic tiles on their glazed side to mark the line of cut.

Steel rule A steel rule is necessary for marking straight lines and for guiding a pencil-type tile cutter or craft (utility) knife to cut a straight edge.

Profile gauge This device, also known as a profile template, is useful for marking awkward shapes to be cut. It consists of hundreds of needles or strips of plastic held in a frame. When pressed against a shaped surface, the tool takes up its exact shape, which you can then transfer to a tile by following the outline with a chinagraph pencil.

Tools for cutting

Ceramic tiles are brittle, which means that once you have introduced a line of weakness by scoring a straight line in the tile, it can be snapped relatively easily. Shaping a hard tile to fit around a pipe or the edge of a basin is more problematic. However, there are various cutting tools to meet both requirements.

Tile cutter A heavy-duty craft (utility) knife is sufficient for cutting flexible tiles, but you will need some sort of tile cutter for cutting ceramic, quarry or other hard tiles. The simplest option is to use a pen-like tungsten carbide-tipped scorer, or scriber, guided by a steel rule to ensure a clean edge.

The alternative is a mechanical platform-type tile cutter, which is more accurate and a better option if the tiles are extra thick or hard. A third option is an electric tile cutter, which uses a water-cooled diamond cutting wheel.

Tile nibblers These pincers are for cutting irregular pieces out of hard tiles, for example to shape a tile to fit around a pipe (see page 63).

Tile saw An alternative to tile nibblers, a manual tile saw is a type of hacksaw and has a circular cutting blade, tipped with tungsten carbide, held in a metal frame. The blade cuts in any direction, and the size of the frame enables you to turn the saw around a tile without obstruction.

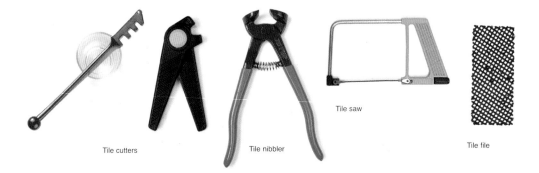

Tile cutters

Tile nibbler

Tile saw

Tile file

Tile file This very hard file lets you smooth the rough edges of cut hard tiles. Alternatively, use coarse sandpaper or carborundum stone.

Protective clothing You will need to wear heavy-duty gloves and safety goggles when cutting or drilling glazed tiles – the glaze can be as sharp as a shard of glass if a piece breaks off.

Tools for fixing

Once you have marked your wall or floor, you are ready to start fixing tiles and will need at least some of the following items:

Serrated spreader The spreader's serrated edge allows you to apply a uniform depth of adhesive to the surface to be tiled. It also applies the adhesive in 'ribbons', which gives it room to move when you press the tiles down so that they adhere well.

Tile spacers Available in different widths to suit different sizes of tile and usually cross-shaped, these pieces of plastic are used to keep the spacing even between hard tiles and are essential for a professional-looking finish. Some spacers are designed to be pressed firmly into the tile adhesive at the corners of tiles and left in place to be grouted over later. Others should be removed when the adhesive is dry.

Alternatively, use ordinary matches or pieces of thick card. Some tiles have specially shaped edges that make them self-spacing, consequently negating the need for tile spacers.

Grout spreader A grout spreader or float allows you to work grout evenly into the joints between hard tiles and force out any trapped air.

Grouting tool Often made of plastic and supplied with tiling kits, this is used to smooth the grout and give a neat finish. A pen top or a small round-ended wooden stick like an ice-lolly stick are just as good alternatives.

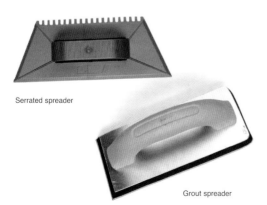

Serrated spreader

Grout spreader

Tiling gauge

Make yourself a tiling gauge, or gauge stick, to help position your tiles on the wall. Mark a long, straight batten with tile widths along its length, allowing gaps for grouting. Then hold the gauge against the wall horizontally, aligning one end with the mid-point of the wall. Move it slightly off centre if necessary, in order to get the right balance and avoid having too many part-tiles at the edges of the tiled area.

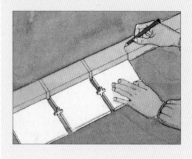

Sponge and clean cloth A sponge is useful for wiping surplus grout from the surface of the tiles. When the grout is dry, you need a cloth to remove any remaining grout and polish the tiles at the same time.

Adhesives, grouts and sealants

Use specially formulated tile adhesive, and choose a waterproof type for condensation-prone areas or those areas that get regular soakings – as in a shower cubicle or splashback.

Grout, for filling the joints between tiles, is sold either ready-mixed in tubs or as a powder that needs mixing to a thick paste according to the manufacturer's instructions. It comes in white and a limited range of colours, or you can colour it yourself to match your scheme. Waterproof grout is preferable, and should always be used on tiled worktops and tabletops, to provide a hygienic and impervious finish. A mortar mix is often used to grout floor tiles.

Where tiling abuts baths, basins or shower trays, you will need to use a silicone sealant to effectively waterproof the joint.

Choosing tiles

Tiles come in all manner of colours, patterns, shapes, sizes and materials. Mostly hardwearing and easy to clean, tiles provide an incredibly versatile and practical covering for both floors and walls. Ceramic tiles are probably the most widely used, but there are plenty of other types of tile for use around the home.

The vast range of tiles available provides you with plenty of scope for mixing colours, designs and styles in any place that a durable surface is required.

Tile sizes

The best size of tile to use depends on the area to be covered and the desired effect. It's obviously quicker to tile an area with larger tiles and they work better for large expanses of wall, whereas smaller tiles work well in small rooms. Small tiles are easier to cut and shape around awkward areas such as built-in fixtures, recesses and window rebates. As for the effect created by different sizes of tile: smaller tiles create a busier look; rectangular tiles are good for creating interesting herringbone and other traditional brickwork patterns; while there are shapes that interlock for special effects.

Ceramic tiles

Ceramic tiles are the perfect protection against water penetration and are great for bathrooms and kitchens. They are made from a thin slab of clay decorated with a coloured glaze, and often with a pattern. There are many shapes beyond the usual squares and rectangles, including hexagonal, octagonal, curved Provençal styles and small 'drop-ins'. The most common square ceramic tiles are either 10 cm (4 in) or 15 cm (6 in). Rectangular tiles are usually 20 x 10 cm (8 x 4 in) and 20 x 15 cm (8 x 6 in).

'Universal' tiles have several glazed edges, which are useful if you wish to avoid leaving an unglazed edge exposed.

You can also buy feature panels – sets of tiles that form a large design. These can be used alone, rather like a piece of artwork, or set into a wall of plainer tiles.

Border tiles

Unless you are using 'universal' tiles, border tiles are the conventional way of finishing off half-tiling. Borders can be chosen to coordinate with the main tiling or to contrast with it and there are some highly decorative deep-profile tiles available. Check that the border tiles are compatible in width with the main tiles and that the colours and glazes work together.

Mosaic tiles

These are tiny tiles supplied on a mesh backing, or paper frontsheet, which is soaked off after the tiles have been laid, usually 30 cm (12 in) square. They may be different tones of plain colours or form a distinct pattern. The sheets are laid in a bed of adhesive and then grouted. Faux mosaics are standard tiles scored to look like mosaic.

Quarry tiles

Quarry tiles are usually used on the floor, but they make a handsome alternative to ceramic tiles on the wall. Although as equally hardwearing as ceramic tiles and requiring similar preparation and fixing, they are unglazed and have more of a country appearance – a look that is emphasized by their earthy coloration.

Cork tiles

Cork tiles are usually fixed as panels, rather than used to cover a whole wall, although cork has good insulating properties. They are ideal for pinboards or feature walls. Most come in 'natural' colours, although some may be stained or dyed. Unsealed tiles are thick and crumbly, so it is better to choose presealed. Cork can be sealed after hanging, but may need many coats.

Metallic and mirror tiles

Metallic and mirror tiles are often used for their reflective value. The metallic tiles are usually produced in a lightweight metal such as aluminium, made to simulate copper, pewter or stainless steel, and some have interesting textures and self-patterns. They are fixed by self-adhesive pads.

Mirror tiles are much heavier, and come in a wide range of sizes. Some are hung using a special adhesive, but heavier panels need to be fixed with special plates or mirror screws. Choose very high-quality tiles for a bathroom, as condensation can cause the silvering on the back of cheap mirror to perish.

You need an especially flat surface for reflective tiles or you will get a distorted reflection. If necessary, fix them to a panel of chipboard or hardboard and then attach this to the wall.

Other types of tiles

Other types of tile include those suitable for flooring (see page 74), namely vinyl, cork, linoleum, rubber and leather tiles. You can use floor tiles on walls, although

Shiny metallic tiles make a perfect splashback in a modern kitchen, but must be laid on a very flat wall to avoid distorting their reflective surface.

they are likely to be heavier and more expensive, but don't use wall tiles on floors because they are not strong enough and may be too slippery.

Where to use tiles

Consider using tiles on various horizontal and vertical surfaces:

- In the dining room, as an integral part of a food-serving surface.
- On the lower part of a hall wall.
- In recesses or alcoves use mirror tiles as a reflective background to glass shelving or to suggest a window in a dark, uninteresting area.
- In the bedroom, where mirror or metallic tiles are useful on wardrobe doors.
- On tabletops or tiled worktops use flooring-grade tiles or special worktop tiles on a base of blockboard, chipboard or plywood. Some have matching edging strips. Alternatively, use plastic trim strips designed to sandwich under the row of edge tiles as they are laid.

Tile examples

It's often difficult to judge how tiles will look when covering a large expanse. Some retailers have comprehensive catalogues showing room sets, while others have samples mounted on display boards. Avoid trendy effects or colours, which you might tire of easily, and be aware that geometric effects will work only where all walls and corners are straight and true.

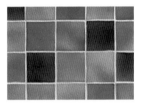

A tricolour mix of blue tiles in gloriously deep glazes of rich azure, sapphire and aquamarine. Show off these intense shades alongside natural woods or modern chromed surfaces in the kitchen. In the bathroom, lay them as a border, or be brave and cover a complete wall, creating a calming environment.

These organic blue stone floor tiles are made by mixing pure clay and water and then covering the surface with pure oxides before firing. An oxidized blue is most effective for flooring and the uneven colour surface gives depth to any room. Use in a hallway or throughout an open-plan kitchen and living area.

Mosaics look fantastic in any bathroom or kitchen – they bring a feeling of Roman grandeur to even the smallest of spaces. If you are feeling truly creative, why not make your own designs? Highlight the areas around mirrors or shower cubicles and have a go at cleverly manipulating the shape of the room.

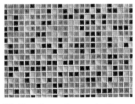

Multi-coloured mosaic tiles are a simple yet stylish solution for all surfaces, even window sills or cupboards and shelving. Mosaics were used by the Japanese, Roman, Greek and Arabic communities to create wonderfully lavish and colourful floor and wall patternings. Today they come in easy-to-handle sheets.

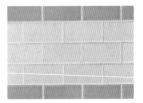

Traditional elongated tiles are an attractive alternative to the more usual square ones. Reminiscent of Victorian bath houses, these pale marble colours would look great in the bathroom or kitchen. Think about continuing them as borders along kitchen work surfaces, or use all over in the bathroom.

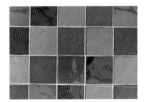

These zinc-look polished tiles are of a relatively new generation of tiles, and are available in both polished and satin finishes. Use in the bathroom and shower as a space-age alternative to coloured tiles. In the kitchen, these tiles are an ideal companion to today's stainless steel appliances and work surfaces.

How many tiles do I need?

Tiles are usually sold in boxes of 25 or 50, or in packs to cover one square metre or yard, but this varies and buying large quantities could be wasteful if you are tiling only a small area. First, you need to know how many tiles you want.

Estimating quantities

Unless you plan your tile design using a scale drawing (see below right), you need to calculate the area to be covered.

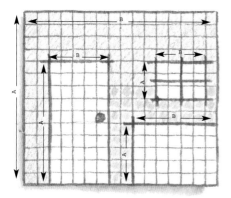

For an unbroken expanse of wall, simply multiply the height of the wall (A) by the width (B). To allow for doors, windows and radiators or other fixed heaters, multiply the height (A) by the width (B) of each feature, add the totals and subtract from the total wall area. This will give you the area to be tiled. For floor tiles, measure the width and length of the room and allow for the area taken up by cupboards, a bath or other features as above.

To determine the number of tiles required, divide the area to be tiled by the area of a single tile. Add an extra 10 per cent to allow for cutting wastage and breakages, and to keep as spares in case you need to replace a damaged tile in the future.

Designing with tiles

Instead of a vast area of plain tiles, try to be bold and create an original look:
- Hang square tiles diagonally for a more interesting, diamond-quilted look.
- Create bold stripes with two or more colours, either horizontally or vertically.
- Halved diagonally, a square tile becomes a triangle for a zigzag border.
- For a patchwork look, use tiles of the same size and thickness in a selection of different colours.

Pattern planning

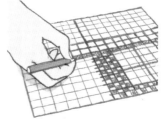

Draw the area to be tiled on a squared grid – if you are using square tiles, one square can equal one tile. Plot your pattern on the grid and colour it in so that you can see the effect and work out accurate quantities.

Centre your design on any feature it relates to, and use your plan to foresee awkward cuts. Whether you choose the middle of a tile or the meeting of two tiles as the mid-point of the area to be tiled (design permitting) can make a big difference to the amount of tile cutting you have to do.

Even if you have planned the design on paper, lay out the tiles in a 'dry run' on the floor. Number them, if necessary, so that you fix them in the right sequence.

How to tile walls

Tiling is perfectly feasible for the average handy person, but start with a small project, such as a basin splashback. Avoid anywhere that requires any tricky tile cutting, and choose tiles that don't need any complicated pattern matching.

Preparation

Tiles must be fixed to a dry, flat surface. Replaster any badly damaged areas and fill small holes and cracks with proprietary filler (see page 20). If the surface is uneven, it may be better to fix the tiles on chipboard or hardboard instead. Then either fix the board to the wall with battens and tile it, or tile the board while horizontal and then fix it with impact adhesive.

You can also tile over existing tiling, as long as the original tiles are firmly stuck down and thoroughly cleaned before covering. In addition, you must stagger the joints so that no new joint is on top of an old one. You will end up with a thick ledge where the tiling ends. Use a wooden trim or edging tiles with quite a deep profile to hide any visible joins between the two.

As long as you establish a perfectly horizontal base from which to work up the wall, your tiles should quite literally slot into place to provide a stunning and hardwearing surface.

Hanging tiles

Hanging tiles is not too difficult, but you need to work out exactly how to position the tiles before you start, otherwise you could end up with a tile cut in an awkward position – or a mismatched pattern. Use a profile gauge to help you, if you like (see page 56). Also make sure that you have to hand all the necessary tools to cut and fix your tiles (see pages 56–57).

1 Tiles are hung from the bottom of the wall working upwards, so you first need to establish a perfectly horizontal base. Measure one tile depth up from the floor, skirting (baseboard) or worktop, allowing a gap for grouting. Attach a temporary batten to the wall with long nails, without hammering them fully home. Use a spirit level to check that it is horizontal and aligned to your measured point. Fix a vertical batten in a similar way, so that its inner edge marks the edge of the last whole tile. If your design has a mid-point, mark the centre of the wall and measure out from this.

2 Apply tile adhesive to the wall using a serrated spreader. Cover only about a square metre or yard at a time, and keep the container covered.

3 Press the first horizontal row of tiles firmly into place against the edge of the batten, inserting spacers

Handy hints

- Try to avoid having to cut pieces of tile less than a quarter of the tile width.
- If planning your tile layout on a squared grid, use a tracing-paper overlay to see where tiled edges will fall best – this is more convenient than having to keep marking and erasing alternatives.
- When using plain or marbled tiles, open the boxes and 'shuffle the pack' to mix the tiles before use to minimize the effect of any colour variation between boxes.
- Remember that tiling will raise the level of the floor and you may have to make adjustments to cupboard doors and the door opening into the room.

A simple basin splashback with an easy-to-follow design that requires no tricky tile cutting or pattern matching is the perfect project for a first attempt at tiling.

between each tile. Work up the wall, row by row, and when you reach an obstacle such as a window, carry on fixing the whole tiles, leaving tile cutting until later. Keep checking that the tiles line up in both directions and that any pattern matches.

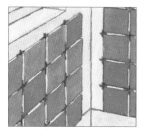

4 Once all the whole tiles are fixed, remove the battens. You can now cut tiles as necessary (see right) and hang them around the edges. You may have to put adhesive on the backs of these part-tiles, rather than on the wall.

5 Once the tiling is done, leave the adhesive to dry for at least 12 hours and remove the spacers if necessary (see page 57). Prepare the grout according to the manufacturer's instructions, then press it into the joints using a sponge or small spreader. Remove the excess with a clean, damp sponge, then use a grouting tool or equivalent (see page 57) to compress and finish the joints. Allow the grout to dry, then polish the tiles with a clean, dry cloth.

Cutting wall tiles

1 To cut straight edges, use a chinagraph pencil to mark on the glazed side of the tile where it is to be cut. Score the glazed surface firmly using a pen-like tile cutter. Place a matchstick beneath the scored line. Press the tile down firmly either side and it should snap cleanly. Alternatively, use a mechanical tile cutter.

2 To cut a curved or angular shape, score the shape in the same way, then nibble away the excess with tile nibblers or use a tile saw. Smooth rough edges with a tile file, coarse sandpaper or carborundum stone.

Tiling tricky areas

With good tools and patience, tiling around tricky shapes is reasonably straightforward. If you are planning a room from scratch, consider the size of tiles to be used to avoid too much tile cutting and shaping later on.

Tiling around corners

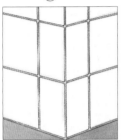

1 Finish external corners with tiles cut to the same size for both walls. Ideally, use tiles with glazed edges so that there is no raw edge facing out, or use a trim strip. With patterned tiles, it is better to use whole glazed-edged tiles and work away to where a cut tile and a pattern break will be less obvious.

2 Internal corners should also, wherever possible, be completed with either whole tiles or part-tiles of the same size meeting in the angle between the two walls. With patterned tiles, use the offcuts from tiling one wall to begin the opposite wall so as to maintain the continuity of the pattern.

Tiling around fixtures

1 Try to tile around washbasins and other fixtures in a symmetrical fashion. Ideally, plan to use a row of whole tiles above fixtures, since cut tiles can look untidy. Where this is impossible, be sure to fill any gaps with a good-quality waterproof sealant.

2 In bathrooms, light fittings must be fitted with a cord pull. Elsewhere, to produce a neat finish around a light switch, turn off the power at the mains, undo the screws in the faceplate and ease the front of the switch clear of the wall. Tile up to the edge of the mounting box so that the faceplate will cover the cut edges of the tiles. Carefully screw the faceplate back into place, hiding the tile edges.

Tiling around doors and windows

The door into a room or the window in a wall are both very much focal points, so try to maintain a visual balance by tiling around them evenly, using whole tiles whenever possible. The door or window frame may not be vertical, so don't use it as a guide for your tiling rows unless it is completely true.

Tiling a recess

For a professional appearance, ensure that the tiles are 'balanced' across a window recess – in other words, that the cut tiles either side of the recess are in symmetry. Tiles that protrude on external corners must have glazed edges or be covered by a trim strip.

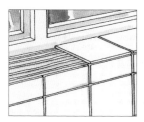

1 To produce the neatest effect, tiles lining a window recess should project to overlap those on the wall. The tiles in the recess should therefore have glazed edges.

2 Make sure that the tile spacings in the recess are in line with those on the wall. Use cut tiles with glazed edges at either end of the ledge to finish it off neatly.

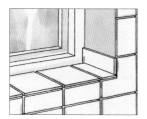

3 Start the sides of the recess with a cut, glazed-edge tile so that the spacings remain exactly consistent with those between the horizontal rows on the wall. Tile the underside of the recess last and tape the tiles in position until the adhesive has fully dried.

Drilling tiles

1 Apply a criss-cross of masking tape over the spot to be drilled to stop the drill bit slipping and cracking the tile during drilling.

2 Drill the hole using a pointed tile bit or a sharp masonry bit, but don't drill right through the tile into stone or brick. If you have a variable-speed power drill, run it at its slowest setting to maximize your control. Never use a power drill set to hammer action – the vibration will shatter the tile.

3 Peel away the masking tape afterwards and the small pieces of drilled tile should come away with it.

To drill holes in a tiled wall for accessories like a towel rail or shelf, use a tile drill bit and drill very slowly and carefully to avoid cracking the tile.

How to tile floors

The technique for laying floor tiles is much the same whether you are using flexible or hard tiles. They require a stable, level surface, so unless the subfloor is perfect, it is best to put down plywood or flooring-grade hardboard or chipboard before laying the tiles.

Handling floor tiles

Flexible floor tiles like vinyl, linoleum, cork and rubber are easier to handle and cut than hard tiles. Some are self-adhesive (see page 83) and simply have a peel-off backing.

Before laying flexible tiles, remove the packaging and leave them in the room where you are going to lay them for 24–48 hours so that they can acclimatize. Make sure that you have the right kind of adhesive for the tile. Most of the harder types of tile are best left to the experts to lay – they are heavy to handle and hard to cut, and some have to be set in a bed of mortar.

Flooring patterns

Floor tiles can be used creatively to make whatever pattern you like and an imaginative design can help to improve the proportions of the room. For example, stripes laid widthways will make a floor area look less long and narrow, while a chequerboard effect will create an impression of greater space.

Like wall tiles, floor tiles need to be centred on the middle of the floor or a dominant feature like a fireplace. If you are creating a pattern, draw up a scale plan of the room on graph paper, so that you can see how best to position the pattern and how many tiles of each colour you will need.

However sure you are of your calculations, always buy a few extra tiles as a contingency measure to allow for accidents and wastage.

Laying floor tiles

It is usual to lay tiles from the centre point and work outwards, towards the edges of the room, but in bathrooms and kitchens where much of the floor space is occupied by cupboards, you may have trouble finding the centre of the area to be tiled. It's important to lay tiles by working from a right angle you have marked on the floor because very few rooms have walls and corners that are completely true. If you started by working from one wall, you could soon find your tiles out of alignment.

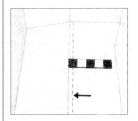

1 Mark the centre line in chalk and check that the edge tiles will be at least half a tile wide. If not, move the line a half-tile width to one side.

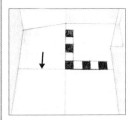

2 Mark a centre line in the other direction, at right angles to the first. Check as before and again move the line if necessary to avoid having small strips of tile at the sides of the room.

3 Spread tile adhesive along the floor, on either side of the centre line chalk marks.

4 Lay the central tiles first, either side of the chalk line, using floor tile spacers if necessary.

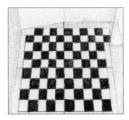

5 Continue working outwards from the centre tiles towards the edges until the floor area is completely covered. Lay a spirit level across the tiles periodically to check that they are level. Adjust the amount of adhesive beneath a tile if necessary to bring it in line with the others. Lay the tiles around the edges of the room last, cutting the tiles to fit as necessary. If using hard tiles, finish off by grouting in the same way as wall tiles (see page 63).

Hard tiles like quarry tiles are a popular choice for kitchen floors. They are more difficult to lay than flexible floor tiles, so probably best laid by experts for the best result.

Cutting flexible tiles to fit

1 To cut flexible tiles for edges, place a tile that needs cutting squarely on top of the last tile, then place another tile on top of it, butted up against the wall. Mark a pencil line along the edge of the top tile on the tile below. Cut the marked tile to this line – it should fit in the gap. Apply adhesive and firm into position, aligning the cut edge against the wall.

2 Use the same technique to cut around an external corner where a single tile is involved. Place two full tiles over the last laid tile and slide the top one over to butt up against the skirting (baseboard) or wall. Mark a pencil line on the tile beneath.

3 Move both tiles around the corner, without turning them, and position over the last laid tile on that side. Mark a line as before, cut out the part that is not required and glue the part-tile into place.

4 To tile around a pipe, first cut an edge tile to fit the space, then push the tile against the pipe and mark the centre of the pipe. Next, move the tile against the wall and mark the pipe centre on the edge of the tile. Draw light pencil lines from both points and cut a hole where the lines bisect. Make a slit in the tile to allow you to feed it around the pipe.

Flooring
basics

Which type of flooring?

There are plenty of different types of flooring, but before you commit yourself to stripping old floorboards or laying a marvellous expanse of marble, consider objectively the look you want, what demands you will put on the floor and how much you can afford.

The options

There are three basic types of flooring:
Hard, which includes brick, stone, wood and tiles (see pages 74–75).
Resilient, such as vinyl, linoleum and rubber (see pages 80–81).
Soft, which includes carpets and rugs, as well as natural floorcoverings like sisal and jute (see pages 86–89).

Practical considerations

Floors take a lot of punishment – feet tramp across, bringing in water, mud and grit from outside; fidgety feet scuff the same patch in front of chairs or sofas; tracks are worn where there is only one possible route across a room. It's heartbreaking to spend time and effort laying a floor, only to find it looks scruffy after a few months or requires tremendous upkeep. To make sure you get it right, think about the following practicalities before making a decision:

- How much wear and tear will the floor receive? Floors that get a lot of heavy use or through-traffic, for example those in halls, on staircases and landings, need to be hardwearing.
- Does it need to be washable? The flooring in halls, bathrooms, kitchens and children's rooms all need to be easy to clean and resistant to dirt and stains.
- Do you want a permanent flooring – a wise choice for kitchens, conservatories and halls – or something that will not be too difficult to change?
- What is the condition of the existing floor? Is it easier to remove it or cover it up? This could affect the options available to you.
- Do you need a type of flooring that you can lay yourself, or is there enough in the budget to pay for it to be fitted? Large pieces of sheet material or rolls of carpet can be quite difficult to handle if you are inexperienced in these matters.

Design considerations

The flooring needs to relate to the style of the room or area. It is a significant proportion of the room's surface decoration, so will not go unnoticed. You therefore need to think carefully about the look that you want in addition to the practical considerations of the flooring:

- Strong colours and bold patterns may appear to hit you in the eye, so avoid these where you want to create a relaxing mood.

Soft flooring is warm underfoot and a comfortable choice for living rooms, although a pale colour is impractical in homes with small children and pets.

In areas like hallways that inevitably take a lot of through-traffic, wood is a good choice for a hardwearing flooring that is easy to keep clean.

Handy hints

- Always buy the best-quality flooring you can afford. Price is usually a good guide – if a good carpet is beyond your budget, look at cheaper alternatives to carpet rather than very cheap carpets.
- To create an impression of space, use a similar flooring, or the same colour flooring throughout – particularly effective in small flats or apartments, and bungalows.
- Where two different floorings meet at a doorway, you may have to install a threshold. Metal ones look very utilitarian; wooden ones are easy to stain or paint to match the floor or décor.
- Try to use manufacturers' own adhesives or sealants where possible.
- Check aftercare instructions, to avoid spoiling a floor with the wrong treatment.
- Some floor tiles need sealing after laying to protect them from stains – check with the manufacturer.

- Where much of the floor is covered up with furniture or equipment, it may be a waste of effort to design a patterned floor that will not be appreciated. Interesting patterns often look best in halls, kitchens, corridors and large, sparse rooms where they can best be shown off in all their glory.
- Consider the size of any pattern in relation to the scale of the room. Pale colours and small patterns can look disappointing on a large floor.
- When planning a patterned floor, whether in tiles or as a painted design on wood, think about how the pattern relates to the room's configuration – you don't want an awkward 'break' in the design at a doorway or in front of a fireplace, for example. Working out the design on a scale plan first is always helpful.
- Collect samples of your proposed flooring and look at them in the room where you plan to use them, to gauge their effect in situ.

Use stencils and floor paints on stripped wooden floorboards to reproduce the effect of a patterned carpet without the expense of the real thing.

Preparing your floor

Whatever type of flooring you choose, it will need to be laid on a subfloor that is smooth, clean, level and dry. Problems such as damp or rot cannot be ignored and will need to be cured before you start work.

Remedying an uneven subfloor

There are several ways to level an uneven subfloor:
- Cover it with panels of plywood or flooring-grade chipboard or hardboard. Lay hardboard smooth side uppermost if covering with adhesive, or rough side uppermost to give a better grip for underlay and soft floorings. Stagger the joins of the new panels so that they do not align with existing boards.

- Use a self-levelling screeding compound. This comes as a powder that is mixed and poured over the floor, where it fills any imperfections and finds its own level to set in a perfectly flat finish.
- Dig up and rescreed. These are both jobs that should be carried out by a professional.

Removing old floor tiles

To remove old cork and vinyl floor tiles, start with a loose tile or one in the middle of the floor and lever it up using a flexible scraper. Remove all the tiles one by one, then use a hot-air gun to soften the adhesive left on the floor so that you can scrape it off. Linoleum can be removed similarly – you may find a floor scraper, which has a long handle, useful for the job.

To remove old quarry and ceramic tiles, you will need to lever them up using a hammer and bolster chisel. Wear protective clothing, such as gloves and goggles, as shards of tile can be very sharp.

Covering an uneven subfloor with sheets of flooring-grade hardboard or chipboard will ensure the best result when it comes to laying the final floorcovering.

It's a shame to remove or cover up original flooring tiles unless you really have to. Consider restoring them if possible using proprietary restoring products.

If you find that draughts and dust are coming up through the gaps between your old floorboards, try filling them with fillets of wood or with papier mâché.

Handy hints

- Never lay new carpet on top of old carpet or underlay, as the worn areas will quickly work through to the new carpet.
- Don't be tempted to pour concrete over an existing hard floor you don't like – this will damage it for ever. Calling in a salvage company will save it for someone who does like it and also boost the budget towards your new flooring.
- When painting, staining or tiling a floor, start in the corner furthest from the door and work back towards the door opening.
- If you are fixing a permanent or semi-permanent floorcovering, bear in mind that you might need to access pipes and cables beneath the floor at some stage in the future. It may be worth marking the position of these on the floorboards to show their layout.

Dealing with old floorboards

Old floorboards are likely to be uneven and may have been cut to install or repair pipes and cables. If they are to be covered with a soft or resilient flooring, the ridges will show through as wear in the new flooring, even with an underlay. So, whether you intend to make a feature of the floorboards or to conceal them, you need to make sure that they are in good condition.

Fill wide gaps with fillets of wood glued on either side and tapped into position, flush with the neighbouring boards; and fill narrow gaps with papier mâché made from paper and water-based PVA (white) glue. Repair or replace any damaged boards. Punch down nail heads – at least 3 mm (1/8 in) below the surface if you are going to sand the boards – and screw down any loose boards (first checking beneath for cables and pipes that you might damage).

Old floorboards can also be turned over – the underside should be smooth and the wood aged and seasoned. Call on professionals to do this, as it is a major job and will involve removing and replacing skirting boards (baseboards).

If leaving floorboards uncovered, you could either sand them back for a light finish or coat them with a dark stain or paint to suit your room scheme.

Hard flooring

Laying a hard floor is usually a job for the professionals, since the materials are heavy to handle and require precise fitting. However, there are some types that you can fit yourself.

Brick

Similar to terracotta tiles but thicker, floor bricks are effective in halls, living areas of period homes and conservatories, but impractical for kitchens. Brick is crumbly and porous if not sealed.

Tiles

Floor tiles come in a huge range of colours and styles:
Ceramic These work well in halls, kitchens, dining rooms and conservatories. They are thicker and stronger than ceramic wall tiles, and without the high glaze that could make them slippery. Never lay wall tiles on floors.
Quarry Made of tough clay in various earthy colours, quarry tiles look good wherever a rustic look is required. They are usually porous, so may need sealing. If left untreated, quarry tiles have a matt appearance. For a more shiny finish, treat them with linseed oil and turpentine.
Terracotta These tiles can be brittle. Buy recycled ones from a salvage company or new ones with a slightly 'distressed' surface.
Encaustic Also called Victorian tiles because they are often found in entrance halls of this period. Encaustic tiles have a pattern, usually geometric or heraldic, constructed as an inlay that never wears.
Mosaic Like mosaic tiles intended for walls (see page 59), these tiny clay tiles are supplied in sheet form and require sticking down and grouting.

Concrete

Concrete is common as a subfloor in modern homes, but makes a hardwearing top floor if smoothed (but not polished) and sealed with special non-slip resin. Concrete can be laid as slabs or poured on site, coloured with pigment and even embedded with decorative materials.

Stone

Original stone flagstones are still found in period homes, which proves their long-lasting quality. Nowadays, many types of stone make practical and attractive flooring. A cheaper option is reconstituted stone slabs, as sold by garden centres, which can be used indoors if they are adequately sealed.

Slate

Slate floor tiles are usually slightly roughened (riven), making them non-slip and safe underfoot, but not so easy to clean. Ensure that the slate is flooring quality, not for roofs or wall cladding.

Wood

The hardwearing resilience and warmth of wooden flooring makes it ideal throughout the house.

In many older houses, suspended floors are made from floorboards fixed to the joists. Old boards can be restored or turned and relaid (see pages 76–77). Wooden flooring can also come as wood-block, laid in herringbone patterns, or intricately patterned parquet. If you have either type, you may have to do some restoration work, but do not paint an old parquet floor.

Wood strips, panels and veneers are alternatives to solid wood. They are constructed of a thin layer (veneer) of wood on a cheaper backing. Some are suitable for laying by non-professionals. Do not confuse manmade 'wood laminate' with real wood.

Laminates

These include woodgrain effects (often called wood laminate), marble and a host of individual designs. They need no sealing or polishing and can be cleaned with a damp cloth. They are suitable for most rooms except bathrooms, where they could swell and start to lift if saturated – check with the manufacturer.

Plywood

Plywood can be used as a floor in its own right, as well as for levelling a subfloor. A birch- or maple-faced plywood can look very stylish in a modern living room.

Some of the options

Tiles offer lots of decorative options and are probably the most commonly used type of hard flooring, but it's always worth considering some of the alternatives.

Terracotta is a popular traditional flooring. In the summer it is cool underfoot and, with the help of underfloor heating, in winter the tiles absorb the heat and keep warm for hours.

These rich red antique terracotta tiles have been rescued from chateaux, manor houses and even barns in Burgundy, France, and are understandably expensive.

Reminiscent of Roman mosaics, these stone mosaic tiles are ideal on both floors and walls – the greater the surface area covered, the better they look.

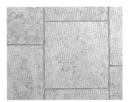

Stone flooring is ideal for a traditional rustic-feel room, but can easily be made more formal or contemporary with the addition of oversized modern stone pieces such as raw chunky side tables.

Real slate is formed over thousands of years, and no two pieces will be the same. Use it in the kitchen for a long-lasting flooring. Varnish regularly to keep it looking good.

Oak, a straight-grained wood characterized by distinctive flecking, is a particularly good material for flooring. Wood floors are a healthy alternative to carpet, as there is no build-up of dirt.

Pros and cons of hard flooring

For
- Hardwearing
- Looks good and even improves with time
- Easy to maintain and stain-resistant if sealed
- Good option for allergy sufferers, as less dust build-up than carpet

Against
- Unyielding underfoot
- Noisy, so rarely practical in a flat or apartment – many leases stipulate soft floorcovering for all floors in flats or apartments
- Heavy. The subfloor or joists may need strengthening, especially upstairs. May become slippery when wet

Facelift for a wooden floor

If you find a wood floor concealed beneath old floorcoverings, why not refurbish it? Sanding is an option for old wooden floors in good condition, while modern paints can bring new life to wooden and other types of floor.

Sanding

If you have an existing wooden floor, you may be able to restore it to its natural beauty by sanding. This involves a lot of physical work, but the rewards can be tremendous. A sanding machine makes the job much easier, although you may need to finish off some areas by hand.

Ensure that the floor is solid wood, since your sander could pulverize wood strip, wood mosaic panels, parquet or other veneers. Sanding is a very noisy business, so work only during sociable hours and warn your neighbours – they would probably prefer to go out for the day!

You can hire sanders for the day or weekend. Insist that the staff show you how to use the machines and provide a full set of instructions. You will need:

- A large drum sanding machine
- A small belt or orbital sander for the edges, or a sanding attachment on a drill
- Coarse, medium and fine abrasive strips for each machine
- Ear defenders, goggle and face mask

Before you start, deal with any loose and damaged boards (see page 73). Sweep up all dust and debris, seal the door with masking tape to keep dust from the rest of the house and open the windows so that you are working in a well-ventilated space.

1 Wearing the safety equipment, begin with the big sander and a coarse abrasive sheet. Work diagonally across the floor, taking care not to knock the skirting boards (baseboards).

2 Change to a medium-grade abrasive and sand parallel with the direction of the boards.

3 Finally, switch to a fine-grade abrasive, again working in the direction of the boards. Empty the dust bag frequently, and vacuum up wood dust from the floor.

4 Use the small sander or the sanding attachment on your drill to deal with edges and corners. Again, work through the different grades of abrasive paper.

5 Finish by sanding by hand any areas that the machines have missed.

You'll need to hire a sanding machine to strip original floorboards. It's noisy, dirty and very hard work, but the end result will be worth all the effort.

6 Vacuum thoroughly, including window sills and crevices between the boards. Wipe over the floor with a soft cloth soaked in white spirit, to remove any remaining dust.

Painting

Floorboards that are in poor condition or heavily filled can be coated with floor paint, which presents endless possibilities for colour use and design. You can create a geometric pattern or an eye-catching border, simulate a rug or give your floor a faux marble or tile effect – the possibilities are limitless. You can also transform a concrete or cement floor with industrial floor paints. A chequerboard effect can look stunning.

1 Start in the corner furthest from the door so that you have a clear exit and begin by applying a thinned coat of varnish to the whole floor. Allow to dry.

2 When marking out your design, use chalk and a rule to keep lines crisp, and low-tack masking tape to delineate the edge of each colour as you work.

3 Now apply the paint, making sure that your brushstrokes go in the direction of the wood's grain (length of floorboards). For any special effect, such as marbling, do a trial run on some spare wood first.

4 Remove the masking tape carefully and allow each coat to dry thoroughly before protecting all paintwork with several topcoats of varnish.

Reviving vinyl and linoleum

Special makeover paint can bring new life to tired vinyl or linoleum. Why not paint a simple border to outline architectural features, or define kitchen units or bathroom fittings? Alternatively, you could try using stencils and stamps (see page 32) – for example, print a Victorian tiled look with sponges cut into geometric shapes or stencil a unique patterned flooring. There is no need to varnish the floor.

Staining and sealing

You can alter the colour of timber floors using a woodstain followed by a varnish to seal, or a varnish stain, which combines the two jobs. Both oils and varnishes darken or yellow wood slightly, and woodstains can come up much stronger than on a shade card, so test first on a spare piece of sanded wood or in an unobtrusive corner. An undercoat of varnish thinned with white spirit will dilute the effect of a stain. Each finish will need several coats. Lightly sand between coats to key the surface for the next coat, and wipe away dust with a cloth and white spirit. For safety reasons, always use a matt or semi-matt varnish on floors to avoid creating a slippery surface.

Painting old floorboards is an easier option than sanding and is recommended if the boards are in poor condition. Choose a light, neutral colour for a modern look.

Laying a laminate floor

Real wood is an expensive option, so if you don't have an existing floor that you can restore or you don't want the bother of stripping floorboards, a popular and relatively inexpensive alternative is a wood laminate, or floating, floor.

What is laminate flooring?

Laminates are formed by fusing an image of a natural material like wood on to a backing board of MDF (medium-density fibreboard) or condensed chipboard and protecting it with layers of transparent laminate so that it looks like a hard floor finish. Laminate boards resemble floorboards, but are only about 1 cm ($\frac{1}{2}$ in) thick. They are tongued and grooved to fit together easily and are glued or clipped to each other, but not to the surface beneath – hence the term 'floating floor'. Wood laminates come in a wide variety of colours, from blonde ash to dark oak or rich cherry, and in different grades to suit different areas of the house.

Laminate flooring boards are supplied in packs that cover a calculated area, usually in the region of 20 sq m (215 sq ft). Divide the area of your floor space by the area covered by the pack to give you the number of packs you need, remembering to allow for wastage.

The pros and cons

A laminate floor is easy to clean and non-allergenic, but as noisy underfoot as most hard floors. If you are laying over a hard floor, and especially in an upstairs apartment, the insulating membrane usually supplied with the laminate may not be enough. You will need to consider some form of extra insulation beneath the laminate or even insulating between the joists. Laminate can be laid over almost any other type of flooring, and if you predict problems with noise, you might consider laying it over a ready-fitted carpet, although this is not ideal.

Although laminate flooring is tough and hardwearing, it should not be saturated with water. Mopping the floor with excess water could cause the boards to swell and push up. Use a damp mop or cloth only, and always wipe up any spills immediately.

Tools and materials

- Strong pair of scissors
- Foam insulating membrane
- Steel measuring tape
- Laminate boards and 2 cm (¾ in) quadrant moulding (quarter-circle wood trim)
- Adhesive, in a glue gun
- Wooden or plastic spacers, 6 mm (¼ in) thick
- Set square or straight edge
- Pencil
- Craft (utility) knife
- Hand tenon or crosscut saw
- Tamping block and hammer
- Damp cloth

A modern alternative to a real wood floor, wood laminate flooring is relatively easy to lay, comprising tongue-and-groove boards that are glued or clipped to each other.

How to lay laminate

The following instructions are for boards that need gluing, which is the traditional method, but the principles are the same for the newer glueless installation systems.

Before you start, ensure that the subfloor is sound and flat (see page 72). You can remove the skirting boards (baseboards) if you like, although this is not essential and they can be fiddly to replace.

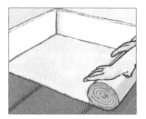

1 Cut the foam insulating membrane into lengths and cover the existing floor with it, abutting lengths as necessary and fitting it neatly into the corners.

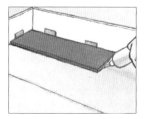

2 Start in the corner furthest away from the door. Lay the first laminate board against the wall, at right angles to any existing boards. Spread glue sparingly on the end tongue and slot on a second board. Work down the length of the room, inserting 6 mm (^{1}/4 in) thick spacers between the boards and the wall to create an expansion gap. This allows the wooden floor to expand and contract with temperature changes, without buckling.

3 To complete the first row with a part-board, carefully measure and mark the board with a set square or straight edge and pencil. Score the mark with the craft (utility) knife and cut cleanly with the saw.

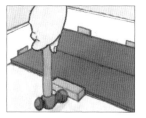

4 To lay the second row, apply the adhesive along the length as well as the end tongue. Tap the boards home with the tamping block and hammer. Wipe off any excess adhesive with a damp cloth immediately.

5 Continue laying the floor, length by length, across the room, staggering the joins to help strengthen the flooring and to avoid a noticeable line of board ends. You can achieve this by always using an offcut from the previous row of boards to start the next row. You may have to cut the last row of boards lengthways to fit – remember to allow for the 6 mm (^{1}/4 in) space between the floor and the wall. Use a profile gauge (see page 56) if necessary to mark and cut boards to fit around pipes.

6 Leave the floor to dry, and make sure that no one walks on it before the glue is completely set.

7 Remove all the spacers. Cut lengths of 2 cm (^{3}/4 in) quadrant moulding (quarter-circle wood trim) to fit around the perimeter of the room, to cover the expansion gap between the laminate and the wall. Glue or nail the skirting (baseboard) face of the quadrant only, so that the floor can still move, or 'float'.

Handy hints

- Atmospheric moisture affects wood, so after buying your laminate flooring, lie the boards flat in the room in which they are to be laid for at least a couple of days.
- A damp-proof membrane should be laid to provide a barrier to residual moisture in a solid subfloor, but must not be used over existing wooden flooring.
- Many manufacturers supply quadrant moulding (quarter-circle wood trim) to match their boards.
- Laminate boards that are locked together can be easily removed.

Resilient flooring

These floorcoverings are less noisy and kinder underfoot than hard floorings, but firmer than carpet. Resilient floors are made in both natural and manmade materials. Some are available in extra-broad widths to fit a large room without seams or joins, while others come as tiles that are easy to lay.

> **Pros and cons of resilient flooring**
> **For**
> - Comfortable underfoot
> - Practical alternative to hard flooring where soft floorcoverings are not suitable
> - Low-maintenance
> - Often easy to lay
> - Many suit a small budget
>
> **Against**
> - Those masquerading as traditional flooring can be unconvincing
> - The cheapest ranges can prove to be a poor buy
> - Many are unsuitable in combination with underfloor heating

Cork

Derived from the bark of the cork oak tree, cork flooring is light, warm and a natural insulator that deadens sound. It is suitable for any room, but does swell when wet, so must not be exposed to extreme damp. Cork tiles are available sealed and unsealed – the latter need sealing with several coats of polyurethane varnish after laying.

Linoleum

First patented in the 19th century, linoleum, or lino, is a natural product made from linseed oil, resin, powdered cork, wood flour and fillers, spread on to a hessian (burlap) backing and cured to create a very flexible, hardwearing flooring.

Available in various colours and effects, linoleum is suitable for any room in the house except the stairs. Sheet linoleum is best fitted professionally (especially if you want a laser-cut inlaid design), but tiles are comparatively easy to lay yourself, and you can buy coordinating borders and strips.

> **Safety note**
> An early type of synthetic floor was the thermoplastic or vinyl asbestos tile. It is essential to call in experts when removing these, as the asbestos content is hazardous to health.

Rubber

Rubber is warm, very resilient and quiet underfoot, and comes in a wide range of colours. Some of the heavily studded surfaces can be difficult to clean. Contrary to expectations, it is not ideal for a bathroom or shower room, as it can perish if saturated with water. Rubber comes in sheets (best laid by a professional) and do-it-yourself tiles, which can be used on stairs (see page 81).

Vinyl

The artificial equivalent of linoleum, vinyl flooring is often used to imitate tiles, wood or other traditional floors, although there is a huge selection of other colours and styles, including modern ranges with interesting effects such as glitter, mother-of-pearl and metallic looks. Vinyl is more vulnerable to scratching, dents and burns than some resilient floorings. Most types are unsuitable for stairs, but vinyl is particularly useful in kitchens and bathrooms. Available in sheet form or tiles, most vinyl can be laid by a competent home owner (see pages 82–83).

Some of the options

Invariably chosen for its practicality, easy maintenance and economical price, resilient flooring comes in different styles, textures and colours.

The iridescent, almost glass-like finish of this resin flooring absorbs and reflects colours around the room, giving off a subtle glow. Hardwearing and watertight, it is perfect for any bathroom.

Linoleum flooring, with its watertight properties and hardwearing, easy-to-clean finish, is perfect for bathrooms and kitchens. Simple designs such as stone and dappled effects look especially stylish.

Items made from reclaimed wood or driftwood have a wonderfully individual quality. The driftwood look is equally appealing for flooring because of its unrefined qualities.

Other types of resilient flooring

Resilient flooring in natural materials includes leather tiles, which are very expensive, and metal decking (stainless or galvanized steel, or aluminium), which is expensive and noisy, but perfect for an industrial look. There are also vinyl and rubber simulations that achieve the same hi-tech look as metal.

Smooth rubber tiles, warm and luxurious underfoot, are the ultimate in tough contemporary flooring and a good choice for bathrooms or kitchens. Mix and match for chequerboard effects.

Durable resin flooring has a tricolour effect in the surface. It is suitable for bathrooms, contemporary kitchen spaces and spectacular entrance halls. The effect varies across the room.

This leather flooring is embossed with a pattern to produce a mock-crocodile effect. Leather flooring is an extremely luxurious underfoot solution, but is surprisingly durable and long-lasting. It gives a sexy feel that is perfect for the bedroom, where tactile materials are particularly desirable.

Resilient flooring combines the durability and practicality of hard flooring with the less noisy and more comfortable aspects of soft flooring.

Laying vinyl

Rigid vinyl is available as tiles and complementary borders, but can be quite unyielding underfoot. Flexible vinyl, available in sheets and tiles (including self-adhesive), can be 'lay flat', which moulds itself to the subfloor and needs sticking down only around the perimeter, or cushioned, which gives extra bounce.

Vinyl tiles

Vinyl tiles are easy to lay yourself – they simply butt up against each other and don't need grouting. Some require fixing with adhesive, while others are the 'peel-and-stick' type. Being smaller, vinyl tiles are easier to handle than vinyl sheeting and can be easily cut to fit (see page 67). They allow you to create borders and panels for design interest, but the joins between tiles mean that dirt and spillages can penetrate. Vinyl tiles range in quality from vinyl coated to solid vinyl.

Tools and materials

- Steel measuring tape
- Chalk line (see page 66)
- Self-adhesive vinyl tiles
- Pencil
- Straight edge
- Cutting board
- Heavy-duty craft (utility) knife
- Profile gauge and sharp scissors

Floor tile planning

Make a scale drawing of the room to be tiled on squared graph paper, where each square represents one floor tile. Mark on the plan all alcoves and other irregularities. In a kitchen, much of the floor may be taken up with fixed units, so include these to scale as well. Shade in the design for the pattern and to determine the quantities of tiles of each colour required.

Vinyl sheeting is more practical than vinyl tiles in a bathroom, as it provides fewer joins through which dirt and spillages can penetrate and ultimately lift the flooring.

How to lay self-adhesive vinyl tiles

The following instructions are for self-adhesive vinyl tiles, which are the easiest to lay, but the principles are much the same for all tiles (see page 66).

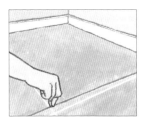

1 Find the true centre of the room by marking the centre of two opposite walls. Snap a chalk line between the two points. Do this between the other two walls and the centre of the room will be marked as a cross.

2 Lay out the tiles in a 'dry run' so that any problems come to light before you start sticking them down.

3 Peel the backing off the first tile and, aligning it with two arms of the central cross, press it down lightly and firmly. Work from the centre out towards the edges of the room, carefully butting the tiles up to each other and checking pattern matches.

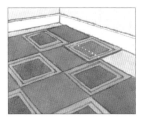

4 You will probably have to cut tiles to fit around the edge of the room. Lay a tile (do not remove the backing) over the last full tile, and mark with the pencil and straight edge where the cut is to come.

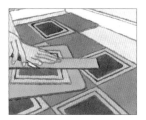

5 Cut the tile on a cutting board, using a heavy-duty craft (utility) knife against the straight edge.

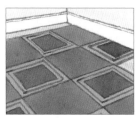

6 Peel off the backing and lay the tile in position with the cut edge against the wall, not abutting the last full tile.

7 To cut a non-rectangular part-tile (walls are seldom perfectly straight), you will need to turn the tile over to mark the fit, or carefully measure the space. For awkward shapes, especially curves, use a profile gauge (see page 56) to template the outline. A fiddly shape may be easier to cut with scissors than with a knife.

Available in styles that provide the look of hard tiles or wood for a fraction of the price of the real thing, most vinyl flooring can be laid by a competent do-it-yourselfer.

Vinyl sheeting

Buy the best you can afford, since cheap vinyl sheeting will eventually crack and does not withstand scratching, staining or spills for long. Although large rolls of vinyl are heavy and awkward to handle, vinyl sheeting does have the advantage of covering large areas quickly and with the minimum of seams. For large rooms use 4 m (13 ft) wide sheet material.

When working out how much you need, allow an extra 5 cm (2 in) all round, as walls are often uneven. Decide which way you want the pattern to run and avoid seams in doorways, where foot traffic is heaviest. Laying seams at right angles to windows makes them less noticeable because the light won't cast a shadow.

Tools and materials

- Heavy-duty craft (utility) knife
- Vinyl sheeting
- Steel measuring tape
- Soft broom
- Wooden block
- Straight edge
- Paint scraper
- Pencil and paper for template making
- Adhesive
- Serrated spreader

How to lay vinyl sheeting

Cold temperatures make vinyl brittle, so leave the vinyl loosely rolled in a warm room for 24 hours before laying to allow it to become supple.

1 Cut the vinyl about 5 cm (2 in) longer than required to allow for trimming. Lay it up against the skirting (baseboard) or wall by 5 cm (2 in). Sweep over the vinyl with a soft broom to ensure that the sheet is in close contact with the floor.

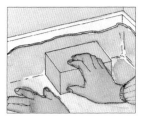

2 Use a wooden block to press the vinyl firmly into the angle between the floor and skirting (baseboard). If necessary, make vertical release cuts into the corner flaps. Don't trim the vinyl or apply adhesive until the fitting is complete.

3 If a second sheet is required to cover the floor area, lay it so that it overlaps the first, matching any pattern. Using a straight edge and a sharp, heavy-duty craft (utility) knife, cut through both thicknesses at the same time. Pull away the waste material and you will be left with a perfect fit.

4 Use a paint scraper to hold the vinyl hard against the junction of floor and skirting (baseboard), and trim off the surplus with the craft (utility) knife.

Cutting safely

Keep a sheet of scrap hardboard at hand on which to make cuts. Use a heavy-duty, sharp craft (utility) knife with a snap-off blade so that you can maintain a keen edge. Position a steel straight edge along the line to be cut and use the knife so that the blade cuts away from your other hand.

Trimming around a door frame

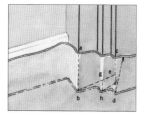

1 Make two 5 cm (2 in) vertical cuts in the vinyl at the projecting points of the frame (**ab** and **cd**). Next, make diagonal cuts to the same points (**eb** and **fd**). Make another vertical cut around the frame (**gh**) and cut diagonally (**ih**).

2 Press the vinyl tightly against the frame and trim off the surplus. Take the vinyl into the doorway and trim it so that it will end up halfway under the door. (Finish it off later by using a threshold strip to prevent lifting.)

External corners

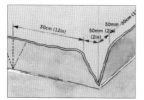

1 Lift the vinyl and make a vertical cut at the corner. Take the blade just to the floor. Make further diagonal cuts from 5 cm (2 in) on either side down to the base of the first cut so that the vinyl rests against each wall. Make other cuts every 30 cm (12 in) if necessary.

2 Hold the vinyl tight against the wall with a wooden block, then position the knife with its point where the wall and floor meet. Cut into the corner, holding the blade at 45 degrees as you proceed. Repeat this process for the remaining flap of vinyl, making sure that you achieve a neat fit on the corner. Bear in mind that it is better to trim away too little rather than too much – you can always pare away a little more if necessary.

Internal corners

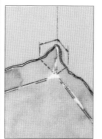

1 Leave 2.5 cm (1 in) of the surplus running up the wall, then cut out a triangle from the corner.

2 This will allow you to press the vinyl against both walls for trimming.

Cutting around a pedestal basin

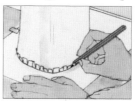

With awkward shapes like a pedestal basin, it is best to make a paper template first and then transfer the shape on to the vinyl to be cut.

Applying adhesive

Finish all the fitting before sticking down the vinyl flooring. It will be too late to make changes once it is stuck into position. Not all vinyl sheeting needs gluing – it may be necessary only near doorways, for example – so check the manufacturer's instructions and use the appropriate adhesive as directed.

Soft flooring

The appeal of soft floorcoverings is their warmth and quiet. As well as conventional carpets and rugs, this category includes 'natural' floorcoverings made from a variety of grasses and vegetable fibres.

Natural-material floorcoverings

Grasses and vegetable fibres have been used for centuries as floorcoverings. Most are strong and hardwearing, and provide a smart alternative to carpets, used wall to wall or in rug form on wooden or concrete floors. They are, in the main, rather harsh or roughly textured, and not really suitable for floors where children might be crawling, or where it is usual to walk around barefoot.

Environmentally friendly and durable, natural floorcoverings are a popular choice in modern homes for their textural interest, neutral colours and ability to work well with other natural materials.

Natural-material floorcoverings stain permanently if water is spilt on them, so they are not suitable for use in the kitchen or bathroom. In addition, some can be slippery and are not suitable for use on stairs. These types of flooring (apart from rush matting) are laid in a similar way to carpet, although some cannot be stretched. They may need to be laid over underlay, although some of the latex-backed varieties can be stuck to the subfloor. When used as a close-covered carpet, all need to be professionally laid.

Coir

Formerly used only for doormats, coir, or coconut fibre, is now woven into coarse but interestingly textured flooring, which is sometimes dyed bright colours. It is usually supplied backed, but some narrow widths – for use in halls or corridors – are unbacked.

Seagrass

A tough tropical grass spun and woven into coarse matting, seagrass is usually left undyed, in a random mix of yellow, beige, green and a hint of russet. It is hardwearing, but not suitable for wet areas. Extra loose-laid mats are recommended as protection from furniture castors and wear in front of sofas. If laid on stairs, the grain should run parallel to the tread.

Sisal

Sisal is a whitish, stringy fibre that is woven into attractive herringbone, bouclé and ribbed patterns in a range of colours; it can also be stencilled. Sisal is not recommended for kitchens or bathrooms. A sisal and coir blend gives a finer weave and texture that is less scratchy underfoot. Sisal can stretch (even with a backing) and may need occasional refitting (a light spray of water can help shrink it back into shape). Like rush matting, sisal is inclined to shed fibres.

Other natural materials

Hemp is soft underfoot, but not as strong as some natural-material floorings. It is woven into attractive herringbone, ribbed and chevron textures. Jute looks similar to sisal and has a textured, ribbed weave. It is best used in areas of fairly light wear. Paper twine is twisted from strong, unbleached paper and made into rugs. Rush matting is hand- or machine-plaited into strips, sewn together to form standard-sized mats.

Some of the options

Coir, seagrass and sisal are widely used, but there are others. The natural fibres are often woven into a variety of patterns and can be bleached or dyed.

The 100 per cent coir from which this herringbone flooring is made is softened by soaking it in lagoons for up to ten months before it is woven.

A seagrass floorcovering is a fantastic alternative to carpet. For best results, do not use in the kitchen or bathroom, but hallways and stairs are fine, as it can take constant traffic.

This sisal flooring looks fantastic in any room, but for the living room or bedroom, combine with sheepskins or rugs to protect bare feet from the rough texture of the fibres.

A bitter chocolate version of sisal flooring, this dark woven matting makes a striking change in any room and would look stunning as a rug on a wooden floor.

Pros and cons of soft flooring

For
- Warm and cosy underfoot, although some natural-material floorcoverings are much less so
- Good insulation from cold and draughts
- Helps deaden sound
- Natural-material floorcoverings are environmentally friendly

Against
- Vulnerable to staining, even if treated
- Impractical in areas that get wet
- Some natural-material floorcoverings can be slippery, so are highly unsuitable for use on stairs

The abaca fibre from which this natural-material flooring is made comes from the banana plant family, and gives a much smoother and more comfortable surface than many other woven natural-material floorcoverings.

This softly golden natural-material floorcovering made from jute gives a warm glow to any room, although it will not withstand very heavy wear and tear.

Carpets

Carpets are a popular option, and the choice – even before you consider colour or design – is immense. What they are made of and how they are made affects their feel and durability. Read labels carefully and take advice from the supplier. Make sure that prices quoted include the necessary underlay and fitting.

Construction methods

Woven carpet has the pile closely woven into the backing to produce a high-density surface – Axminster and Wilton refer to weaving methods, not the source of the carpet. Woven carpets are beautiful and durable, but can also be expensive. The majority of carpets in the mid-price range are non-woven. Most are tufted, made by 'needling' the pile into a backing, with a secondary backing for strength and stability.

Types of carpet pile

Density of pile refers to the number of tufts per square centimetre or inch – the thicker the pile, the more hardwearing the carpet – and for areas of heavy use, a looped or kinked pile is a sensible choice.

- Close, or velvet, is luxurious, but will show 'tracking' where it has been walked on.
- Hard-twist has an extra kink in it, like curly hair. This adds to its wearability, but can make it slippery, so it is best not used on stairs.
- Long, or shag, is usually looped or twisted. This creates an interesting texture, but is very difficult to keep looking good.
- Looped has a characteristic nubbly texture. When made with mixed fibres, this may 'pill' into small balls of loose fibre, so choose a 100 per cent wool – often called Berber-style.
- Saxony is a dense, mid-length pile, best for areas of light to medium use.
- 'Sculptured' or 'carved' pile is a mixture of cut and looped, creating a heavily textured effect; for medium to light use.

Carpet fibres

Some fibres are more resistant to stains than others. However, whatever the carpet manufacturers claim, carpets are not truly washable, even when treated with a stain inhibitor.

Wool The traditional fibre for carpets, wool has a natural resilience. A mix of 80 per cent wool with 20 per cent easy-care synthetic (usually nylon) is considered to be the best fibre for carpets.

Synthetics Acrylic is the synthetic fibre that most closely resembles wool, but other synthetics include

Wall-to-wall carpet is hard to beat for sheer comfort and warmth, and a neutral colour allows plenty of scope for redecorating when you want to change the room's colour scheme.

nylon in various forms, polyester, polypropylene and viscose/rayon, either on their own or combined with other fibres.

Cotton This is used for washable rugs and to bulk out other fibres.

Silk This is still used in hand-knotted oriental carpets and rugs.

Underlay

Carpet lasts much longer and is more comfortable underfoot if it is cushioned by an underlay. Underlay will also minimize dust travelling up from floorboards. It can be the felted hairy type, or a rubber or plastic foam that increases the 'bounce' factor. Foam and rubber underlay are not suitable for stairs or heavily seamed areas. Underlay should be professionally fitted at the same time as the carpet.

Sizing up

Narrow 'body' or 'strip' widths are used as runners for halls and on stairs. Broadloom (woven on a wide loom) comes in multiples of 1 m (3 ft) up to 5 m (16 ft), so you can usually avoid having joins in a carpeted area.

Stair coverings

Stairs do not have to be covered. You could leave them exposed as natural wood, or stain or paint them – simulate a runner, for example, and carry the design down into the hall, and paint the floor to match. If you do decide to cover the stairs, however, safety is paramount – whatever you choose must be non-slip and non-trip, as well as hardwearing. Here are a few appropriate options to consider:

Close-carpeting Close-carpeting on the stairs is definitely a job for the expert. Not all carpets are suitable, so take advice from a professional. Carpet or matting is a good choice, as it helps deaden the sound of noisy footsteps on the stairs.

Carpet runner A runner leaves some of the stair on either side uncovered and is much simpler to fit than close carpeting because it is held in position with stair rods, which slot into clips or eyes screwed to the base of each stair riser. The carpet can be moved up or down the stairs occasionally to even out the wear – tuck under the excess at either the top or bottom of the stairs when laying.

Rubber tiles These can look very effective on stairs, with some design input. Choose, for example, two contrasting colours for the tread and the riser, or have nosings (the front edge of the tread) in a different colour. Alternatively, you could create a striking patchwork effect by using several different colours of tile.

Ceramic tiles Especially suitable for a Mediterranean or North African style, ceramic tiles on the stairs are noisy, but could inspire an interesting design feature. They need to be professionally laid.

A thick rug softens both the look and feel of wooden floorboards in the bedroom, providing a touch of luxury to bare feet and textural interest to the décor.

Carpet tiles

These can be cut easily to fit around awkward shapes, making them useful for small or irregularly shaped rooms. Individual tiles can be lifted for cleaning or replacing, but, despite claims to the contrary, this does not make them ideal for wet areas. They should be fixed either with a flexible adhesive at each corner or with a special double-sided tape. Carpet tiles present interesting design possibilities, such as chequerboard and chevrons, borders, stripes and checks – and even, with precise cutting, inlaid motifs.

Rugs

Rugs add colour and interest to a room, as well as providing protection for carpet or wood – and you can take them with you when you move home. Match your rugs to your style: ethnic alternatives to expensive oriental rugs include a wide variety of kelims, dhurries and animal skins, while felt, cotton and rag rugs suit a cottage style.

For safety reasons, especially in a household with children, lay rugs on a non-slip backing so that they do not slide on smooth floors or ruck up on carpets.

Working with colour

Understanding colour

The most powerful decorating tool of all, colour is usually the first thing we notice about a room. It creates mood, atmosphere and impact, and allows you to express aspects of your personality. It can be used to stimulate or to relax, and can bring a touch of sunshine into a dark, dismal area. Colour can also be used to effect some visual tricks and help disguise the proportions of a room.

The colour wheel

The colour wheel shows how the spectrum of colours turns full circle, each colour graduating into the next. It is made up of three sets of colours:

Primary colours These are red, yellow and blue, which cannot be obtained by mixing.

Secondary colours Obtained by mixing equal parts of two primary colours, the secondary colours are orange (red and yellow), green (yellow and blue) and violet (blue and red).

Tertiary colours These are mixes of a primary and a neighbouring secondary, for example blue-green and orange-red.

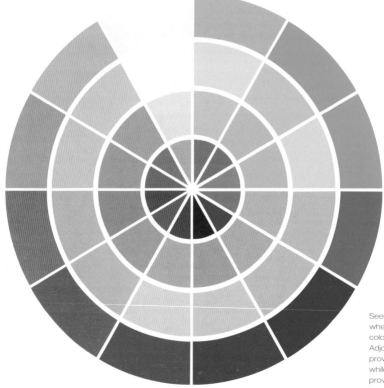

Seeing colours as spokes of a wheel enables you to judge how colours relate to one another. Adjoining colours on the wheel provide subtle colour schemes, while those opposite each other provide dramatic contrast.

Different tints and shades of the same pure colour are always a safe option when deciding which colours to combine in the same room.

Tonal variations

The infinite subtleties of colours are obtained by the addition of black, grey and white. These do not feature on the colour wheel in their own right because, strictly speaking, they are not colours at all but an absence or saturation of light.

You will find colours referred to indiscriminately as hues, tints, shades and tones, but these actually have specific meanings:

- Hues are pure colours, without the addition of neutrals.
- Tints are hues of one colour with varying degrees of white added.
- Shades are obtained by adding black to a hue.
- Tones, sometimes called mid-tones, result from the addition of grey.

Warm and cool colours

The colours on the red/orange/yellow side of the wheel are considered warm and appear to advance towards you, and are often used for intimate spaces, while the colours on the blue/green side are cool and appear to recede, and can be used to make a space look larger (although a strong blue can be enclosing). The warmth or coolness of a mixed colour varies greatly according to the predominance of the hue used in the mix – some greens can be warm, if there is more yellow in them, or cool if there is more blue, for example.

Handy hints

- Colour is affected by light, so consider your chosen colours by natural daylight at different times of the day, and also by the room's artificial lighting.
- The amount of colour used affects its apparent intensity, be it on the walls or floor, so try to see a colour on the scale at which it will be used to judge its impact.
- Our perception of colour is affected by neighbouring colours. A small red and white print, for instance, will appear pink from a short distance away.
- Neutrals are invaluable in the colour palette (see page 102). Use them in effective ways to provide harmony or to tone down a strong scheme.

Although traditionally thought to clash with each other, pink and red are next to each other on the colour wheel and so can work together very effectively.

Since adjacent hues on the colour wheel are pleasing on the eye, blues and violets are always a successful combination. Touches of pale gold prevent the scheme appearing too bland.

Choosing colours

Since the visible spectrum is huge, colour possibilities are almost limitless. A red scheme, for example, can vary from crimson to scarlet, or terracotta to shocking pink, and it can be adapted for very different living areas. In a formal dining room, lit for evening entertaining, rich crimson tones can be very romantic; in a sunny family kitchen, the warm tones of terracotta tiles and accessories can appear friendly and inviting. In a bedroom, combining deep and pale tones of rose in the wallpaper, bed linen and curtains can produce a country-style look. For something unusual in the bathroom, consider teaming shocking pink flooring with wallpaper decorated with a sugar pink design.

For a colour scheme that is strikingly different, you could decorate areas of your home in bold blocks of primary colours. Think how a spacious and sparsely furnished sunny hallway or living room could look warm and welcoming with a daffodil yellow ceiling, bleached wood floors, orange curtains and turquoise cushions and accessories set against deep blue-grey walls. But this is only one possible colour scheme from the myriad of options available – use the colour wheel to help you select suitable hues.

Colour inspirations

You might like to build an entire colour scheme around a single item such as a rug, a ceramic piece or an item of furniture. For example, your imagination could be inspired by a wooden dresser painted a rough apple green colour. This colour contrasts wonderfully with brown, and so is ideally suited to a room with a natural wood floor, unpainted brick walls and bare pine furniture. The effect could be further heightened with additional touches of the same green – in cushion covers, painted window frames and a few accessories.

Stencilling lively motifs on walls and furniture (see page 32) is another way to add bold splashes of colour. The subject of the motif could vary from room to room – to reflect changing uses and activities – or stay consistent throughout, and so act as a unifying decorative element. In this way, you can begin to build bridges between the decorative approaches in different areas of your home.

The importance of your choice

As you will see in more detail on the following pages, your choice of colours can make a room seem smaller or larger, cramped or spacious, warmer or cooler, brighter or more subdued. Knowing which colours to

Warm red suggests intimacy and can be effective in the bedroom, providing you take care not to swamp the room and make it too dark. Neutrals always provide a good counterbalance.

Regarded as an appetite-inducing colour, red is ideal for dining rooms, but it must not be allowed to overdominate. Using it on just one feature wall is an ideal compromise.

intimacy, use plenty of deeper tones and bold colours in the warm red range, and include lots of colourful patterns and textures.

Decorating in rich, bright colours will help to enliven a dull, predominantly shady room, while subtle colours and darker tones will subdue a sunny room. Warm, bold colours and strong contrasts create a lively and inviting atmosphere, while cool tones and subtle contrasts create more of a calm and relaxed environment. The effects created, however, do depend on the intensity of the colours you choose, and whether you use them in their pure forms or mixed in the form of tints, tones and shades.

Despite all these 'rules', using colour is a very personal matter. Like music, colour varies enormously in the mood and atmosphere it creates. So allow your own style to develop as you plan and have confidence in whatever colours appeal to you. Remember, if you have a favourite colour you are wary of using all over, there are plenty of less obtrusive ways to incorporate it in your scheme – in the accessories (see page 103), on a feature wall or by way of an item of painted furniture.

select to achieve the precise effect you want is not always an easy task. The secret of success lies in the skill with which the fabrics, furniture, wallpaper and decorative objects are selected and mixed. So it is vital to look, learn and plan as much as you can before actually buying anything.

Developing a colour sense

Everyone can develop an eye for successful colour combinations, and become aware of how colours and patterns work together. To explore your own taste and style, observe the colour combinations in everyday life. Take note of your surroundings wherever you are and study window displays, magazines and advertising brochures. Make notes of what you like and don't like, cut out interesting pictures and make yourself a mood board (see page 106). You will soon develop your own personal preferences and discover the combinations you find most pleasing.

Learning the 'rules'

Besides consulting the colour wheel (see page 92), there are some broad guidelines to help you choose colours for your home. For example, to emphasize spaciousness, choose a limited range of white, pale pastels or shades of blue. To suggest cosiness and

Whites and neutrals suggest spaciousness and airiness, but can be too dull used alone. A touch of pale blue in the accessories can lift and complete the colour scheme.

Reds, oranges and yellows

Warm colours will make a room seem cosy and intimate, but use with care, because if the colour values are too strong or bright, the result can be overpowering – even claustrophobic.

Red

Red is the colour of vitality, passion and energy – it is bright, exciting and dramatic. As it's also the strongest advancing colour, it can be overpowering and will make a room seem smaller if the stronger hues are used. The strength of its warmth works well in cold bathrooms and kitchens, and, because it is a welcoming colour, it is good for halls. Red is also an appetite-inducing colour, and because it makes food (especially meat) look appetizing, it has long been a favourite choice for the dining room.

When red is tinted, it becomes pink. Often regarded as a feminine colour associated with love and romance (pastel pinks and deeper rose will help you create a really romantic bedroom), pink is in fact a very versatile colour with many different shades. Warm pinks, like shell and salmon pink, help thaw the chill of cool rooms and are a good background for dark furniture. Although all pinks bring some warmth to a colour scheme, cool pinks are those with a degree of blue in their makeup, for example raspberry pink, fuchsia and pinky-mauve – a mysterious, sophisticated colour, ideal for bedrooms and bathrooms. Deeper tones and shades of red are more subtle, for example rose, plum and claret. These create an elegant look in traditional living rooms, hallways, dining rooms and studies.

Orange

A warm, friendly and happy colour, orange is almost as strong and advancing as red, and can be used in a similar way. It can be highly stimulating, especially if combined with black, grey, white or with its complementary colour, blue (see page 100). These are combinations that can work successfully in children's playrooms, bathrooms and kitchens. Orange combined with bright red and a touch of cactus green or turquoise provides a Mexican or 'ethnic'-themed colour scheme; orange teamed with lilac or purple produces a modern funky-looking room, while orange used with yellows and browns creates a restful rustic look.

Tinted oranges become peach, coral or apricot – delicate, feminine and romantic colours that work well in bedrooms. When it is greyed down, orange becomes terracotta, tan or chestnut brown, producing very versatile decorating colours that can be used with white or cream to create an elegant, warm, inviting scheme for a hall, living room or home office.

From the warm side of the colour wheel, reds, oranges and yellows appear to advance towards you, making a room seem smaller. They are therefore safest used in a large room.

The touches of blue and lilac in the stripes provide a cool contrast to the warmth of the predominant red, yellow and orange colours in this living room.

Use reds, oranges and yellows to...

• Warm up rooms that appear chilly – particularly cold bathrooms and kitchens, and any north- or east-facing rooms.
• Promote a cosy and intimate atmosphere, for example in bedrooms or dining rooms.
• Brighten rooms with limited natural light (see page 104).
• Make walls and ceilings advance towards you, thereby making large rooms look smaller or high-ceilinged rooms look cosier.
• Make rooms such as hallways appear inviting and welcoming.
• Counterbalance or add warm contrasts to cool colour schemes.
• Draw attention to a particular feature, such as an attractive chimney breast or alcove.

Note: Many tints, shades and tones of these colours will perform the above functions.

Yellow

Yellow is a joyful colour associated with sunshine, warmth and summer. It is also the colour of the mind, intellect and creative energy. Bright yellow will bring light and sunshine into the darkest room, but it is highly stimulating, so use with care. Neutral backgrounds, and the classic Scandinavian mix of yellow with blue, will help to ensure that it is not overpowering. Yellow is a good colour for hallways, bathrooms, home offices and children's rooms – in nurseries, especially where the sex of the baby is not known in advance, and in older children's rooms to provide an intellect-stimulating environment to help them with their homework!

Greyed yellow becomes mustard, rich gold or subtle honey brown. These are the colours to use in sophisticated schemes for traditional drawing rooms, bedrooms and studies. A yellow with a hint of olive green can be elegant – but take care as it can look grey under artificial light. Pale yellow has a highly reflective quality and will make a small space seem larger and brighter. When it goes towards green, it becomes lime, which can be stimulating and is a good accent colour.

This cheering, sunny yellow colour could be overpowering on its own, but it works well with the reflective metallic finishes and glassware in this compact kitchen.

Greens, blues and violets

Greens, blues and violets are on the cooler side of the colour wheel, but often appear far from cold. Many of them mix easily together and there are fewer strident colours, making them a 'safe' choice on which to base a scheme.

Green

Lively and invigorating, true green is the 'balance' colour, halfway between the warm and cool colours of the spectrum. In all its many guises, which allow it to be a restful, vibrant or zingy colour (compare grey-

Use greens, blues and violets to...
- Alter the perceived dimensions of an area. Cool colours, especially the paler values, make walls and ceilings appear to go away from you, thereby making the space seem larger than it actually is. For example, you can make a narrow area such as a landing look wider.
- Balance the feel of a room that receives a lot of light (see page 104).
- Create a feeling of airy spaciousness.
- Add contrasting cool accents to a warm colour scheme.
- Make an unattractive feature fade into the background.
- Create a calm and relaxed environment.

The use of grey-green in a decorative scheme results in a subtle and sophisticated look that can help soften the potentially stark appearance of some modern décor.

green with apple green or citric lime), it's an easy hue to live with and a popular choice for decorating schemes. The colour of nature and guaranteed to suggest 'landscape', green is a particularly good choice for a city apartment or dull townhouse to bring a sense of the outdoors indoors.

Some greens can be very cold, but mix well with contrasting warm colours to ward off the chill. Pale tints of green create a very spacious look for small bathrooms and bedrooms, and when green goes towards blue, it becomes minty, which is very refreshing in a kitchen, and on to aqua, an ever-popular colour for marine-themed bathrooms.

Dark shades of green are rich and sophisticated – deep malachite or forest green work well with both traditional and modern styles of décor. Used as the main colour, they work best in rooms with bright natural light and need balancing with white or cream and reflective surfaces. Alternatively, use dark green as an accent colour with pastel pink or yellow.

Blue is a versatile colour that combines well with most other colours. Here, pale blues are teamed with white and pale violet for a particularly pleasing scheme.

The greyed tones and shades of blue can be subtle. They look very effective teamed with crisp neutrals – white or cream – or warmed up with contrasting accents of orange, yellow or bright pink.

Violet

In its strongest value, a regal purple, this is a vibrant and demanding colour that needs neutral contrasts. It works particularly well with its adjacent colours on the wheel – blue, blue-green and pink-violet.

The pale tints of lilac and lavender are delicate and feminine, giving a romantic feel to a bedroom or bathroom, or a sophisticated look to a living room. Lilacs teamed with lime greens are very contemporary.

Greyed lighter tints give subtle heathers that are changeable in different lights, while the darker shades yield rich plums and aubergines. These work well in period settings, teamed with golds, cream and pale yellow in drawing rooms or dining rooms.

Greyed values of green can be very subtle. Sage, rosemary and olive greens are elegant, and look good in country-style drawing rooms, classic hallways or modern dining rooms, but, like yellow-greens, need to be well lit so that they don't look gloomy at night.

Blue

Blue is the colour of harmony, peace and devotion. It is associated with the sky and wide vistas, and creates an impression of space. But because it is basically a cool colour, use it with care. Blue is fairly low in reflective value, and will diffuse and soften strong sunlight, calming down over-bright rooms. However, clear bright blue can also be very cheerful, which makes it ideal for children's rooms or a basement kitchen.

The pure values of blue, especially as it starts to go towards green – peacock or turquoise – can be very demanding, so use these in small amounts if the room is small. Lightened to aqua, its freshness works well in bathrooms and kitchens.

Another decorative scheme proving that pale lilac and lavender combine well with blue, working together here to give a romantic yet sophisticated feel to a seaside room.

Using harmonious and contrasting colours

The colour wheel is an invaluable tool. It illustrates the natural neighbours and contrasts of each colour, and is a ready reminder of how colours relate to each other. Use it as a guide to which colours work well together as well as to inspire unusual combinations.

Harmonious colours

Harmonious colour schemes are based on neighbours on the colour wheel and always create a relaxing atmosphere. Pick colours that directly adjoin each other on the wheel or are very close to one another, for example choose three or four colours of a similar value that originate from a single primary colour, or team a primary colour with one or more of its neighbours for a more striking effect.

A monochromatic scheme

A tighter variation of a harmonious colour scheme is to work within a single colour, from its lightest tint to its darkest shade, but without straying sideways into the next segment of the colour wheel. This results in a monochromatic, or tonal, scheme.

Paint colour cards comprising strips of different tints and shades of the same colour are readily available from paint stockists and are ideal for helping build a monochromatic scheme. There will probably be several cards to cover all the possibilities within a single colour, giving you a wide range to play with. You might use the palest value of the colour for the woodwork, a slightly stronger tint for the ceiling, a mid-tone for the walls and a deeper shade for the floorcovering. Look for patterned wallpapers or fabrics that use different tones of the same colour to help prevent the potential boredom of using just one colour.

Most monochromatic schemes need brightening up with accent colours – look back at the colour wheel to see which hues contrast with your chosen colour.

A harmonious colour scheme like this one relies on using colours that are neighbours on the colour wheel – in this case soft, pale violets and blues.

Contrasting colours

Contrasting colours (also known as complementaries) produce colour schemes based on direct opposites on the colour wheel – red and green, yellow and violet, blue and orange. The special relationship between contrasting colours means that each brings out the best in the other. By choosing contrasting colours, you automatically team a warm colour with a cool one. If you focus on a strong hue of a warm colour (red, for example) for a minute or so, then look away, you will see an 'after colour' of its opposite (green) – the eye plays strange tricks!

When used together, contrasting colours can be stimulating and exciting, but if the colour values of both are too bright, the effect can be disturbing.

The pink of the sofa and scatter cushions are a welcome addition to this living room, bringing some life and warmth to the understated, neutral colours.

Handy hints

• For the most successful colour scheme, choose a harmonious, a monochromatic (tonal) or a contrasting (complementary) scheme, rather than picking colours from the wheel at random.

• Colours on opposite sides of the colour wheel fight for dominance and tend to clash if used in their 'pure' intensities, so use them in extremely unequal proportions or mute one or both of the colours as lighter or darker tones.

• As a general rule, in a monochromatic scheme, lighter tones produce subtle harmonies, while darker tones give bolder and more dramatic results.

• Using furnishing fabrics and materials with various different textures is particularly important in a monochromatic colour scheme (see opposite).

However, contrasts include the colours in all their tints, tones and shades – so a scheme based on sugar pink and olive green or turquoise and terracotta, for example, will still be contrasting, but not overpowering. Such 'diluted' contrasts work well in rooms where you don't want to relax too much, but don't want to be continually stimulated either.

A contrasting colour scheme can also be split-complementary, by using a primary colour combined with the two tertiary colours that flank its opposite on the colour wheel – such as blue with red-orange and yellow-orange.

You can create an equally successful contrasting colour scheme without actually using direct opposites, as long as you combine warm and cool colours, for example blue with yellow, orange with jade-green or green with violet.

Don't use your chosen contrasting colours in equal amounts in your decorating scheme, as the colours will all fight for attention and cancel each other out. Instead, feature on one predominant colour. You could introduce a third colour if you like, but certainly use no more than three.

A few accessories in hot orange introduce interest and touches of warmth to this monochromatic room scheme, which showcases the tints and shades of violet.

Working with neutrals

The only three true neutrals are white, black and the in-between of grey, but there are also the accepted neutrals – or naturals – the broken whites, creams, beiges, taupes and soft browns of stone, wood, undyed linen or wool.

Just neutrals

Neutral colours on their own create a harmonious scheme, and are often effective for a very contemporary look, but the pale neutrals can be difficult to keep clean. A basic rule of interior design is to consider the practical alongside the aesthetic. It would be impractical, for example, to decorate a hallway in pale cream with an off-white carpet and expect it to cope with a regular flow of visitors, muddy feet and even bike or baby-buggy wheels. On the other

Subtle contrasting accent colours in warm orange and brown, teamed with rough-textured fabrics and smooth, polished wood surfaces, add interest to this neutral living-room scheme.

A pale neutral room scheme, devoid of any other colour, creates a very contemporary, elegant and restful grown-up look, not really practical for homes with small children and pets.

hand, such a pure and simple colour scheme would provide a pleasing atmosphere of calm in a main bedroom or a living room.

Black and white, especially used together to create a bold pattern, is the most stimulating and disturbing of neutral combinations, and needs to be used with care.

Importance of texture

If using neutral colours on their own in a room scheme, a good mixture of contrasting textures – smooth, rough, hard, soft, shiny and matt – is important for providing visual interest and stimulation (see page 124), to avoid the scheme looking too bland.

Untreated wood, bamboo, rattan, wicker, bare brick walls, rough plaster, natural floorcoverings, unglazed terracotta, paper lampshades, undyed muslin and faux fur are just some of the rough textural possibilities in neutral colours. Smooth and shiny textures available in neutral colours include stone and ceramic surfaces, glossy leather furniture, laminate flooring, polished wood and gloss paint.

Neutrals in a mixed scheme

On their own, neutrals can be rather boring, so it is a good idea to enliven them with contrasting accents (see box, right). Follow the basic rule of relating these accents to the overall style of the room, and choose warm or cool colours according to the atmosphere you want. With a predominantly neutral scheme, you could use several different accent colours, mixing cool and warm, or different tonal values of one or two colours.

Neutrals can also make a major contribution to other colour schemes. They form a good background for printed fabrics and wallcoverings, and provide an element of quiet contrast, often unnoticed.

When is white not white?

Many so-called neutrals, especially near-whites, are actually very pale tints of a 'proper' colour. Creams can have hints of yellow or pink, while 'greiges' (grey/beige) and browns can have undertones of warm orange or cool blue. These origins may not be apparent until placed near another colour or neutral. Pure white woodwork can make an off-white carpet look dirty, for example, and a subtly shaded tweed fabric can just appear grey in the wrong company.

A neutral room scheme of whites and off-whites provides a good backdrop for dark wood furniture and a subtly coloured but boldly patterned wallcovering.

Adding accent colours

Use accessories to add accent colours, together with a patterned fabric, wallpaper or flooring. The dominant colour should relate to the main scheme, with secondary colours echoed in other plain accessories. To vary the tonal balance, add warm accents to a cool scheme, cool ones to a warm scheme and strong, rich colours to neutrals. Look at the following ways to introduce accent colours:

In a living room or dining room:
- Cushions or padded seat covers
- Rugs
- Plants and flowers
- Pictures, prints and photographs (including interesting frames)
- Glass or china
- Lamp bases and shades
- Table covers
- Candles and holders

In the kitchen:
- Pots and pans
- China, pottery and glass
- Tea towels, aprons and oven gloves (pot gloves)
- Pictures
- Herbs in decorative pots

In the bathroom:
- Towels and bath mats
- Boxes and baskets for toiletries
- Pictures
- Plants

In the bedroom:
- Bedside lamps and shades
- Pictures
- Rugs
- Cushions and throws

Note: Bed linen should be an integral part of the scheme, not an accessory.

Creating a colour scheme

The colour scheme you choose for decorating any area of your home may be determined by a number of factors – the size and shape of the room, existing furnishings and furniture, the lighting, the mood you wish to create and the function of the room.

Working with existing features

In an ideal world, you would be able to create a colour scheme with absolutely no constraints at all. But in reality, most of us have to work a new colour scheme around an existing item such as a bathroom suite, kitchen units, curtains, a fitted carpet or a sofa. As a basic rule, choose one colour of an existing item and use it as the cornerstone of your colour scheme.

Room size is an additional factor when it comes to colour schemes. For example, small rooms can feel claustrophobic if strong colours are used (see pages 96 and 110). The room's architecture and natural light may also affect your colour decisions.

Architectural factors

The architecture can suggest an overall style for the room, and any interesting features should be enhanced. An attractive fireplace is worth emphasizing – colour the chimney breast a rich dark tone to 'bring forward' a light-coloured fire surround, or paint it a pale colour to contrast with a dark surround. If the room has beautiful windows, give them a very simple treatment to enhance their natural shape.

Natural light

The orientation of the room will affect the daylight that it receives. For rooms without much morning light, choose colours from the warmer side of the colour spectrum. For those bathed in morning sunlight, which are cooler and darker in the evening, try to work with the paler 'sunshine' tones. Rooms that are bright and warm from midday onwards work best with cooler, receding colours.

Function and mood

When choosing a colour scheme, you must also consider the purpose of each room and how much it is used. For example, do you have a busy living room with a lot of activity in a small space? If so, lots of strong colours may add to the confusion. Instead, plan a scheme that provides a fairly neutral background.

Don't make the mistake of picking a colour simply because it is currently in fashion – you'll soon regret it! Whatever your colour scheme, think about how

Attractive architectural features can be emphasized by clever use of colour. For example, this pale painted chimney breast contrasts with the darker walls around it to make the fireplace stand out.

If you have to work around the colour of existing furniture, make this colour the basis of your scheme and match it with various closely related tones for a harmonious look.

frequently you may need to redecorate and how much you may want to spend. If you want to be able to create an entirely different atmosphere at minimal cost, keep the room's basic colour scheme fairly light and simple. You can then introduce strong colours with the curtains, blinds, painted woodwork, prints, plants, accessories and lighting – all of which can be changed with minimal disruption.

Balancing colours and patterns

It is important to relate the strength of colours and size of pattern to the scale on which they will be used. Bright colours and bold, jazzy patterns will look at least twice as strong on a large expanse of floor or wall, so always try to see as large a sample as possible. If you plan to paint a wall, use a tester pot on a length of lining paper and hang the painted paper in the room for a few days, moving it on to different walls to see how it looks in the varying light at different times of the day. If in doubt, choose a shade lighter than you think you want, since paint colours are notoriously difficult to assess from a small sample.

Combining patterns is one of the trickiest schemes to pull off successfully (see page 122). Use a mood board (see page 106) to experiment with different effects. It is often too broad a colour range that makes

pattern mixes look messy, so carefully study the colours that make up each design and aim for patterns that share a common palette.

Don't overlook the important part that neutrals play. Even a rich, colourful scheme will rely on white or cream for contrast, to emphasize the brilliance of the other colours and to avoid sensory overload.

It can be tricky mixing different types of pattern, so it helps to restrict pattern to small areas like cushions and to choose patterns with a common colour palette.

Making a mood board

Good colour schemes don't just happen – they have to be planned. Since nobody can 'carry colour' successfully in their eye, this means taking samples of decorating materials home, placing them together and looking at them under both daylight and artificial light.

What is a mood board?

A mood, or sample, board is a collection of visual ideas, colour swatches and sample materials for a specific project. The display of samples of all the proposed furnishings gives the effect, almost, of a miniature room, and professional interior designers always work up mood boards for their clients.

It is both useful and fun to create one yourself when planning a decorative scheme, as it's an excellent way to visualize your colour scheme and design concept, and avoid costly mistakes. The process of collecting ideas allows you to crystallize your thoughts and decide which ideas to develop further and which ones it would be best to drop.

How to make a mood board

Start by browsing through magazines and catalogues (they don't have to be on interior design) for inspirational images and design ideas you might like to consider for the room you intend to decorate. Cut out any pictures you like and once you have some ideas in mind and a starting point – this could be a main base colour, a favourite texture or a patterned fabric that you like – start collecting images and samples. Include colour cards from paint charts; swatches of fabric for curtains, upholstery and scatter cushions; pictures of lighting and key furniture; pieces of wallcoverings and samples of carpets or other floorcovering.

Handy hints

• Time spent planning the room to be decorated and making a mood board allows you to budget properly and helps avoid making decorating mistakes.

• Bear in mind that a room scheme you've seen somewhere else – perhaps in a plush hotel or restaurant – that you want to copy might not be totally practical for your lifestyle or size of room. It is important to be prepared to modify and come up with your own ideas rather than slavishly copying someone else's.

• Don't rush into completing your mood board. It's not something to be compiled in one go, but needs to evolve over a period of time as your ideas take shape, and you'll invariably change your mind several times along the way!

• Don't think about one aspect of the room in isolation. Everything should work together – colours, pattern and texture; furniture; wall, window and floor treatments; lighting.

Get yourself a large piece of cardboard or mounting board and lay your samples next to each other on the board. Arrange them in the general order of the room – with floorcovering at the bottom of the board and ceiling colour near the top – and make sure that the materials are more or less in the correct proportion. For example, wall and floor samples should be larger than the upholstery or curtain fabric.

Paste your pictures and samples on to the board and review how all the elements look together. If you decide that something doesn't work, remove it and keep looking for alternatives. It is better to spend a lot

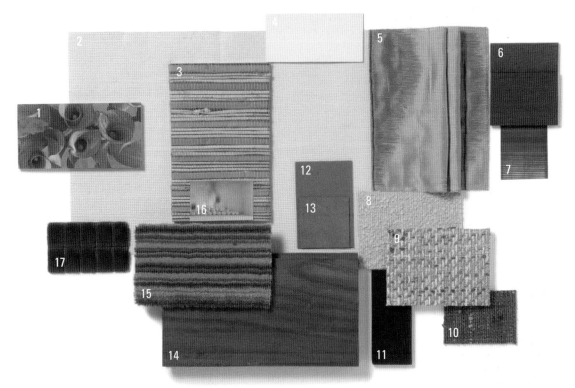

Elements of a mood board

1	Picture	7	Blinds: overall look	13	Tub chair 2
2	Main wallcovering	8	Sofa 1 fabric	14	Wood flooring sample
3	Covering for chimney breast	9	Sofa 2 fabric	15	Rug sample
4	Ceiling paint	10	Single chair fabric	16	Contemporary fireplace
5	Curtain fabric	11	Wood sample for shelving	17	Cushion fabric
6	Blinds: wood type	12	Tub chair 1		

of time and effort at this stage, researching and compiling a mood board, rather than completing your decorating and then deciding that you don't like the overall look of your new room.

Putting it into practice

The starting point for the mood board pictured above is the rug (15), which is striped in golds, greens, yellows and terracottas. It will be placed on a wooden floor in a living room and is the centrepiece around which the rest of the mood board is put together, providing an inspiring starting place for colour and texture.

Wallcoverings The main wallcovering is soft yellow-green, with a bolder texture and deeper colour on a grasscloth for the chimney breast to enhance the

modern fireplace. A paler yellow-green paint has been selected for the ceiling.

Window treatment A silky, textured fabric for curtains in a darker tone than the walls, but of a similar colour, has been chosen to enrich without distracting. Rattan blinds are to go under the curtains, providing privacy and filtering the light.

Upholstery Upholstery fabrics in contrasting textures in green, gold and terracotta complete the theme. The tweedy texture for the sofa cover contains some turquoise, which could be used, with terracotta, for extra accessories.

Decorative elements Paintings or prints can be introduced at the final stage to pull together all the elements of the design, including any accent colours.

Visual tricks with colour

As well as creating an atmosphere with colour, and visually heating or cooling a room, you can use colour together with pattern and light to play decorating tricks that appear to alter a room's proportions (see also pages 110 and 112) – far less expensive options than any structural alteration!

Lowering a ceiling

There are several options here. The most obvious is to paint the ceiling with a warm, advancing colour and the walls with a cool contrast. Alternatively, consider colouring the floor to match the ceiling, or at least use the same tonal value for both. If you prefer darker walls, then you can team them with a brilliant white ceiling, as it is a misconception that white ceilings always make a room look higher.

When choosing wallpaper, you could put a horizontal pattern on the walls, or divide them up using a picture rail or frieze. Other options include tenting the ceiling with fabric, investing in tall items of furniture or simply painting the cornicing/coving to contrast with the ceiling.

Adding height

There are a variety of useful techniques for dealing with a low ceiling, which can be tailored to suit any colour scheme. The first is to paint the ceiling a pale receding colour – sky blue is particularly effective. Otherwise, you could colour the ceiling a slightly lighter tone than the walls or match it to the background of any wallcovering. Using a light-reflecting finish on the ceiling may also be effective, but only if the plasterwork is in good condition. In addition, vertical stripes for wallpaper, curtains and blinds will help to direct attention away from a low ceiling, as will low-slung furniture.

Making a small room look larger

Pale receding colours – such as blues, greens and lilacs – and small patterns will create an illusion of space, as will light-reflecting shiny surfaces and textures, and mirrors. It is wise to avoid too much contrast in colour, choosing instead a harmonious, neutral or monochromatic scheme. Keep accessories simple, and avoid clutter.

Making a large room cosier

Warm, advancing colours and contrasting textures will bring instant warmth to a large room. Emphasize different features or areas with lighting and use bold patterns. Using complementary colours, for example curtains that contrast with walls and furniture that contrasts with the floor, will also draw a room in.

A large room can appear a little unwelcoming, but the use of warm, advancing colours will help to bring the walls in and make the room seem cosier.

This faux fireplace, in a contrasting colour that makes it stand out from its surroundings, helps distract attention away from the boxy shape of the room.

Camouflaging or enhancing features

Paint or colour unsightly features the same colour as the background – this is a particularly effective trick if you have unattractive radiators or built-in cupboards in your home. Otherwise, use receding colours, from the cooler half of the colour wheel, on both the feature and the background.

Conversely, paint or colour attractive features like an imposing chimney breast to contrast with the background, for example use neutral colours against a white background or an advancing colour (warm) against a receding one (cool). Otherwise, simply light your favourite feature dramatically.

Tricks with lighting

• A free-standing lamp placed in a corner can make a room appear larger, as can a central ceiling light because of reflection from the ceiling.
• Using table lamps makes a room feel more intimate and therefore smaller.
• Varying the height of the light sources in the room creates separate areas of light and shade, and makes rooms more interesting.

Adding width

This will really depend on the size, shape and purpose of the narrow area. Try painting or papering end walls in a bold, advancing colour or with a strong pattern, or if it's on a long corridor, paint or paper both long walls in a cool, receding colour. If there is a window at the end, try dressing it with floor-to-ceiling curtains in a companion fabric to the wall treatment. Other options include putting a well-lit, eye-catching piece of art or group of pictures on an end wall; hanging mirrors on one of the long walls; and making the floor seem wider with widthways stripes or a chequerboard effect. You could also try painting the skirting board (baseboard) to match the floor.

Making a box room less square

This is a very common problem, for which there are several very easy solutions that will instantly transform the space. Consider colouring one wall in a bold contrast to the other walls. Or, create a focal point in the centre of one wall such as a fireplace, opulent window treatment or bold drapes above a bed to contrast with the surrounding wall. You could even create a trompe l'oeil effect. If storage is an issue, use one wall for built-in furniture, decorated with contrasting panels or beading.

Painting the walls to match the sofa allows the natural light that floods through the imposing windows during the day to be the room's focal point rather than the angle of the walls.

Using colour in small rooms

Whatever main colour you choose for your decorating scheme, it will have greater dramatic impact on a small space than on a large one. Since you can decorate a small room relatively quickly and inexpensively, why not take the chance to experiment? You can try more unusual colour combinations and explore different textures and effects.

Illusion of spaciousness

Very pale colours make surfaces recede and seem less noticeable, thus creating the impression of spaciousness. The simplest way to ensure an uncluttered and restful effect in a small room is in fact to limit the basic décor to white. However, although white is a good choice for small rooms, it can be stark and boring if used in its pure form. By using just a hint of colour, you can begin to make more of a statement. For a start, walls can be painted in one of the enormous range of almost-whites – from warm peach to soft, cool blue. Texture, too, can add interest and warmth to a predominantly white scheme.

Incorporate curtains, cushions, small prints or rugs as a way of introducing colours in occasional splashes. When the time comes for a new look, all you need to do is change the accessories. However, if you have a lot of furniture and accessories, it may be better to select plain fabrics and muted tones to avoid a cluttered feeling in the room.

Experiment with colour

Despite the oft-quoted guidelines, don't feel limited to white and the off-whites just because you are decorating a small room. Why not start with a strong colour, such as yellow or purple? There is no basic problem here, as long as you limit your colour scheme to different tints and shades of a single colour. You can

Using just a hint of colour in a small room can offer a good alternative to plain white. The use of muted colour can be continued in the soft furnishings to add additional interest.

even incorporate dark colours in a small room as long as you avoid creating too many colour contrasts or combining them with bright, richly coloured or patterned furnishings. If you include too many competing colours, a small room can end up looking cramped and cluttered.

If you are painting in bold colours, be aware that when applied to the wall, paint always ends up darker than the colour suggested by the swatch card.

Limiting the colour of walls, floor, furniture and accessories to a restricted range of pale neutral tints helps make a small room appear larger than it is.

Handy hints

- If you use dark colours in a small room, make sure that the lighting is adequate so that they don't look dull and gloomy.
- Since mirrors reflect both light and space, they can dramatically transform a small room. They are particularly effective in small spaces and corners, where they can be angled in specific directions to highlight interesting features.
- Experiment with indirect lighting, such as uplighters. It influences subtle colours and gives an extra dimension to small spaces, particularly in alcoves and corners.
- Introducing texture in accessories and fabric can help give a small room interest, dimension and depth.

Illusion of height

In a small room with a low ceiling, you can use colour to give an illusion of height and space. If the room has no decorative features, simply paint the ceiling white and the walls a single almost-white tone, from skirting boards (baseboards) to ceiling. If the room has traditional mouldings such as dado or picture rails and cornicing, you can 'shade up' by painting each horizontal 'band' of the wall a subtle tonal variation of white.

For example, start by painting the ceiling white, the cornice an almost-white tone, then the area above the dado rail with a touch more colour. Carry on like this down to the skirting board (baseboard). The floor will be the deepest colour, but avoid very dark floor tones, which will make the room look even smaller than it is.

Rooms within rooms

Many houses have deep alcoves, recesses or even a box room, which can be modified to make a room within a room. If the area is reasonably large, then an en-suite bathroom may be a possibility. If the space is smaller, it could be ideal as a walk-in closet. Natural light will probably be restricted, if not absent altogether, so you need to pay particular attention to the colours used and the way they are affected by different types of artificial lighting.

You don't have to stick to pale colours in small rooms. Here, a feature has been made of a deep alcove by wallpapering it in a bold, contrasting colour.

Using colour in large rooms

Making a small room feel spacious is a familiar decorative challenge. Less frequent, perhaps, but equally challenging is the task of making a large, high-ceilinged room feel warm, intimate and friendly. In both of these situations, colour is a vital tool for producing the particular effect you want to achieve.

Which colours?

Warm-coloured surfaces in reds, oranges and yellows and other deep, rich colours give the illusion of advancing towards the viewer, so they are an ideal choice when you want to make distant walls seem nearer and the room cosier. In contrast, cool blue and green tones give a feeling of movement away from the viewer, so they can make an already large space seem larger and airier. There are a few decorating solutions that will guide you towards a suitable scheme.

A large room can withstand – and even benefit from – strong, pure colours. In fact, decorating it in a variety of colours, tones and textures is another way of making it appear intimate. All the vivid contrasts break up large expanses of space, creating interest and a feeling of warmth. It is a good idea to link these strong colours with their very pale equivalents – or neutral colours such as tones of grey – to avoid garish results.

Using pattern

Not only can large rooms take strong, pure colours with ease, they can also be made to appear more welcoming or intimate by the use of bold, flamboyant pattern on the walls (see page 120). This might be desirable in a large living room or bedroom.

Lowering a high ceiling

As outlined on page 108, there are a number of simple decorating tricks for reducing the apparent height of a high-ceilinged room. One method is to paint the ceiling in a dark, rich hue such as a brick red, possibly matching the floorcovering, then paint the walls in a complementary pale colour. This will add intimacy and, at the same time, avoid a drab or dull atmosphere.

If the walls of the room have dado rails or other interesting features, paint these in a contrasting lighter tone to create another focal point and further break up the expanse of wall surface. Alternatively, paint both the ceiling and the top of the walls down to the dado rail in one dark colour, the dado rail in the contrasting pale colour and the lower walls in a medium hue that complements the ceiling and upper walls. This will give the illusion of a much more compact room with a lower ceiling height.

The dark-painted pillar in the middle of this large, light room helps both anchor the high ceiling and break up the space so as to unite the distinct living and dining zones.

Creating zones

In a very large, open-plan room that needs some sense of unity, one way to achieve a feeling of intimacy is to create several clearly marked zones within the space. Each zone can be defined by its colour scheme, as well as by its furniture and lighting (see page 196). For example, to break up a large living room, choose perhaps four complementary hues – one for a dining corner, another for studying, another by the windows for daytime work and another for evening relaxation and socializing. (In the same way, you can use colour to define the separate functions of dual-purpose rooms like a home office/spare bedroom or a kitchen/diner.)

Choose colours that are sufficiently different to provide the desired contrast, but not so far apart in the spectrum that they clash and compete for attention. Link the colours together by interspersing some neutral tones, such as beige or grey, and use these in shared features such as the flooring or colour of the skirting board (baseboard).

Orange-coloured walls evoke a sense of warmth and intimacy – ideal for a cosy dining area – while the contrasting picture rail helps break up the walls and creates a focal point.

Creating areas of interest

• If you decorate a room in predominantly warm, dark colours, introduce furnishings in pale tones of the same warm colours for harmony and brightness.
• Create two well-defined but linked areas in a large room by decorating one area in subtle warm tones and the other in similarly subtle cool tones.
• Try painting just one wall of a large room in a dark hue to create an area of intimacy.
• Experiment with lighting to create different areas of interest in a large space, such as recessed lights for soft background effects, spotlights for work surfaces and display lights for focal points.

Working
with
pattern

Choosing patterns

Like colour, pattern can serve many functions. It can be a focal point or a backdrop, and it can alter the apparent dimensions of a room. Patterned wallcoverings can soften angles and are more effective than plain surfaces for disguising an odd-shaped room or covering uneven walls.

Where to start?

When choosing a pattern, consider how effectively a large area of pattern will complement or contrast with your existing or proposed colour and design scheme. **Mood and function** Patterns influence the mood of a room, so start by considering the room's function. Large, bold patterns – like deep, rich colours – are intense and active, and work best as focal points in large living areas. Small, subtle patterns – like pale, neutral colours – offer a less-challenging backdrop.

The predominant colours in a pattern influence mood. Reds have a warm, welcoming quality; blues are restful and calming; browns and oranges are warm; yellows are bright and reflective; greens have a natural, cool and spacious feel. Patterns in pale, neutral tones of these colours act like texture to add depth and interest. **Colour scheme** Think about the basic colour scheme with which the pattern will contrast or harmonize. If the pattern is fairly small, it will take on the appearance of a single colour when seen from a distance. You can then use the principles of colour matching (see pages 92–95) to decide whether it works with the rest of the décor. **Style of pattern** A common mistake is to choose a pattern that is either too dark or too fussy. Don't forget to consider both the lighting and the size of the area you are decorating. If you are not certain what pattern to choose, opt for one with an off-white background and colours that subtly contrast with or complement the other colours in the room.

Striped patterns in just two colours can appear quite formal, whereas multi-coloured stripes like those on the walls, bedding, floor and furniture in this bedroom produce a fun, modern look.

Balance Balance is all important. Too little variety of colour, tone, pattern or texture and the room may seem lifeless. Too much and it can look chaotic. If you already have a neutral colour scheme, you have the scope to balance it with a variety of rich patterns. But if you have heavily patterned, richly coloured curtains, consider a plain wallcovering in a muted tone of the predominant colour in the pattern.

Types of pattern

Just as there is an infinite range of colours, there is a huge variety of patterns from which to choose. Patterns are either static or dynamic. A static pattern is one where the eye remains within the design – geometric checks, or a small repeated motif, for example. With a dynamic pattern, the eye is constantly travelling from one part of the design to the other – these include damasks and twining floral and leaf designs.

If you are mixing patterns, think carefully about the combinations (see page 122), and consider the atmosphere and style you are after.

Stripes

Depending on the combination of colours used and the width of the stripes, a stripy design can be subtle (like candy stripes) or bold (like deckchair stripes). Stripes work well on walls, floors, upholstery and soft furnishings, but take care to use the correct width of stripe for the size of the area. Regimented stripes in two contrasting colours can provide a formal look, which is particularly effective on blinds, and on walls

A mix of gingham and different-sized floral patterns is typical of a country-style look and these fabrics work well together as long as they share similar colours.

up to dado rail height in period rooms. Stripes with blurred lines in muted colours create a very different, more relaxed effect.

Use stripes to alter the perceived dimensions of an area. For example, bold, vertical stripes increase the apparent height of a room, while horizontal stripes make walls appear longer and lower, and can make a narrow room appear wider. A striped hall carpet looks smart and welcoming as it draws the viewer in.

Checks

Checks can vary in size from large-scale bold squares and trellis-style diagonal checks to a minuscule two-colour check design that gives the appearance of a solid colour from a distance. Checks work well with both solid colours and stripes.

Gingham (white checked with another colour), once regarded quintessential country kitchen and often mixed with florals, looks equally good in modern rooms with surfaces not usually associated with it, like a stainless steel kitchen or in a bathroom with a steel basin and towel rails.

Spots

Bold spots work particularly well on rugs and furnishings, while spots in subtle colours can look good on walls in children's rooms and family rooms. Spots and stripes in the same colours work well together.

Geometrics

Regular geometric patterns (any regular design other than spots, stripes and checks) tend to be static and formal. They are particularly good on rugs and in

masculine rooms. They make a great style statement, but need careful use if you want to mix and match patterns on walls or fabrics.

Pictorials

Pictorial designs range from French-inspired toile and traditional chinoiserie patterns to oriental-style prints and fun themed designs for bathrooms and children's rooms. Pictorial fabrics make fantastic roller blinds, as the lack of pleats and folds allows the design to be seen fully when the blind is in use.

Florals

Floral patterns range in size from busy sprigs to huge dramatic flower heads, and encompass both traditional and modern styles. Traditional interior floral fabrics have recently enjoyed a resurgence of favour. Contrast them with ginghams for country cottage appeal, or team them with modern accessories and metal surfaces for a contemporary take on a classic look.

Floral wallpaper needs more care. It can be overpowering, but is ideal on feature walls (see page 126) or used on the lower half of walls, up to dado rail or even picture rail height. Repetitive floral patterns give a sense of movement and flow.

Abstracts

This is a huge category, which includes ethnic patterns and faux animal skin prints, plus anything else not covered above. An abstract pattern often works best if it's the main attraction, so it could be a good starting point for a room scheme.

The large, bold pattern of the wallhanging set against a white wall provides a focal point for this living room yet works well with the fabrics in smaller patterns in coordinating colours on the sofa.

Examples of pattern

Using pattern is one way to add interest to a design scheme. The swatches below are just a tiny sample of the hundreds of patterns available in fabric and wallpaper; there are many more patterns to be found in furnishings, accessories and carpeting, and even prints and pictures.

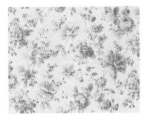

Green and pink are a much-loved classic floral combination. Coordinate such florals with stripes for an ageless combination that rarely goes wrong in any light, airy room, or with gingham for a timeless country cottage look.

Faded summer stripes are simple and timeless, and this pale pink colour gives an antiqued feel to any room. Stripes are effective alongside both miniature and large-scale floral patterning, checks, abstracts and geometrics.

Combine African-style or animal print patterns with modern striped designs and textures to create a striking 'ethnic', contemporary environment. Stick to a simple colour palette of warm stone or terracotta and chocolate brown, and mix and match patterns.

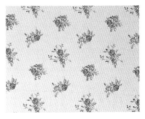

This classic, floral design is perfect for creating an inviting, comfortable environment. To keep such traditional patterns from becoming too sentimental or overly fussy, combine and contrast them with brighter colours and bold plain surfaces or simple checks or stripes.

This distinctive overscaled poppy design is from the classic house of Finnish design, Marimekko. Made famous in the 1960s with its bold and simple prints on cotton fabrics, ready-made products are widely available.

This paisley pattern is an excellent example of modern-style yellows – limed tones mixed with fresh white and pale mint green. Use the colours in the pattern for inspiration for accessories such as mint-coloured glassware and oversized plain white tableware.

Japanese-inspired patterns always look elegant and classic – mix with natural surfaces like dark wood and bamboo for a pared-down oriental feel.

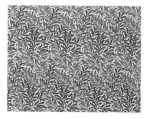

William Morris print designs, based on flowers and foliage, are instantly recognizable and ever popular, and have a timeless quality suited to any interior.

French pictorial patterns, once the preserve of Marie Antoinette and the Palace of Versailles, are now widely available for wallcoverings and soft furnishings. Contrast this pictorial print with a plain coral red for a lighter note in an opulent interior.

Powder blues always work well in simple geometric shapes. Polka dots look good with stripes if kept within the same colour group and the combination works particularly well in bedrooms, bathrooms or kitchens. Alternatively, team spots with florals.

A new interpretation of classic textile designs, this pattern would look great for the upholstery fabric of a large sofa or overstuffed chairs. More and more interior design is taking reference from the world of fashion.

In this stylish interpretation of classic deckchair striping, muted ochre and burnt orange are an appealing combination. This pattern would work well teamed with modern furnishings and used with a plain colour for scatter cushions and small accessories.

Size and scale

The scale of patterns in your decorating scheme can vary from enormous repeats that dominate a room to minuscule mini-prints that are hardly visible from a distance. Don't be afraid to use pattern – sometimes the bolder the pattern, the better the effect.

Large patterns

Large-scale patterns require careful planning. If the design contrasts highly with its background, it will create a basic colour scheme around which the rest of the décor must revolve.

Usually, large bold patterns emphasize form and movement. They look most attractive when used on open, uncluttered areas such as on the floor of a large

A balance of large- and small-scale patterns is achieved here by the use of boldly patterned floor-length curtains teamed with a few cushions in relatively small-scale patterns.

A large-scale pattern on the wall makes an effective background for plain white furnishings in this apparently simple yet striking monochromatic colour scheme.

room, on bed covers or on the walls of a stairwell, where the design can be seen in its entirety without the interruption of furnishings.

Like dark colours, large-scale patterns can also be effective on a single wall of a large room, as a focal point (see page 126) or a backdrop to plain furnishings. Large patterns advance and tend to make a small room look smaller; they are less suitable for rooms with lots of windows, doors or alcoves, since the motifs will be constantly interrupted. However, you can emphasize the intensity of a small space by using a large pattern in a small room.

Avoid placing a large-scale pattern on furniture where it will not be seen at its best and where it may need to be kept a specific way up. It is more practical to choose a small self-pattern for a sofa, which allows the cushions to be used any way up, thereby distributing wear evenly. If you are unsure which size of pattern will best suit your room, err towards the larger side, as this will at least look distinctive.

Handy hints

• Large patterns tend to have much the same effects and uses as vivid colours, while small patterns function like muted colours.
• In general, select smaller and more subtle patterns for small areas, and bolder patterns for more spacious areas. This applies to fabrics as well as wallcoverings – use large-scale patterns for full-length curtains and bed linen, and smaller patterns for scatter cushions, lampshades and curtain tie-backs.
• To incorporate a large-scale design in a small room, choose a pattern in muted colours on a non-contrasting background.
• Too many large-scale patterns in one room fight and overwhelm each other, while a room decorated in only small-scale patterns looks insipid. A contrast of large scale plus small scale will bring a room alive, and yet still look balanced.

Mixing small, regular patterns, such as this pretty floral sprig, with a larger, bolder pattern can be successful as long as the patterns share a common colour.

A small-scale patterned wallpaper is ideal in rooms with multi-angled surfaces. Here, it helps to visually enlarge a small attic bathroom with a sloping ceiling and inset alcove.

Small patterns

Small patterns suit smaller spaces. They are particularly effective in rooms with lots of surfaces at different angles, such as an attic room. Here, miniature designs, such as small floral patterns, can give the illusion of a larger, cohesive space.

Small patterns produce a quite different effect when seen on a large scale, so don't judge them from a small swatch. Some mini-prints lose all definition and give the impression of a texture rather than a distinct pattern when applied to the whole wall. Others take on a single colour and tone when viewed from a distance, making them the easiest to match to a colour scheme. Whether you allow a small-scale pattern to function as a single tone throughout a room or coordinate it with areas of plain colour is a personal decision. In general, however, a balance of plain colour and patterned areas is easy on the eyes. Avoid using small designs in large rooms, since they can look spotty. Steer clear of a fully coordinated look that uses only small-scale patterns. Instead, mix small patterns with larger-scale prints or weaves to add depth and variety.

Patterns that work together

Contrasting a single pattern with a limited number of plain colours requires thought and planning. The size, style and colours of the pattern all need to be selected carefully so that they harmonize with the rest of the décor. When it comes to combining two or more patterns, the challenge is that much greater.

Don't be afraid to mix patterns – the similarity of pattern on the walls and chair and the common colour palette guarantees a successful mix.

Size, shape and colour

Pattern mixing and matching is often a matter of personal taste, but you do need to keep some continuity of colour or theme for a successful, balanced look. With regard to pattern size, colour and shape, there are three options:

- Patterns of the same size and form but in different colours, for example varied floral designs.
- Patterns of the same form and colour but in different sizes, for example different widths of stripe.
- Patterns of the same colour and size but with varied forms, for example a mixture of geometrics and florals in the same colour.

Successful contrasts

The first option above is probably the easiest way to match patterns – pick patterns of the same size and design that differ only in colour. In this context, you then really have only to choose colours that contrast or blend well together, following the colour guidelines established earlier (see pages 92–103).

If you want to combine small, regular patterns with large, bold ones, make sure that the two patterns are linked by colour. If the overall colours of each pattern are close to one another on the colour wheel (see page 92), the effect of them in combination will be successful. Pleasing results can also be obtained by matching large, bold patterns with small-scale versions

of the same or similar designs in the same colour scheme. This can be very effective in a child's bedroom, for instance.

Very different patterns – such as toile with checks – can also work together, if their main colours are linked. As a general rule, the more complex the patterns, the simpler the colours should be, to avoid clashes. Choose patterns with a single main colour and small amounts of contrasting accent colours; or patterns with two main colours that are very close in tone; or mix complementaries and link them with neutral tones.

Another possibility is to introduce texture into the equation. For example, you could combine fabrics that have a similar pattern like checks but that have completely different textures.

Handy hints

- If you are using a variety of patterns, create visual continuity by relating their predominant colours throughout the house.
- Link areas of your home by limiting the wallcoverings in the halls and stairways to a single pattern and colour, or by having fitted carpeting in a single colour and texture throughout the house.
- Don't mix too many patterns in one room. On the other hand, avoid a completely coordinated look, which can look uncomfortably twee.
- When you mix or match patterns, if their main colours are complementary, they will work well together, and also if they are lightened or darkened in tone and used in unequal amounts.
- Static and dynamic patterns (see page 116) in related shades combine very successfully, such as classic florals with checks and stripes in the same colours.

Continuity of colour and fabric accounts for the success in mixing and matching these very different patterns, none of which dominates the others.

Mixing geometric patterns like these checks and stripes creates a clean modern look that relies on the use of the same colour in the patterns for its success.

Themed patterns

A trickier alternative to the 'safe' pattern-matching options described opposite is to go for themed patterns – think of bedding and décor featuring children's characters – but team your own ideas together for an individual-looking room with distinction rather than buying the ready-made and fully coordinated look.

Start by choosing a theme that suits the room's function, for example herbs for a kitchen, wine bottles for a dining room, jungle animals for a young child's bedroom or moon and stars for a bedroom.

Make your theme the continuous common thread, mixing completely different patterns together, while bearing in mind the general guidelines on room size, colour combinations, pattern scale, texture and lighting. Do have fun locating patterned wallpaper, fabric, ceramic tiles and accessories for your themed room, but take care not to get carried away so that the end result is an over-the-top riot of confusion. Remember, less is more, and you'll need some plain colour for balance. Making a mood board (see page 106) is highly recommended here to test your ideas.

Texture

Like pattern, texture is often used for decorative effect – adding interesting focal points to a room. Using textured surfaces, whether on walls, furnishings or flooring, is also a useful device for concealing underlying imperfections.

Texture and colour

Texture affects how we see colour – for example, a rough, bobbly fabric will appear different from a light-reflecting gloss paint in the same hue. Texture is therefore an important element to consider when planning a decorating scheme. Rough surfaces scatter light and make colours appear darker and duller. They can, in some situations, create interesting shadows. By contrast, smooth surfaces reflect light and make colours look lighter and livelier. Even black or very dark walls reflect some light if decorated in gloss paint.

Achieving a balance of colour, pattern and texture can be tricky, but you can rarely go wrong with natural colours and textures as the basis for your scheme.

Tricks with textures
- Warm, rich colours and hard, shiny surfaces appear to come towards you. Cool colours and soft, matt textures give the appearance of receding more into the background. Bear this in mind when you want to alter the apparent size of a room.
- Break up large spaces into intimate areas by using different-textured hangings or rugs.
- Create contrasts by regularly interspersing textures and patterns with areas of plain, smooth colour.
- Combine 'rough' textures like untreated wood, stone or sisal flooring, wicker and hessian (burlap) with 'smooth' textures like glass, metal, polished wood, finished leather, shiny chintz and fine silk.

Creating a mood

Smooth surfaces create a cold, clean, sparse mood – especially when combined with black or white. Such a scheme may be ideal for the bathroom, and could also work well for a business-like study. However, for a bedroom or candle-lit dining area, textured surfaces such as brick, wood and coarse fabrics create a more preferable, softer mood. When used with a combination of muted colours and tones, they impart warmth and intimacy to the overall scheme.

Combining colour, pattern and texture

Just as the predominance of a single colour can be overwhelming or dull, so, too, can the overuse of a single texture or pattern. However, it is best to limit the variety of textures and patterns if you have a complicated colour scheme or the effect can be confusing. For example, if you have a range of textured surfaces in natural tones of brown and beige, it is a good idea to limit the patterns and stick to smooth surfaces for the other colours in the room.

Examples of texture

Texture is not only found in woven fabrics, but on virtually any surface from walls to floors, from rough, natural fibres to smooth tiles, as can be seen from the small selection of different products below.

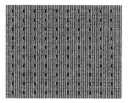

This geometrically textured flooring is a great modern alternative to traditional woven carpeting. Precise and structured patterning gives a contemporary feel to any interior style.

Here, raised geometric stripes have been created in a synthetic suede by using clever textile techniques to give a simple weave that would look impressive as cushion covers or curtains.

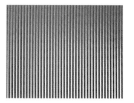

This textured natural flooring is almost like tweed, with many different colours woven together. Because it is undyed, the soft greens and toffee colourings are completely organic.

The interesting surface quality of this wallcovering adds a new dimension to simple décor. It offers a gentle background, which would be particularly suited to a living room or bedroom.

This ribbed-lead-effect resin flooring gives an industrial look. Durable and ultra-modern, it works well in open-plan flats teamed with metal staircases and polished bare concrete.

The intricate surfaces of fabrics that are pleated, naturally creased, ruched, smocked or embossed are either woven in or permanently set, keeping fabrics textured even after washing.

Ceramic tiles introduce a smooth, glossy texture into a scheme. This reproduction Delft tiling can be used in the kitchen or bathroom, or, for a more traditional approach, around a fireplace.

This matt, delicately textured wallpaper is highlighted with soft pin-stripes of pale gold. When using metallics, choose tarnished or antiqued finishes for a subtle, more elegant feel.

Focal patterns

If the room you are decorating has a special feature, you might like to use pattern to emphasize it and treat it as a focal point. Alternatively, use pattern to *create* a focal point – single walls, alcoves, sofas or even curtains can all become focal points if patterns are used carefully.

Focal features

The most obvious focal points are fireplaces, large bay windows and unusual recesses. Any of these could be accentuated by applying pattern to the surface. For example, to highlight a fireplace, use a wallcovering in a warm-toned complementary style on the surrounding wall, or turn an alcove into a focal point with a splash of colourful pattern; offset these by keeping the adjacent walls plain. Similarly, you could enhance a bay window with richly patterned, floor-to-ceiling curtains.

In this bedroom decorated in mostly plain colours, the eye is immediately drawn to the room's focal point – stunning, full floor-length curtains with a rich gold-on-blue pattern.

The opposite can also work successfully. For example, you could decorate most of the room in subtle patterns, leaving an expanse of plain colour in a featured alcove as a backdrop to shelves of attractive ornaments or a display of framed pictures.

Feature walls

Unlike older properties with striking fireplaces, interesting nooks and crannies, exposed beams, panelled walls or doors, ceiling roses or bay windows, most modern homes lack any architectural detail on walls and ceilings. In any size room, deliberately creating a feature wall by using an interesting patterned wallpaper, for example, is a good way of overcoming this plainness. Similarly, a feature wall in a room can help draw the eye away from an unattractive view outside the window.

Using patterned wallpaper on one wall in this large room makes a feature of the bed, while also helping to zone the room by visually separating the sleeping and washing areas.

These striking bold curtains are the focal point in a plainly decorated room with its large, relatively pattern-free areas of walls and furniture.

Handy hints

• For maximum effect, use the most flamboyant patterns in the most simple settings – bold floral prints, for example, give a boost in plain, uncluttered rooms. Enhance a sense of coherence by picking out a single colour from the pattern design for the plain colours in the room.

• Patterns look more exciting than plain fabrics, but bear in mind that you can quickly tire of a powerful design, and it can soon dominate a room or start to look dated.

• Upholstery and curtains need to last a long time – it would be a shame if your curtains still have many years of use left in them, but you are simply tired of an over-dramatic or outdated design. Use simpler, neutral patterns on the more expensive items such as curtains and large pieces of upholstery, and save the exciting patterns for items that can be changed more frequently such as cushions and tablecloths.

In large rooms, consider using patterned wallpaper on one or two walls or on a chimney breast. Large-scale geometric patterning, for example, could become a real feature within a room.

Similarly, multi-functional rooms such as kitchens, living-dining areas or bedrooms that double as studies can be divided into sections through clever use of patterned and non-patterned surfaces. Keep the colours simple and coordinated, and use pattern to direct the eye away from work areas.

Working with existing patterns

If you have no choice but to work with a fitted patterned carpet, patterned curtains or a patterned suite of furniture, stick to plain contrasting-coloured walls as the backdrop and plain-weave fabrics for the other soft furnishings.

Too many large-scale patterns in a room can appear to fight, but this boldly patterned piece of furniture looks great teamed with plain walls and accessories.

Soft
furnishings

Furnishing your home

Before you decide what to put in a room, think about what you will use it for, and create a scheme that is specific to you and your lifestyle – not other people's expectations and conventions. Don't choose furniture and furnishings until you have decided on the final effect.

Design versus fashion

Interior design is a careful decision-making process. It is not just a question of filling a room with bits and pieces, however chic and modish. Distinguish between design, which is creating interiors that work for you, and fashion, which is the latest craze in styles and colours (and which may not last very long).

Bear in mind that different fabrics have different textures, qualities and price tags, which make some fabrics more suited to a particular project than others.

You may not want to go to the trouble of creating a mood board (see page 106), but it is well worth finding an undisturbed spot like the corner of a noticeboard where you can arrange your choices of fabrics together and live with them for a while. Something that appealed to you at first sight may not be so attractive after a couple of weeks, and you will be able to see easily whether your colour and pattern choices are working, or whether they need some adjustment.

Choosing fabrics

Not all fabrics are the same, so the first thing you need to know is whether or not the fabric you have fallen in love with is suitable for what you are trying to achieve.

It is well worth buying just a metre or yard of a fabric you like before committing to a soft furnishing project. You can then find out how it drapes and handles, how the pattern suits your home and whether the colours work for you and in their intended space.

Draping

Some bulky fabrics, such as velvets, tapestries and chenilles, make excellent insulating curtains, while very heavy fabrics are best used flat for seating and cushions, because they can be too stiff for curtains,

List your activities

Perfection is probably impossible, but you will get a lot closer to designing the ideal room if you first list all the activities that will be taking place there. The list may be longer than you think! It won't just involve the obvious things like eating, sleeping, watching television and cooking, but also many other varied activities such as storing things, exercising, listening to music, reading and indoor gardening.

The bulky fabric used for these curtains drapes well and has good insulating qualities, retaining the room's warmth when drawn for the night.

which then won't fold or drape easily. Heavier fabrics give presence to roman blinds, however, where a lightweight fabric can appear flimsy.

Letting light through

You can vary the amount of light that comes into a room by the thickness or translucency of your curtain fabric – achieving either a soft light to work by, or a comforting twilight to help you go to sleep.

Reaction to light

Some fabrics, such as silks, are particularly susceptible to strong sunlight, and will fade quickly. For bright rooms, consider fitting additional roller blinds or inner sheers to protect a precious fabric from the light.

Price

A budget fabric tends not to last as long as a more expensive one. But you can create great effects with a large quantity of a cheaper fabric, then replace it later.

Fabric widths

Most furnishing fabrics are approximately 140 cm (54 in) wide. Some cottons and voiles may be wider than this, and some fabrics – eastern silks, for example

Hoarders beware!

Homes frequently fill up with furniture and soft furnishings that are not actually needed and it is important to watch out for this. It may not happen immediately, but if you begin to feel irritated by the state of your home, it's time to take stock of your possessions. In fact, every home should be audited once a year, as needs and expectations change – what suited you a few years ago might be less appropriate now.

– are appreciably narrower. A bargain price per metre or yard of fabric may not always prove to be an economy if the width is very narrow, as you may have to buy a greater total length of fabric to get the effect you want.

Colour variation

Just as with rolls of wallpaper, dye colours may vary slightly from roll to roll of fabric, so make sure that you buy enough fabric to complete your project, as it could prove difficult to match later.

Sheer fabric at the window allows light in, while still providing daytime privacy from the outside world. The textured fabric in the room adds interest to the all-white colour scheme.

Soft furnishing fabrics

The range of soft furnishing fabrics is extensive – just make sure you work with your chosen fabric appropriately to avoid shrinkage and damage. You *can* use dress fabrics for soft furnishings, although they are not usually as strong as proper furnishing fabrics, and certainly not as resistant to fading in strong sunlight.

Natural fabrics

The range of natural fibres used for furnishing fabrics is limited, but the textures and patterns they produce are almost infinite. Weavers have developed many ways to create texture, making the same fibre soft, stiff, supple, smooth or rough.

Cotton

Cotton is relatively economical to produce and extremely versatile. It can be dyed; it produces a smooth surface for printed patterns; and it can be woven into heavy upholstery cottons or light transparent muslin. It is not luxurious, but very tough and practical.

Linen

More expensive than cotton because it is more time-consuming to produce, linen has a distinctive crisp, dry texture that is very appealing. Despite being strong and smooth, it creases easily, so you have to appreciate the rumpled look that is its hallmark. It is often combined with cotton to make 'linen union', which gives you the best of both fabrics. It is commonly used for tablecloths and napkins.

Wool

Sheep's wool has a natural crimp to it, which makes a soft, warm fabric that drapes beautifully and can be dyed in deep, rich colours. It has a tendency to shrink, so is often blended with other fibres for furnishings.

Silk

Silk is the finest and smoothest natural fibre and is derived from the cocoon spun by the silkworm larva. The fibre has a unique sheen that gives the woven textile, also called silk, an instant look of luxury. The cheaper, lightweight Indian or Chinese silks make beautiful curtains, although they usually come in narrower widths than European silks.

Hemp and jute

Jute is quite a rough fibre, while hemp has very similar qualities to linen in that it is lustrous and extremely hardwearing – it also tends to crease. It is not in common supply, although manufacturers are currently experimenting with mixing it with cotton or silk for both curtain and upholstery fabrics.

Natural fabrics like cotton and linen (woven from the fibres of the cotton and flax plants, respectively) are good, hardwearing options for soft furnishings.

Artificial and unusual fabrics

Synthetic fabrics, such as nylon and polyester, are often easier to maintain than natural ones. Polyester sheers, for example, will wash without shrinking, and require little or no ironing compared with sheers made from cotton muslin or lace.

Manmade fibres were originally devised as a cheap substitute for expensive natural fibres, such as silks. However, a new generation of textile designers has exploited the strength and versatility of these fibres in producing fabrics that are magnificent and innovative in their own right. Furthermore, many natural fibres benefit from having a small percentage of strong nylon or polyester added to the weave, which produces a fabric that will withstand modern wear and tear.

Markets and antique outlets are good sources of unusual fabrics. You can quite easily transform an old tapestry or beautiful silk brocade panel into a blind or cushion. Just remember that older fabrics need to be treated with care, and they may not be strong enough to withstand a lot of stretching and stitching.

Leather and suede

Leather and suede make excellent furnishing fabrics. Covering a sofa or armchair in real leather is a job for the experts, but the beginner can successfully cut hides into simple shapes to make a smart cushion cover. Artificial leather and suede are now almost indistinguishable from the real thing, and you can buy them by the metre or yard, which makes them much easier to use.

Real, or artificial, leather and suede can be tough to sew, so keep the construction simple. Use a heavy cotton thread and a specialist three-sided hand or machine needle for leather, designed to make a clean hole. Hold the pieces together at the seams with masking tape or paper clips and press with a warm (not hot) iron.

Plastic-coated fabrics

Plastic-coated fabrics make cheerful and robust table covers for multi-purpose rooms. They need the minimum of stitching – just cut and use in simple shapes. All puncture marks made by pins and needles remain permanently, so it is impossible to pin or tack these fabrics together, and any alterations show. Always use a long machine stitch, as these fabrics can tear where perforated by a stitching line. Pressing with a hot iron will melt the fabric, so use your fingers or a heavy book to flatten any seams.

Handy hints

Natural fabrics bring few problems in sewing, either by hand or machine, and are excellent materials for beginners:

• Use a matching cotton thread and a medium needle for cottons and linens. Polyester thread is better for wool, as it has a slight stretchiness.

• Many silks are easy to handle, but fine ones can prove difficult – use a new, sharp needle and a fine polyester thread rather than cotton.

• Press pure linen carefully on the wrong side, as the iron can leave shiny marks.

• Press silks with a dry iron, as the fabrics can watermark badly if pressed damp, leaving a permanent stain.

Furs

Fur fabrics make fun cushions, or cosy and luxurious throws for beds and armchairs. Like all unusual fabrics, pattern pieces need to be kept to simple shapes. Pin all the seams first, as the fur pile will make the layers slip as you stitch. You may have to use a pin to pick free the fur pile along the seam lines on the right side.

Faux fur cushions are currently a popular choice in decorating schemes, introducing thick, luxurious texture as well as a sense of fun into contemporary living rooms and bedrooms.

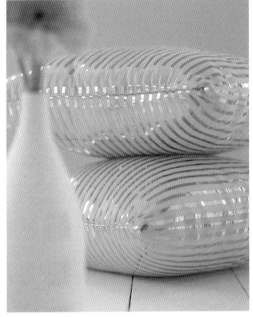

Since cushions require only small amounts of fabric, they are ideal showcases for luxurious or unusual fabrics that would be both visually overwhelming and too costly if used in larger quantities.

Unconventional and techno fabrics

Contemporary textiles may incorporate extraordinary weaving and knitting techniques, giving openwork or three-dimensional effects, sometimes interlocking several layers, or interweaving small, delicate items like beads or sequins.

Use a synthetic sewing thread when stitching these fabrics, as they can fray badly when cut and, because of their structure, can be difficult to sew inconspicuously. Allow for wide turnings in seams and for deep hems, and avoid any design that needs a lot of detailed and tailored structuring.

Voiles and sheers

Sheer fabrics can be light and airy, billowing in the breeze, or darkly dramatic in rich jewel colours. They have a magical quality of filtering harsh light and can provide screening from the world outside during the day, but when lights are on in a room at night, most sheers offer little privacy and you may need additional curtains in a heavier fabric, or a roller blind. Sheers should be used simply, without complicated stitching and construction, in order to emphasize the intrinsic beauty of the fabric.

Working with sheers

• The transparency of sheers means that all seams and turnings show through on the right side, so simplicity in making up is best. Neat selvedges at the side of the fabric mean you can usually avoid side hemming.

• A deep, double bottom hem of at least 15 cm (6 in) looks better than a narrow, single one. Allow for this in your fabric calculations.

• Some sheers are available wider than ordinary furnishing fabrics so that vertical seams can be avoided. If you need to join panels to fit a large window, hang them side by side rather than stitching them together.

• You can buy transparent heading tapes, which avoid an opaque or coloured band showing at the top.

• Always use sharp scissors to avoid ragged edges and snags on these lightweight and slippery fabrics.

• Use fine dressmaking sewing thread (polyester or polyester-cotton) to match the lightness of the fabric and avoid puckering.

• Always fit a new machine needle before stitching these fabrics, and loosen the top tension slightly. Ease the fabric gently through the machine with one hand in front and one behind the needle to stop it bunching and becoming damaged. Experiment on a scrap of the fabric, doubled over, until you get your stitching right before you attempt any long seams or hems.

Sheers vary tremendously in the effect they have, and it is advisable to check them against the light before you buy, as this affects both their colour and their apparent texture. Some have shine and polish, and are available in bright colours and daring techno weaves. Others have the soft, gauzy look of traditional cheesecloth and cotton. Linen-based sheers always have that appealing, slightly rumpled look. Many contain artificial fibres, such as polyester, which makes them easier to maintain.

Available in a huge range of colours, sheer fabrics filter light and provide some privacy. For night-time screening and warmth, use an additional window dressing like a roller blind.

Lace

Often based on historical patterns, laces are most effective when hung almost flat, as panels, so that the design can be seen clearly. Heavier laces can be stiffened and made into roller blinds, while other sheers can be treated this way if they have a high cotton or linen content.

Hanging sheers

These lightweight fabrics are simpler to handle than formal curtains, as they don't need lining or robust tracks and fixings. Avoid old-fashioned expanding wires for hanging, however, as these tend to sag. Tensioned wire cables are perfect or you can sew a simple casing along the top of a sheer fabric and ruche it on to a pole or a café-style rod. Sheers on any type of pole attached with rings, ties or clips always look good, and are an economical way of dressing up a window.

Sheer care

Some, but not all, sheers are washable. Loosen gathering tapes, remove any clips or hooks and use a delicates machine wash with a limited spin to avoid creasing. Artificial fibres absorb little water, which means you can hang the curtains back up straight from the washing machine. Laces and sheers of cotton and linen may shrink, need ironing and can become limp with repeated washing. You can wash the fabric before you make it up, to preshrink it, but always test-wash a sample to be sure. If in doubt, have it dry cleaned.

Muslin

Muslin is the name given to soft, matt, sheer fabrics, often embroidered or printed. Inexpensive butter muslin and cheesecloths are excellent when used in large quantities and can create a dramatic effect, although they are not very durable. They shrink and become limp on washing, and are best used for short-term effects and thrown away when shabby. Slightly more expensive cotton and cotton mix sheers will have a longer life.

Organza

Stiffened sheers are known as organzas. They have an appealing party-dress quality and often include metallic or opalescent threads, which shimmer as they move in the breeze of an open window.

Sheer fabrics are not only useful at windows. This length of embroidered muslin makes an effective room divider in an open-plan area without detracting from the available daylight.

Bed and table linen

Most bed and table linen is very easy to make, because it is largely based on rectangles and squares with straight seams and simple hems. If you feel like it, you can add embroidery – by hand or machine – or decorative edges.

Suitable fabrics

Although the terms bed and table 'linen' are frequently used, the more suitable fabrics for these items are, in fact, cottons or polyester-cottons – anything that will withstand constant washing and ironing.

Some materials shrink slightly when washed for the first time, so it is a good idea to prewash any fabric before you cut and hem it. Dress fabrics, shirting or polyester-cotton bed linens can also be made up into tablecloths and napkins.

Sheeting It is possible to buy sheeting fabric by the metre or yard in cotton or polyester-cotton, and in widths larger than usual. This means that you can make up sheets and duvet (comforter) covers without seams for both single and double (full-size) beds.

Cotton fabrics Although these are very good and hardwearing, like linen, they need ironing.

Cotton/synthetic blends These have very similar qualities to cotton, but are easier to care for, needing little or no ironing.

All-synthetic fabrics These wash and dry very quickly, but they can feel unpleasantly slippery, and tend to build up static electricity. They are non-absorbent, which makes them hot and uncomfortable to sleep in when the weather is warm.

Patterned or plain?

Bed and table linen have traditionally been white for a good reason – white fabrics can take constant washing and ironing best, particularly the high temperatures to which tablecloths may need to be subjected. And pure white linen, well cared for, has a look of effortless class.

Because linen fibres were traditionally used to make the fabric used for sheets and pillowcases, 'linen' has become the generic term for such bedding today.

It is worth taking the trouble of cleaning and starching small pieces of beautiful white linen or embroidery to accessorize tables and beds.

You can make bed linen out of dark-coloured or patterned fabrics, but these will inevitably fade with frequent washing, and may look drab before they have reached the end of their useful lives. Brightly coloured borders on pale fabrics may be a better option.

Making bed covers

A throw-over bedspread is easy to make and can cover either the whole bed, touching the floor at the foot and sides, or just the duvet (comforter). Bedspreads can be made of less durable fabrics than other bed linen, because they don't need to be cleaned so often.

You can use standard-width fabrics for bedspreads, but this means that you will almost certainly have to make a join or two. If this is the case, use fabrics of similar weights, and position the seams so that there is a whole width in the centre of the bed, with smaller part-widths on either side. If you do have to join fabric, either try to make the seams unobtrusive or use them to contribute to the design in some way – a band of lace can be sewn between the edges, for example. Just make sure that these decorations will wash as well as the fabric itself.

Heavier-weight fabrics make the best bedspreads, but if you want to use fine fabrics, you can make the cover more substantial by backing it with a lining fabric and finishing the edges with a binding.

You can leave the corners of a bed cover square, or you can round them off to stop them trailing on the floor. Leave them plain or finish with a decorative trimming as a border or edging.

Making a three-panelled cover

The generous cover pictured here (right) is made from three contrasting fabrics, stitched together lengthways along the selvages, with a double-hemmed edge.

2 Cut the fabrics to the desired lengths. With right sides together, machine stitch the panels together, allowing for a 2 cm ($^3/_4$ in) seam. Make a few reverse machine stitches at the beginning and end of each seam to give a strong finish. (If you cut off the fabric selvages, you will need to neaten or finish the raw edges.) Press the seams open.

3 Press under a double hem with 2.5 cm (1 in) in each turning, and stitch. Note: If the fabrics contrast strongly, it is worth taking the time to stitch each one with its own matching thread for a professional finish.

You will need
- Basic sewing kit
- Three contrasting fabrics for the bands
- Matching thread for each of the fabrics

1 Take measurements over a made-up bed, using a fabric measuring tape. Measure from the top of the mattress at the head, over the pillows to the desired length at the foot. Add 8 cm ($3^1/_4$ in) to your calculations to allow for the two seams. Measure the width from the desired length on one side over to the same length on the other side. Add 5 cm (2 in) all round for the hem.

A bedspread allows you to disguise bed linen – perhaps a duvet (comforter) cover and pillowcases – that doesn't match the décor of the room, but is too costly to replace.

Table linen

Since eating and entertaining have become more informal activities, it is no longer necessary to load the table with the traditional intimidating collection of matching cutlery and formal accessories. Instead, dressing up a table for entertaining now offers a great opportunity to be creative, even if you're on a budget. Your table can be cool, crisp and white, or bright, fun and funky. One easy decorative option is to place a second cloth over a plain one. This can be a piece of dramatic fabric that is not big enough to be a tablecloth or a long strip of silk, embroidery or brocade used as a runner down the centre of the table.

Measuring up

Tablecloths There are no standard sizes for tablecloths. If you already have a cloth that fits your table, simply measure its width and length. Otherwise, measure the dimensions of your tabletop and, for a short cloth, sit on a chair and measure from the top of the table to your lap. If you want a floor-length tablecloth (handy for disguising very ugly table legs), measure from the top of the table to the floor. Remember to add the measurement to each side of the tabletop measurement, plus a further 5 cm (2 in) all round for a narrow hem, or 10 cm (4 in) for a wide hem.

Napkins Napkins are usually square, and can be anything from 30 cm (12 in) square for tea size to 60 cm (24 in) square for dinner size. A good all-purpose size is 40 cm (16 in) square, which fits economically into standard-width fabrics, allowing for turnings and avoiding wastage.

To estimate fabric for a napkin, take the finished size and add 1 cm (⅜ in) on each side for the hems. A metre or yard of 90 cm (36 in) wide fabric will make four 40 cm (16 in) square napkins. A metre or yard of 140 cm (54 in) wide fabric will make six napkins of the same size.

The contemporary dining experience is likely to be funky and informal, mixing bright colours and patterns in the glassware, crockery and table linen.

Mix and match

A stunning piece of printed fabric over a table can have the effect of decorating an entire room. It's not necessary for all the table linen to match perfectly, and you can buy remnants of relatively expensive designer fabrics for a good price, because they are too small for regular curtains and upholstery. A mixture of colours and patterns can be charming, and will act as a perfect foil for plain plates and dishes. There is an art, however, to putting different fabrics together successfully, no matter how casual the finished effect appears to your guests. For a scheme to work, there has to be a common denominator behind your selection:

- Base all the fabrics on a similar design motif, such as stripes, checks or florals.
- Choose fabrics that are closely related in colour, even though the designs may be different.
- Purchase fabrics that have a similar texture – all rough matt linens, all light and gauzy or all with a metallic trim.
- Opt for fabrics of a similar tone – rich, vivid, jewel-like colours or soft, pretty and pastel.

Making tablecloths and napkins

Making tablecloths and napkins with your own chosen fabrics and colours is a good way of using small pieces of attractive fabric not large enough for other projects.

You will need
- Basic sewing kit
- Fabric
- Matching thread

Pastel-coloured striped fabric used for placemats and table runners is a perfect foil for plain coloured crockery with a pearlized finish, as seen here.

1 Cut out your chosen fabric to the calculated size, including the hem allowance (see box, opposite), making any joins that may be necessary in order to make the fabric wide enough. Finish the edges with a double hem.

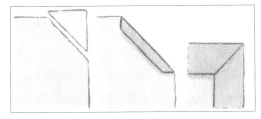

2 To make neat hems on tablecloths and napkins, cut off each corner diagonally. This cut should be about 10 cm (4 in) long. Press a narrow turning to the wrong side along this diagonal, and then press the edges over all round so that the corners meet in a neat mitre.

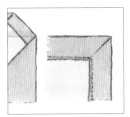

3 Open the pressed sides, and turn the raw edges under by about 1 cm ($^3/_8$ in). Press. Turn the hem back in place all round and pin or tack if necessary. Machine stitch close to the inner edge of the hem.

Protecting the table

Wood and other surfaces can be badly marked by hot plates and pots, or left with unsightly rings from drinks glasses. If you have a quality table, it needs protecting. Traditional, individual table mats can look fussy and are often quite slippery or awkward. Softer, woven mats are more attractive, but a really hot casserole straight from the oven will need significantly thicker insulation, perhaps even a metal trivet.

A layer of padding under the cloth gives a calmer, less-cluttered table. You can buy table-saver materials, often with a rubberized base, by the metre or yard.

Oilcloth and similar plasticized fabrics wipe down in seconds and need no sewing at all – just cut them to the required size.

Cushions

Getting the seating right goes a long way to making a home feel more comfortable. Cushions of various kinds are important, not only for decoration, but also to soften functional and uncomfortable furniture.

Making cushion covers

Making a cushion involves creating a cover to fit over a ready-made cushion pad – an inner cover containing the filling – so that the outer cover can be removed for cleaning. The best pads contain a feather filling, but budget cushions stuffed with acrylic wadding or polyester are almost as good. Decorative cushion covers can be made using any fabric, while seating and floor cushions need a robust and washable furnishing fabric. You will need a zip (zipper) or buttons, unless you're making the envelope-style cushion cover (right).

An easy sewing project, most cushions require only small quantities of fabric and some method of opening and closing such as a zip (zipper) or buttons.

Making an envelope-style cushion

All you need for this simplest of cushion covers, which involves no fastenings, is fabric for the front and back.

You will need
- Basic sewing kit
- Square cushion pad
- Covering fabric and matching thread

1 The width of the fabric should be the cushion pad width plus 4 cm (1$^{1}/_{2}$ in) for seam allowances, and the length of the fabric should be twice the pad width, plus 18 cm (7 in) for the overlap.

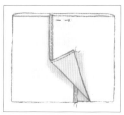

2 On the two short sides, press a turning of 2 cm ($^{3}/_{4}$ in) to the wrong side, and then fold it again to make a double hem. Stitch along the edge.

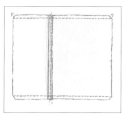

3 With right sides together, wrap the fabric around so that the short edges overlap by 10 cm (4 in) on the back. Pin together the raw edges of the cover at the top and bottom. Stitch along these edges with a 2 cm ($^{3}/_{4}$ in) seam allowance. Trim the corners diagonally. Turn the cushion cover the right way out and press. Insert the cushion pad through the slot at the back.

Making tie-on cushions

Tie-on seat cushions add comfort to wooden dining chairs and are tied to their backs to keep them in place.

You will need

- Basic sewing kit

- A square cushion pad for each chair, approximately the same size as the seat

- Covering fabric, plus extra for making four 30 cm (12 in) long ties per cushion

- A zip (zipper) the same length or slightly shorter than the back edge of each cushion

- Matching thread

1 To make each tie, cut a strip of fabric approximately 33 x 9 cm (13 x 3^1/$_2$ in). Press in half lengthways, right sides facing out. Turn the raw edges into the fold and press again. Stitch the open edges together on the right side. Trim the raw ends neatly with scissors.

2 Next, measure the size of your cushion pad from seam to seam. You will need to cut two pieces of fabric per cushion, each one the size of the pad, plus 2 cm (^{3}/$_4$ in) on one side (for the zip/zipper), and plus 9 cm (3^1/$_2$ in) on the three other sides (for the decorative Oxford edges).

3 Lay the two pieces of fabric together, right sides facing. On the zip (zipper) side, pin together two short seams of 12 cm (4^3/$_4$ in) from each corner, along the seam allowance.

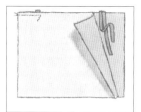

4 Slip two pairs of ties into the seams, each one 10 cm (4 in) in from the edge, then stitch the seams with two lines of stitching to secure the ties.

5 Press the short seams flat, and press the seam allowance to the wrong side along the opening between the sewn seams.

6 Lay the zip (zipper) face up on a flat surface and centre the cushion cover on top of it, with the wrong side of the fabric to the zip (zipper) and with the opening over the zip (zipper) teeth. Tack the zip (zipper) in place.

7 On the right side of the fabric, stitch along both sides of the zip (zipper) and across the top and bottom ends using the zipper foot of your machine, or as close to the teeth as you can get with a normal sewing foot.

8 Remove the tacking and open the zip (zipper). With right sides facing, fold one side of the cushion cover on top of the other, and pin and sew the three raw sides. Trim the corners diagonally for ease of turning.

9 Turn the cushion the right way out and press the seams flat, using a pin to pick out the corner points.

10 To make the Oxford edges, stitch around three sides of the cover (the ones without the zip/zipper) 7 cm (2^3/$_4$ in) from the edge. Insert the cushion pad, close the zip (zipper) and tie the cushion to the chair.

It's worth adding ties to seat cushions, as it stops them sliding around uncomfortably and always ending up on the floor. Either make matching fabric ties or choose a plain or contrasting colour.

Window dressings

Curtains and blinds can perform a variety of functions and the success of any window dressing relies on careful planning. Where is the window? What shape or size is it? What is your aim? What is your budget? Is there an outside view to enhance or obscure? These considerations give you plenty to think about before making a decision on style.

What are you trying to achieve?

Think about what it is you want your intended window dressing to do in each situation. A style or design you admire may not give you what you need, so decide first what function the dressing is being asked to perform and the options will become clearer:

Insulation Curtains keep heat in and control draughts, particularly in older homes without double glazing.

Excluding light Controlling the amount of light in a room is important, especially for a bedroom.

Protection from light Sunlight can damage your furnishings, so a light screen is useful in sunny rooms.

Camouflage An ugly view will be less conspicuous if you have a bold and imaginative window dressing.

Privacy To avoid being overlooked, some form of permanent filter between you and the outside world is often essential.

Decoration Curtains and blinds can tell a fashion and style story better than almost anything else in a room.

Budget considerations

Curtains can be an expensive item, but a room will look unfinished without them. Grand curtains are labour- and skill-intensive, so making your own can bring very useful savings. It is preferable to use more of a cheaper fabric than to skimp on an expensive one, and plain fabrics are more cost-effective than patterned ones. You can always buy ready-made curtains – they are more limited in range and style, but are less

A high window like this one, where privacy is unimportant, can be left permanently uncovered and just softened with a pretty yet unobtrusive frame of draped sheer fabric.

expensive than having them made to measure. If they are longer than your windows, you can easily hem them to the correct size.

Soft blinds like a roman blind add colour, folds and softness to a window and are economical with fabric at the same time. A money-saving roller blind can be used to give privacy, perhaps with an inexpensive sheer curtain draped to one side to add style.

Other considerations

Curtains give an additional frame to a window – as you think about how and where to hang them, look at the window in the context of the wall around it. Use the wall space above and around the window to improve the shape and proportion of your window dressing.

Wall space Always make sure that there is enough wall space for the curtains to stack back on – curtains don't look good if they are cramped and will block light. If you have wall space only on one side, a single curtain may be a good solution. If there is no wall space for stacking, then a blind may be a better idea.

Eyelet headings hold curtains in perfectly even folds and are particularly suited to more formal curtains, like those in this high-ceilinged room with period architectural details.

Framing Curtains can frame a beautiful view, or obscure an ugly one. To keep the eye in the room, use strong colours and a bold design. To make the most of a splendid outlook, frame the window with unobtrusive colours and a plain or simple pattern, and allow the view to take centre stage.

Toning colours Use fabric colours that tone with the wall colour if the windows are awkwardly placed, not balanced, or if you have used very different treatments on other windows in the same room. The lack of symmetry will then be less obvious.

Formal or informal? High ceilings and large rooms can take very formal curtains, while in smaller, irregular rooms, the focus should be on a beautiful fabric used simply for a cosier effect.

Avoiding problems Check for pipes, power points and switches when you are planning your window dressing. Their presence indicates that electricity cables run in the wall, which could be a safety hazard when fitting curtain track. In addition, think about whether you will be able to open the windows once the dressing is in place. Blinds often get in the way of casement or tip-and-tilt windows, in which case curtains will be the preferable option.

Shape Round or unusual-shaped windows are often difficult to dress. By hanging a conventional set of curtains, you ignore the shape completely, while shaping the top of the curtains to fit means that you won't be able to pull them back and forth. One solution is to hang a length of voile or sheer fabric over the window, so that the architectural shape and light still shine through.

Size Very small windows may need no dressing at all except, perhaps, for a painted border around the outside, or a piece of lace or embroidery as a tiny valance across the top. Tall windows are easier to dress than horizontal ones – some treatments don't work when stretched out across a whole wall, while modern 'picture' windows need modern styling. In both cases, emphasize the beauty or texture of the fabric you have chosen, and keep construction to a minimum.

Curtain length Short curtains – to the sill or slightly below – are appropriate if you are trying to create a cottage or rustic-style interior. Otherwise, try to fit floor-length curtains if you can, as they are more elegant. However, if you have a radiator beneath the window, you must decide whether you want to cover it with full-length curtains, or whether short curtains or a blind would be a better choice.

When drawn across the full width of the bay, these eyelet-headed curtains threaded along a tensioned wire completely disguise the shape of the bay window behind.

Curtains

Few things have greater effect on a room's appearance than what is put at the window, so your choice of curtain style, colour, accessories and method of hanging are important. If you are making your own curtains, an essential part of the process is measuring up accurately.

Curtain poles and tracks

There is a huge range of curtain tracks and poles to choose from, and you may find the task daunting at first. Hardware (houseware) and department stores will have a basic range of tracks and poles, but it's also worth locating a few of the many specialist companies making individual poles and finials in varied and often exquisite materials.

Curtain tracks

Most curtain tracks are made of metal or white plastic and tend to be inexpensive and functional, but not particularly attractive. Generally, however, they sit behind some kind of pelmet, swag or valance and are not on show. A plastic track is often the only budget option for a bay or bow window, as it can be bent into the correct shape at home.

Curtain poles

Not only do poles support the curtains, but they also make a style statement in their own right. You will find poles in all styles from traditional to modern – and at all prices. You can commission exquisite handmade poles for your windows, in beautiful decorative finishes including gilding. You can also create such effects yourself by decorating a budget pole from a do-it-yourself store.

When buying a wooden pole, always opt for the largest diameter you can afford – narrow poles look flimsy and can sag across a large span. Metal poles are stronger, and so can be thin and slender with small, delicate finials, in finishes from wrought iron to brass and stainless steel. The sleekest system of all involves tensioned wires, which carry the curtains on fine rings or clips.

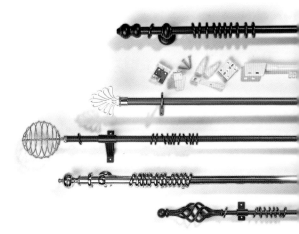

You'll encounter a tremendous range of styles and materials for curtain tracks, poles and finials, which means that making your final choice can be quite difficult.

Calculating length and position

It's important to get right both the required length of the curtain pole or track and its position in relation to the window. Too short a pole/track will leave the curtains covering the sides of the window and blocking daylight when drawn open, while one that is fixed too close to the top of the window will let light shine through along the top edge of the curtains.

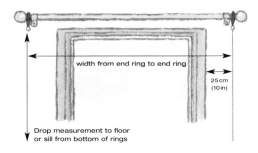

width from end ring to end ring

25 cm (10 in)

Drop measurement to floor or sill from bottom of rings

For an average window, make the track or pole approximately 25 cm (10 in) wider than the window on either side, and take the track or pole at least 10 cm (4 in) above the window.

Measuring for curtains

For each pair of curtains you need two measurements: the complete length of the curtain track or pole, and the finished length (or drop) of the curtains. Use a long steel measuring tape, as fabric tapes can stretch and are unlikely to be accurate. This is a job that is much easier with two people. Sketch your window first, and fill in the measurements around it.

Fix the pole or track in position, then measure its length. Next, take the measurement for the length of the finished curtains from the bottom of the rings, where the curtain hooks will go. (For tab-top curtains, take the measurement from the top of the pole – see page 147.) The curtains should end 1 cm ($^3/_8$ in) from the floor or window sill.

Fullness

Curtains always have more fabric in their width than the length of the track or pole, so that they fall in folds when drawn closed. Depending on the look you want, you can allow different quantities of fabric:

One-and-a-half-times fullness This is where the fabric is one-and-a-half times as wide as the finished width of the window dressing and is useful for contemporary styles where you want only a little folding. It is also the most economical option.

Curtains have a major impact on the look of a room. Without a window dressing of some sort, a room can look unfinished and the windows appear cold and stark.

Calculating fabric requirements

1 Once you have decided on the curtain fullness you want, multiply the width of the track or pole by the required fullness (two, or two-and-a-half, for example). This will give the total width of fabric you need to make the curtains.

2 Divide this figure by the width of the fabric (see page 131), and then round up to the nearest whole number. This will give you the number of widths you need to sew together to make the curtains.

3 Add 25 cm (10 in) to the finished length of the curtains to allow for turnings at the top and a hem at the bottom. (Don't forget to allow for pattern matching – see below.)

4 Multiply this figure by the number of widths obtained in Step 2 to give the total amount of fabric required.

Twice fullness This is a good average amount, especially for contemporary curtains. It gives fullness, while allowing the pattern of the fabric to be displayed. **Three-times fullness** This gives an extremely full, designer look, but may be too bulky for smaller rooms.

Pattern matching

When you join two widths of a patterned fabric, you must match up the design at the seam, adding an allowance for this to the fabric calculation (see box, above). Common pattern repeats are 15 cm (6 in), 30 cm (12 in) or 64 cm (25 in) and they are given on the fabric labels. Add the amount of the pattern repeat for each width of fabric you are putting in the curtains. This will also allow you to place the design so that it looks good along the hemline of the curtain, without cutting through an important motif or design element

No-sew curtains

It is possible to make good-looking curtains simply by hanging a number of single, unstitched panels of fabric on a pole, using accessories like curtain clips or by attaching ties. You can use instant hemming web to strengthen the top edge of each panel and to make a hem at the bottom. Hemming web can also be used to shorten ready-made curtains without sewing.

Making tie-top curtains

Tie-top curtains (see top picture, page 135) are simple to make – you could even use lengths of ribbon if preferred instead of making your own ties. They suit an informal look and the style can be used for heavy-duty fabrics as well as for voiles and sheers. You could attach the ties directly on to a curtain pole or track, but they work much better tied on to curtain hooks or rings, which allows the curtain to be drawn freely.

You will need

- Basic sewing kit
- Fabric for the curtains (see page 145 for calculating quantities)
- Fabric for ties and a facing
- Matching thread

1 Cut the fabric into lengths for the curtains, remembering to allow extra fabric for hems and turnings. If the curtains require more than one width of fabric to achieve the desired fullness (see page 145), machine stitch the widths together and press the seams open. Press a double hem on the outside long edges of each curtain about 4 cm (1¹/₂ in) wide, and machine stitch.

2 Next, make enough ties to fit along the top of the curtain, bearing in mind that they need to be spaced approximately 15 cm (6 in) apart and that you need two tie lengths at each point. For each one, cut a strip of fabric 40 x 10 cm (16 x 4 in). Press each strip in half lengthways, wrong sides facing, fold the raw edges into the centre and press again. Machine stitch along the open edge to secure.

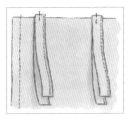

3 To attach the ties, pin, then tack pairs of ties along the top of the curtain, pointing downwards, making sure that there is a set at each end.

4 To make the facing, cut a strip of fabric 8 cm (3¹/₄ in) wide and the same length as the top of the curtain, plus an extra 4 cm (1¹/₂ in) (you may need to join strips). Press under 1 cm (³/₈ in) along one long edge.

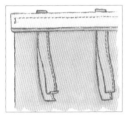

5 With right sides and raw edges together, pin the facing along the top of the curtain, enclosing the ties, and leaving a small turning at either end. Machine stitch through all the layers, 2 cm (³/₄ in) from the top of the curtain.

6 Remove any pins and tacking stitches, turn the facing to the wrong side of the curtain and press flat. Turn in the short edges and press again. Stitch along the short edges and the bottom turned edge of the facing to hold it in place.

7 Check the final length of the curtain. Turn up the spare fabric into a double hem and machine stitch.

Making tab-top curtains

If you make up the curtains entirely by machine, add the tabs following the instructions for the ties in the project opposite.

1 Cut the fabric into lengths for the curtains, remembering to allow for hems and turnings. Machine stitch any widths together and press the seams open.

2 To make the lining, cut the lining to the same length as each finished curtain, and the same width, less 10 cm (4 in). (Sew panels together if necessary.) Sew a double hem by pressing under 2.5 cm (1 in) along the bottom edge, followed by a further turning of 2.5 cm (1 in). Machine stitch.

3 To attach each lining, place it on the curtain fabric, right sides together, so that the top and left-hand edges are level. Machine stitch down the left-hand edges to within approximately 5 cm (2 in) of the bottom edge of the lining, making a 2 cm (³/₄ in) seam. Rearrange the two fabrics so that the right-hand edges are level, and sew in the same way. Turn each lined curtain through to the right side and press so that an equal margin of the front fabric shows on either side.

4 The tabs need to be spaced along each curtain top with 15 cm (6 in) gaps between them. To make each tab, use a piece of fabric 36 x 14 cm (14 x 5¹/₂ in). Fold each piece in half lengthways and, with right sides

facing, machine stitch the long edges together to make a 'tube'. Press the seam open, then turn the tab through to the right side and press flat with the seam running down the middle of the tab.

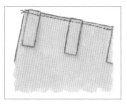

5 Fold the tabs into loops (with the seam to the inside of the loop) and place them along the top edge of each curtain, on the right side, hanging downwards. Make sure that there is a tab at each end of each curtain. Pin, then tack in place before machine stitching 2 cm (³/₄ in) from the top edge of the curtain to hold everything in place.

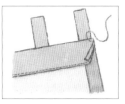

6 To make the facing, cut a strip of fabric 15 cm (6 in) wide and the length of the top of the curtain, plus 4 cm (1¹/₂ in). Press under 1 cm (³/₈ in) along one long edge and stitch. With right sides together, pin the raw edge of the facing along the top of the curtain, sandwiching in the tabs, and machine stitch through all the layers, 2 cm (³/₄ in) from the top.

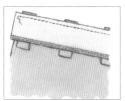

7 Turn the facing to the back of the curtain and press. Turn in the side turnings and stitch in place carefully.

8 Check the final length of the curtain. Turn the spare fabric to the wrong side, making a double hem. You may need to unpick a little of the stitching holding the lining in place to do this neatly. Fold in the ends of the hem to make a shallow angle and hem stitch.

Blinds

Blinds can be divided into two basic types: soft blinds, which include roman and similar blinds, and hard blinds, such as roller and venetian blinds. Soft blinds can be made at home out of many different fabrics, while hard blinds are usually ordered from specialist manufacturers or bought ready-made from decorating stores.

Ready-made blinds

Buying ready-made blinds is cheaper than having them made to order and they are available in many different sizes to fit most windows. There are a few different options, all of which are readily available.

Roller blinds These are most often used on their own, but they can look rather plain. For a more effective treatment, use one behind a set of curtains – the blind can be functional, while the curtains add style and grace. If your window is an unusual size and you cannot find a ready-made roller blind to fit, it may be possible to cut one down to size using a ruler and sharp scissors on the fabric, and a hacksaw to cut the roller. Light-resistant, or blackout, roller blinds are made of a plasticized fabric that blocks light. They are useful in bedrooms, particularly for young children, and for sloping roof windows in attic rooms, and come in a range of plain colours and patterns.

Lace or voile fabrics Blinds made from stiffened lace or voile can be very useful for blocking just a little light in a room and providing privacy.

Venetian blinds These are extremely flexible and can control the light coming into a room in a number of ways. There is a huge range of colours and widths available for the slats. It is advisable to avoid dark colours, which show the dust quickly and are difficult to clean.

Vertical blinds These are most commonly used in offices, although they can be a good solution in a very modern house. They are made of stiffened fabric and, like venetian blinds, offer various options for controlling the light at a window.

Custom-made and do-it-yourself blinds

Several large manufacturers produce pattern books, which you can find in department or curtain stores. They showcase a range of stiffened fabrics that can be made up into a blind of your choice.

Alternatively, you can take your own fabric to a manufacturer, who will make up a roller blind by stiffening the fabric in some way. In most cases, this involves gluing the fabric to a backing, which can be light-resistant if you want. You need to supply the fabric on a roll, not folded, as any creases will show up in the finished blind.

It is also possible to make your own roller blind from a kit, which comes with a spray-glue stiffener. This can be quite successful, but the spray has a powerful solvent and has to be applied outdoors, and it is not always easy to apply an even coating of stiffener to the fabric.

Customizing roller blinds

• Stick a length of lace, braid or ribbon along the lower edge using craft glue.

• Replace a nylon and plastic centre pull cord and acorn with either a length of coloured cord, string or ribbon, or a leather thong, attached to a tassel, a pebble or a shell. Remove the existing cord holder from the back of the lath. Thread the new pull cord through, tie a knot to hold it and replace the holder.

• Cut small designs and shapes from the blind fabric using a sharp craft (utility) knife on a cutting mat, or use decorating stencils to create quite complex designs. Even a simple pattern of small 2 cm (¾ in) cut-out squares spaced around 20 cm (8 in) apart is extremely effective.

will give the recess size (width is customarily given before drop). Deduct 1 cm ($^3/_8$ in) from the measurements for clearance.

Most recessed blinds work well only if the recess is straight and true, and you can check this by measuring the diagonals of the recess. If there is more than 1 cm ($^3/_8$ in) difference between the two diagonals, then the recess is likely to be skewed and you will have to fit the blind on the outside of the recess.

Fitting a blind outside the recess

If the blind is to hang outside the window recess, add 5–10 cm (2–4 in) to the measurement of the width of the window each side and at the top. The bottom edge can touch the window sill, but if the sill is not level, overlap it by 5–10 cm (2–4 in). (The overlap can be larger or smaller. For example, if you want the fabric of the blind to show, but not obscure too much light, the blind can be fitted well above the window, and left partly pulled down.)

Blinds are useful in bays where the room shape can cause problems for curtains. They also help keep window sills and floors uncluttered and are ideal in rooms with limited space.

Measuring for blinds

You can fix a blind either inside or outside the recess of a window. Whether you are making a blind from scratch, ordering a ready-made one or cutting one down to size, accurate measuring is paramount – measure twice, cut once.

Fitting a blind inside the recess

Using a steel tape, measure the width at both the top and bottom of the window (these measurements are often different, even in modern buildings), and use the smaller measurement. Similarly, measure the drop in several places, and use the smaller measurement. This

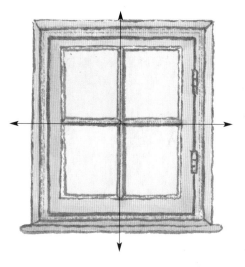

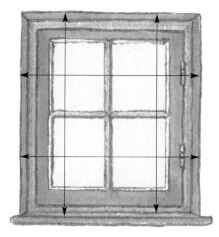

Hanging roller blinds

With a roller blind, the fabric is always narrower than the overall width (pin width) at the top, because you need space for the brackets and mechanism. When buying a roller blind, therefore, it is important to find out whether the measurement you need is the fabric width, or the pin width.

Also decide whether you want a spring-pull mechanism, the classic centre pull cord under tension, or a sidewinder mechanism. This operates the blind by a continuous chain or cord at one side, and tends to be harder wearing.

Find your style

Contemporary style

The combination of light and space, form and function and colour and texture are the basic elements that create contemporary style. A refreshing alternative to overcluttered nostalgia and outdated period style, contemporary is a look that can be adapted to streamline and create the illusion of space in almost any home.

The look

You don't have to be an architect or design purist with cutting-edge furniture and intentionally bare surroundings to live with contemporary style. Although it can be minimalist and stark, it can also be adapted to combine all the basic elements but with a softer approach. With its trademark open-plan layouts and seamless looks, it is an ideal choice for anyone wanting an organized home that is practical, hardwearing and clutter free, yet without sacrificing a sense of comfort.

Contemporary style does, however, demand a certain rigidity for pared-down living and banished mess, so that the overall effect is neat and precise. This requires clever space planning in every room to ensure that there is a place for everything. This can create a practical and easily maintainable living solution, even for a busy family. With effective storage facilities, belongings can be quickly and easily hidden away behind closed doors in built-in cupboards so that the carefully planned silhouette of the room and its contents are both comfortable to relax in and soothing to the eye. Accessories are kept to a minimum and the few that are used are large scale and given room to breathe by a zone of empty space around them.

The materials used in the fabric of the décor are of paramount importance. The focus is on surfaces – walls and worktops, floors and furniture. These should be carefully chosen to create areas of uninterrupted space with hardwearing contemporary surfaces throughout teamed with sleek-styled furniture with clean, smooth lines.

The streamlined shapes and bold statement pieces in this living room are typical of contemporary style, but the neutral colour palette with its accents of ice blue helps create a more relaxed approach.

Why it appeals

The clean lines and attention to detail of contemporary style appeal to those who love sleek, sculptural design and light, airy open spaces, and who want to streamline their possessions with structure and organization. Not suited to those who love intimate surroundings, a hotchpotch of possessions on display or a cluttered mix and match of furniture, contemporary style is a careful and considered approach to design and decorating where every item and surface in the home is included only after much thought and planning.

Although often considered unsuitable for a busy family home with its hard surfaces, sharp edges and minimal style, contemporary interiors can be surprisingly practical, durable and luxurious. Hard floors can be non-slip and underfloor-heated, well-planned storage allows for plenty of space for toys and other kids' paraphernalia and innovative contemporary surfaces are often surprisingly durable and easy to keep clean. There's no need to compromise on comfort or colour either – sculptural lines and hard

Key characteristics

• **Seamless open-plan living** Keep colours and surface styles consistent to link the spaces together and make the rooms look larger and lighter. With a neutral scheme, complementary colours will blend and harmonize throughout the space; if using a bold colour palette, introduce bright splashes of colour from zone to zone.

• **Hard surfaces** Surfaces should blend seamlessly, so think of them as planes of colour and texture and choose hardwearing materials such as glossy granite, reflective glass, shiny marble and practical hardwood, Corian or stainless steel.

• **Good storage** Storage must be well organized to hide away clutter yet make it easily accessible. Choose floor-to-ceiling built-in cupboards with flush doors or neat free-standing units with sleek lines.

• **Streamlined and simple fireplace** Opt for a contemporary hole-in-the-wall-style fireplace complete with remote control. Or, room permitting, invest in a huge statement piece such as a state-of-the-art log burner, which can be placed in the centre of the room.

• **Spotlights** These are a versatile and practical solution for a sleek, minimal scheme, as they are unobtrusive yet provide a variety of lighting effects – mix low-voltage spot lighting with statement pieces like geometric-shaped side or table lamps.

• **Less is more** With plenty of fitted storage, furniture can be streamlined and elegant and accessories minimal but right – a few dramatic-shaped vases grouped together or a statement piece of art to add that all-important personal stamp and final flourish.

• **Neutral-coloured walls** Walls should be in soothing neutrals, either plain painted or with sophisticated finishes from polished plaster to wood veneer panelling.

Floor-to-ceiling glass windows and a neutral wood floor contrast with contemporary statement furniture in a vibrant colour to create a slick, fresh dining area.

surfaces can be softened with luxurious cushions, throws and soft tactile rugs, and contemporary furniture and furnishings come in a riot of vivid colours guaranteed to add a dramatic look for those who want to make a bold statement in their home.

Key colours

With modern open-plan living, the immediate reaction is to use pure brilliant white as a background colour, although this can look cold and rather clinical, especially if combined with huge floor-to-ceiling glass windows. It is more effective instead to use softer shades of white or a tonal colour palette on the walls to create a flow of colour throughout the space rather than to complicate the look by adding a variety of colours. Architects often use a monochrome palette of greys to define different areas in a room and create a sophisticated finish. This trick also works with colour palettes of white, taupe, eau de nil and sand.

A neutral background colour allows a wide choice of furniture and accessories. Choose furnishings in tones that blend and harmonize with the background colours, and add interest around the room with texture and interesting surface details. Alternatively, a neutral background is the ideal contrast for statement pieces of contemporary furniture in bright, vibrant colour or as a backdrop for colourful pieces of modern art.

Walls

In a contemporary decorating scheme, walls are generally in soothing neutral tones or natural materials such as limestone, marble, slate, concrete or polished plaster, all of which create a gentle, easy-on-the-eye background for sleek, streamlined furniture and furnishings or bold, colourful works of art. Although pure white is a popular choice for contemporary style, it can look cold and jarring on the eye and a softer off-white or creamier tone may be more effective, especially in a living room or bedroom. Wallpaper is an unusual yet worthwhile consideration for contemporary style, but it must be in big, bold and eye-catching designs that make a statement or luxurious textured surface papers like metallics, suedes, leather or wood effects (see page 40).

Kitchen and bathroom walls should mix practicality with style. Identical horizontal and vertical surfaces create the most effective and cohesive-looking finish. Choose sleek-looking surfaces such as limestone, marble, slate, concrete, glass or even mirrors and use liberally for walls, floors and bath surround. Although expensive and heavy, these choices create a sophisticated and seamless blend with adjacent surfaces for cutting-edge contemporary style.

A vibrant blue glass lampbase adds a splash of colour to a sleek white decorating scheme. Accents of colour in your accessories will lift a neutral scheme.

Window dressings

Contemporary style is ideally suited to houses with large, floor-to-ceiling feature windows or architect-designed houses where glass plays a major part in the design of the house. Since this is not always possible, make the most of the available light by keeping window styles as simple and streamlined as possible.

Blinds (see page 148) are the most obvious choice, as they are unfussy and come in a variety of styles, designs and fabrics to suit all shapes of window, from practical rollers to roman, venetian and vertical blinds. Where privacy is paramount, frosting the windows is an effective solution – you can do this yourself with a transparent film or spray, or you could replace the glass with special frosted or sandblasted glass panels.

If curtains are a must, opt for very simple structured styles – floor length are best to make windows look longer and more streamlined, and choose tactile fabrics such as felt, suede or wool with simple tab or eyelet headings or sheer curtain panels in luxurious voiles and silks.

Lighting

Plenty of natural light is key to creating a contemporary look, and in open-plan homes with their clean-coloured walls and reflective surfaces, light will bounce around, making the space look larger and feel lighter and brighter. Artificial lighting should be

Geometric-patterned wallpaper in vibrant contemporary colours makes a bold statement in any room. Use large patterns carefully, interspersed with plain neutrals to subdue the effect.

introduced in clever ways in a contemporary home to provide either unobtrusive or feature lighting, both of which need to create a cohesive look around the space without compromising on style.

You should always try to include the lighting requirements in the basic room plans from the very start so that the lighting can be incorporated into ceilings, floors, walls, fitted furniture and decorative features in the room. With free-standing lighting, go for floorstanding and table lamps in wood, metal or leather, and team with simple-shaped plain shades in suede or linen. Sleek chrome and glass lighting or bold coloured perspex are also good choices for modern lighting materials.

Floors

Flooring materials can be very varied, but the required effect is of a seamless space where even if two contrasting floors meet they blend harmoniously and are a major part of the decorative scheme. Hard flooring could be soft, creamy limestone, black, shiny granite or glass, colourful resins, utilitarian cement or ceramic or porcelain tiles. Soft flooring could be luxurious shag pile carpets, rugs, leather or rubber. All types of wood are a possibility and can be sleek, shiny and lacquered or soft-toned and mellow.

Check that the surface you choose is practical for your needs. Limestone and granite, for example, look and feel wonderful, but are extremely heavy and floors

For a more informal touch, hard contemporary lines can be softened by adding accessories in tactile textures such as silks and satins – a luxurious throw can add a welcoming touch to a sofa.

may need strengthening. It is also worth considering underfloor heating with cold, hard surface floors – this not only makes the flooring warm and much more appealing underfoot, it also eliminates the need for other more visually prominent forms of heating such as radiators.

Soft furnishings and fabrics

With such a strong emphasis on simple outline and structured shape, soft furnishings are often disregarded as a major element of contemporary style. However, a few clever touches can make all the difference to a scheme by injecting a splash of bold colour into a neutral room with cushions or throws, drawing attention to a window with a decorative fabric panel or softening the lines of a sculptural bed with beautiful toning linens in tactile textures. The addition of soft furnishings can add those all-important touches that bring your character and personality to the room to prevent it from looking too cold and clinical. Fabrics should be soft suedes and leathers, felt and wool or silks and linens. Alternatively, in contrast, they can be bold, flamboyant prints or textures with oversized pattern and vivid colour.

Wooden boards with a shiny polished surface look streamlined and sophisticated, yet provide a mellow modern backdrop for furniture and furnishings.

Country style

A perennially popular look, country style draws its inspiration from the simple elements of the countryside and its eclectic mix of natural materials, functional furniture and soft earthy colours. All of these elements combine to create a cosy and informal look with timeless appeal.

With its warm, golden tones, pine furniture is the perfect traditional choice for a country-style bedroom. A fresh colour palette of pastel blues and creams prevents the room from looking dark and dingy.

The look

It's a mistake to think that country style should be confined only to homes in the country. Generally, because the style mixes antiques, comfortable furniture and fabrics with lots of natural materials, it is easily adapted to suit almost any home. Country style is the perfect solution if you want a homely and welcoming look and, with its mix and match of old and new and collection of cosy clutter, it captures the nostalgia of a bygone era. It is a look that should constantly grow and evolve over time, absorbing a kaleidoscope of pattern, colour and texture as you pick up an antique at a sale, collect a pretty fabric or set of linen or paint and transform an old chair.

Depending on the colour schemes you choose and how you interpret the theme, country style can be pure classic country with its traditional lived-in rustic feel, rich, earthy colours, cosy clutter and mix of floral prints and patterns, or given the more simple approach of a fresh modern country look. The latter has the essence of country style, but without the frills and flounces, incorporating a lighter, softer colour palette and a more streamlined approach to furnishing.

Why it appeals

Comfort, simplicity and relaxation are the key words that explain why country style is so appealing. Country style is a way of life with a mix and match of possessions collected over the years, which you love and feel comfortable living with, and the style is constantly evolving. Unlike many of the other popular styles, the country look is timeless. It can work equally well in a small cottage or a large house, as the aim is

the same – to create a haven where you can retreat and relax. It is also particularly well suited to large families and lots of pets, since its cluttered style and no need for perfect finishes or surfaces needs little order to look good. Clutter and mix-and-match possessions simply add to the character of the look and are an intrinsic part of its charm and popularity.

Key colours

The ingredients that make up the colour palette for country style are instinctively taken from nature. Soft earthy tones such as terracotta, ochre and burnt umber are a popular choice and create a warm, cosy decorating scheme, while fresher shades inspired by leaves and flowers such as pretty pale greens, pastel blues and primrose yellows and creams add a lighter and softer background colour – particularly good for bedrooms and kitchens or to prevent small rooms looking too dark.

For a modern country approach, opt for the same elements that make up traditional style – wood furniture and simple furnishings, but with more streamlined lines and a softer colour palette.

Since traditional cottage-style proportioned rooms have small windows and low ceilings, it is tempting to paint them white to try to make them look larger and lighter. Always avoid bright whites, which can be stark and cold, and instead opt for off-whites, creams and neutrals for a softer effect – the key to success is to create a calming, relaxing environment by building up layers of soft colour, pattern and texture.

Fresh flowers are essential for adding a pretty touch to a country-style room. Display them in simple ways to make them a feature – a row of flower heads in night light holders has immediate impact.

Key characteristics

• **Wooden furniture** Country furniture has always been made from materials local to the area, so wood is the most obvious and practical choice. Choose chunky pieces of stripped pine or darker oak furniture, or pieces with a matt painted finish in deeper rustic shades for a more traditional look or fresh pastel colours for a modern country look. A dresser (hutch) is a key piece for adding country style to your home – use it to display a selection of china.

• **Natural-looking floors** Keep floors in simple natural materials in soft earthy colours, for example pine and oak planks, rustic terracotta or stone tiles or matting. Rugs are ideal for adding a soft and colourful touch – choose traditional rag rugs and runners for an authentic look.

• **Fabrics** Patchwork, embroidery, natural weaves and pretty cottons all add to the homespun character of the style.

• **Open fire** The open fire and kitchen stove with their cosy glow were traditionally the hub of the home. Incorporate an open fire or woodburning stove into rooms for an authentic country touch – as well being a practical feature, they also provide a focal point and character. A range cooker is also an essential ingredient of country style and adds to the romantic image of the nostalgic country kitchen.

• **Simple lighting** Since country cottages were often small with tiny windows and low ceilings, lighting was limited to wall lights and candles. Overhead lighting is generally too harsh for a soft and shadowy country look, so keep styles simple with the soft glow from wall lights throwing light from wall to ceiling. Position table lamps in dark corners and add a mix of decorative candlesticks and lanterns in a variety of materials.

Walls

For country-style walls, forget pristine finishes and perfect corners – any imperfections and uneven textures only add to the character and charm of the style. While plain painted walls in soft country colours are the most obvious choice, it is worth considering a variety of alternative wall finishes that add traditional character and charm to a room.

Textured plaster finishes painted with a soft wash of colour mimic traditional country-style walls – plastering over a layer of lining paper will make it easy to strip off when you fancy a change. Stencilling and stamping (see page 32) are also a simple and effective way of bringing a classic country feel to a room in an instant, while floral sprig wallpaper is a perfect choice for a pretty country-style bedroom or living room.

Panelling is another option – as well as adding character, it adds impact and proportion to a room, while being tough and durable. Panelling is especially versatile for adding country style to a bathroom.

Window dressings

In large houses, chintz has long been the quintessential fabric of choice for creating country style, with its bold printed floral patterns made up into sweeping and elegant curtain styles. In smaller country cottages,

Wooden flooring is a versatile choice for a country-style interior. Avoid laminates and wood-effect flooring with their uniform appearance and opt for wood boards, which mellow with age.

A creamy white painted wall provides the perfect backdrop for country collectables. It creates a fresh, bright look which is ideal for a small room.

however, simple-styled curtains predominantly made from patterned cotton or natural yarn fabrics have always been more practical.

To replicate such country-style window dressings, choose lightweight cotton fabrics with either small sprigged patterns or checks, or opt for fashionable yarns such as natural textured linens or soft wools. Keep curtain styles unfussy with short curtains for tiny windows, and long flowing curtains for larger windows with simple gathered or slot headings. Fabric blinds are also a suitable country-style solution to prevent windows from looking too fussy or cluttered and are a practical solution in kitchens and bathrooms where privacy is paramount but curtains would be impractical. Keep blinds streamlined and simple in a lightweight cotton fabric either with a roman, roller or pretty roll-up blind with fabric ties.

Lighting

Country-style lighting is primarily about creating a warm and welcoming atmosphere, with soft mood lighting provided by the romantic glow of a real fire and the flicker of candlelight and lanterns. Although practicality must be taken into account, not only for safety but also to provide lighting for specific tasks around the home, you don't need to install bold spotlights or powerful bulbs in every light source. With modern technology, it's easy to install dimmer switches for controllable light and to create an even and effective balance of light around each room by

A junk shop lamp has been revamped with a lick of cream paint and a matching pleated fabric shade to add a pretty touch to a country bedroom scheme.

combining a mix of wall uplighters or downlighters, pendant fittings, table and floor lamps. Choose fittings in traditional country-style materials such as wrought or cast iron, brass, tin, carved wood or chunky stoneware and team with pretty fabric or card shades. Junk shop ceramics and collectables are often converted into decorative table lamps that have an original and unique look.

Candles and lanterns add the perfect finishing touch to a country-style interior and exterior. For a special occasion, a row of lanterns lighting up a pathway or on an outside wall adds an effective display.

Floors

Country-style floors need to cope with a constant stream of children and pets to muddy boots, wet shoes and a wide variety of household paraphernalia without showing the dirt, so hardwearing and practical materials are the only solution.

Natural flooring such as quarry or stone tiles are an effective choice for a kitchen and hallway, as they are both highly durable and easy to keep clean, although

You can mix and match patterns and textures for country-style furnishings, but stick to a complementary colour scheme using two or three contrasting shades to make it work.

they can be cold and hard underfoot. Wooden floors are also a practical and popular choice. If you are lucky enough to have good-quality floorboards in a good condition, you could restore them to their former glory (see page 76) by sanding and sealing. Reclaimed timber is also a worthwhile although relatively costly investment, but can add instant character and personality to a home.

Natural floorcoverings such as coir and sisal (see page 86) are particularly hardwearing and durable, and do add the perfect rustic touch, but they are not suitable for some areas in the home such as stairs (as they can be slippery) or bathrooms and kitchens (as they don't like getting wet). Being a natural colour, matting also provides a neutral base for colourful rugs.

Soft furnishings and fabrics

Country-style fabrics are all about simplicity. Patterns and textures are cleverly mixed together to create an eclectic yet inspirational result. Plain slubby cottons and tactile linens are mixed with polka dots, ginghams and checks, with a printed floral cushion or two thrown in for good measure – and it works! Providing you stick to a simple palette of two or three harmonious or contrasting colours, a mix of pattern and texture in these colours will work together successfully.

Homespun furnishings are essential for adding character and those all-important personal touches to the scheme – beds and sofas covered with patchwork quilts and cushions, crisp embroidered linens, warm woollen throws and handmade lace will add to the quintessential country feel.

Classic style

Drawing inspiration from periods in history, the key to successful classic-style decorating is to create rooms that are formal, symmetrical and elegant, and to achieve the feeling that they have been lived in for generations.

The look

The quality of the interior elements is paramount – from architectural details to furnishings and finishing touches. Each item has a specific place and so there is little flexibility once the scheme is designed.

Symmetry is vital in each room scheme – a bed flanked by two matching side tables and lamps with a mirror or print centred over the bed; a living room with two identical chairs opposite a contrasting sofa yet with matching proportions or a display of prints perfectly balanced on a wall. The effect is designed to be sophisticated and elegant, yet easy on the eye. Although a classic-styled interior can include contemporary elements, these are still incorporated using classic guidelines with the same end result.

Furniture can be a mix of antique, reproduction or more modern pieces. It must, however, be based on classic styles – imposing beds, huge-scale mirrors, ornate statues and elegantly shaped furniture with decorative detailing. Teamed with authentic period colour, plain and elegant furnishings and carefully chosen accessories, the elements combine to create a look that will add timeless appeal to your home.

Why it appeals

If you want to live surrounded by luxurious things displayed simply and elegantly, then classic style is the look for you. This very grown-up look demands not

Rooms inspired by a classic period should be sparing in their use of colour – take a look at the modern ranges of authentic heritage paint colours to recreate a classic look with ease.

You can't go wrong with classic white accessories. From simple white china to crisp linens and fluffy white towels, they can be an essential and timeless addition to the classic interior.

Painting your home in 'period' colours has never been easier thanks to the widely available special 'historic' paints – ranges of heritage colours based on archive material.

Key characteristics

• **Symmetry** Balance each room by using matching chairs or side tables and add impact with pairs of pictures in matching frames or a duo of table lamps.

• **Architectural features** Use architectural features to add proportion and definition as well as instant classic style – from a main focal point such as a fireplace to mouldings such as a dado, picture rail and cornice.

• **Good-quality materials** Essential for classic looks that will stand the test of time – solid hardwood or marquetry floors, marble fireplaces, polished wood furniture and luxurious fabrics from damasks to silks.

• **Grand windows** Opt for generous curtains in traditional styles such as swags and tails or with pelmets to emphasize and accentuate window proportions, making them look larger and longer.

• **Elegant furniture** Upholstered furniture is generally in straight-backed styles with wooden frames. Choose pieces with elegant proportions and team with furniture in dark polished woods, leather or glass.

only structured living, formality and attention to detail, but also the very best quality in furniture and furnishings and strict discipline in arranging them so that they create a streamlined formal interior.

The classic look works better in homes with traditional features and roomy proportions. A larger room gives the space to appreciate how the scheme works, adding to the elegance of the look. In the classic interior, the home is divided into separate areas, each with a particular role to play. A classic living room may not be suited to the modern paraphernalia of busy family lifestyles, so consider establishing a separate informal family room, or incorporate clever storage solutions without compromising on either looks or practicality.

You don't need to confine the décor to a single period to create a classic style that works. Rather than create a pastiche and overworked interior, it's best to choose a mix of pieces that work well together, but also suit the requirements of your lifestyle. A children's bedroom, for example, could include a wonderful antique bateau-style bed and traditional soft furnishings, but be teamed with modern built-in cupboards painted in classic colours to provide practical and concealed storage for clothes and toys.

Key colours

If you are a purist, you might want to track down and use exact replicas of authentic paint colours to capture and recreate a particular period. However, most paint

manufacturers now produce special 'historic' ranges with specific period colours based on archive material, which makes the job of choosing colour much simpler.

Originally, the classic colour palette was derived from natural pigments and so produced a diverse range of tones from soft creamy whites and golds through to shades of taupe, brown, red, green and more exotic shades of blue. While the colour shades vary dramatically, rooms should be decorated extremely simply with a sparing use of colour on walls teamed with either white or a darker shade used to highlight skirtings (baseboards), mouldings and panelling. Contrast with beautiful ornate wood flooring to provide a sophisticated backdrop.

Paint effects (see page 28) can also be used – scumbling, dragging, sponging and marbling were traditionally used to make inferior surfaces look as good as the real thing and are still popular today.

Walls

From historic colours in rich matt paint shades to panelling and heavily patterned wallpaper, the colour and pattern you choose for your wall surfaces (which are often divided by mouldings and features) can make or break the decorating scheme. They not only pull a scheme together and set the tone for the furniture and furnishings, but are also key to creating the mood in the room by playing with the combination of colour and proportion.

It is easy to select a paint colour to suit your requirements from today's specialist heritage ranges. Classic-style painted walls are generally decorated in a plain, flat matt single colour, and the aspect of the room should be a major determining factor as to which colour to use – avoid using pale blues and greens in north-facing rooms, as they can look cold and rather harsh. Soft creams and richer golds make an effective background colour that works with most furniture styles and can be teamed with rich gilt or dramatic black accessories.

Authentic panelled walls and decorative features add instant character and classic looks to a room, but when adding features yourself to a room, pay attention to the divisions of the wall, adapting the proportions to suit the scale of your room. Authentic-looking panelled walls can easily be created using softwood or MDF (medium-density fibreboard) and painted in a colour to match your walls.

Wallpaper is an effective choice for classic style – opt for wide vertical stripes, large-scale damasks or classic-style prints in tone-on-tone colour.

Window dressings

Large windows are more suitable for classic-style window dressings, since they should be elaborate designs using generous amounts of fabric, which would swamp and overpower the proportions of a small window. Choose floor-length curtains topped with a pelmet, valance or elaborate swags and tails. Curtains can be used on their own or, for a really luxurious look, teamed with roman or roll-up fabric blinds in a contrasting fabric.

The classic-style window relies greatly on elegant shaping and correct formal proportions and in the most elaborate interiors were frequently left undressed, relying on shutters for keeping in the warmth. Traditional-style shutters are still a practical and effective choice today, left in natural wood or painted, and work especially well in rooms where you want to avoid fussy curtaining.

Although you can make windows look larger by disguising their proportions – for example, use a wider curtain pole and place it higher than the window – in small rooms, pare down the style and opt for simple floor-length curtains in a pale colour with a plain or subtle patterned fabric. Choose a complementary wall tone to avoid drawing attention to the windows.

Lighting

Good lighting is key to a successful classic-style interior – a badly lit room will distort the proportions and balance in the room, whereas good lighting can reapportion space beautifully and to great effect. With large rooms and big windows, natural light and soft colour schemes will only add to the feeling of space and elegance in a room, and it's easy to accentuate this with large mirrors above mantels and on walls.

Supplement the natural light source with flattering ceiling lights with dimmer switches to adjust the ambience in the room, then add task and feature lighting to complete the look. Symmetrical features are vital for adding grandeur and formality to the look – for example, a pair of carved wooden wall sconces, matching sleek glass table lamps with silk shades or ornate bronze candle holders.

Classic style demands quality materials for lighting – a decorative glass lampbase adds a smart, sophisticated touch to this classic scheme, echoing the unusual tabletop.

Wooden floorboards add character and there is often a glorious floor lurking under years of paint – renovate flooring to its former glory by sanding and sealing it, then adding a coat of varnish.

Floors

Most suitable for hallways, bathrooms, kitchens and dining rooms, the most classic-looking floors are black and white squares in tile or marble or terrazzo (marble chippings set in cement), all of which look wonderful and are extremely durable and hardwearing, but are heavy and expensive. If installing a traditional marble or tiled floor, consider installing underfloor heating at the same time to prevent the surfaces from being cold underfoot.

For living rooms and bedrooms, polished wood flooring, in dark rather than light tones, is also a wonderful-looking classic choice and looks just as good on its own or topped with rugs – hardwoods are the most effective solution and improve and mellow with age. Traditional parquetry and marquetry designs are as popular as ever and original designs can still be found in reclamation yards. Alternatively, existing softwood boards can be made to look fairly authentic (see page 76) by sanding, sealing, finishing with a stain and polishing to a glimmering sheen.

Wall-to-wall carpet is another option for a classic-styled room, but it must be of a really luxurious quality and the carpet colour needs to enhance the overall decorating scheme.

Soft furnishings and fabrics

There is no point in skimping on either quality or quantity with classic-style furnishings. Linens, cottons, silks, satin damasks, velvets, wools and tapestry are all classics and can be introduced in a variety of soft furnishings, from upholstery and curtains to cushions and bedcovers. In complete contrast to contemporary style, trimmings are key, too – finish upholstery with decorative piping or gimp, and curtains with fringing or braiding.

In general, plain colours and subtle patterns work best to emphasize the simple, elegant look of the interior and to highlight the quality of the fabrics – sweeps of plain fabric take the eye from plain to plain, while bold pattern will distract the eye. If you do want bolder patterns and colours, opt for richly coloured brocades, watered silks, embroideries and tapestries, all of which can add impact to a classic scheme, but they should work with it instead of overpower it.

In the bedroom, invariably the look should be luxurious white bed linen and in the bathroom piles of fluffy white or crisp linen towels and a luxurious deep-pile bath mat.

Crisp white linens add a luxurious touch to any room in the home. Look for the most exquisite linens, embroidered cottons and handmade lace.

Global style

It is easy to see why global-style decorating has become so popular. It is all about creating your own style and incorporating a multi-cultural blend of pieces. Whether you are adding a few simple touches or transforming entire rooms with different themes, it's fun to create rooms with personality and individuality that are unique.

The look

With the huge selection of global products in many high-street ranges and the ease of internet shopping, it has never been so easy to access a variety of furniture and furnishings from around the world. With its exotic looks and myriad of regional styles teaming unusual shapes, textures and colours, global-style decorating is a fascinating new world to us and breaks all the rules of creating a formulaic interior.

In complete contrast to the mass-produced items of the west, global style offers handmade and homespun designs using traditions that have been handed down through the ages, giving each item a unique personality of its own with individual characteristics.

Global style can work in any size and style of home and with any budget. A few simple 'ethnic' accessories teamed with a bold colour palette can add unexpected touches to a room without costing a fortune, while a complete transformation with furniture and furnishings creates an exotic mood and a very different way of living.

Why it appeals

Global style has widespread appeal that can be used to transform any style and size of interior, and is a look that can be introduced in a variety of ways. As well as the more confident and exotic approach of combining traditional design, vibrant pattern, bold colour and unique creations, the look can also be restrained and orderly with a more classic approach. For example, a beautiful carved Indonesian cupboard topped with a

An antique teak daybed makes a dramatic statement in this room and is topped with textiles in a medley of bright, tropical colour that picks out the primary tones of the dish.

collection of wooden boxes or a colonial-style four-poster bed are feature pieces in a room that can be juxtaposed with a more traditional decorating scheme.

The key to creating a successful interior is to choose items that you love and ensure that your home is practical for the way you live – think of inventive ways to use more unusual pieces of furniture. A Thai rain drum, for example, can make a dramatic coffee table, while a handcrafted pottery jug can be transformed into a lamp. With its fusion of styles from around the globe, you make of the theme what you want and, depending on your budget, you can add small inexpensive accessories or splash out on antiques.

As well as using dramatic colour, the style is also a great way of introducing a variety of textures to a scheme. Handcrafted items are often made from unusual materials and have a wonderful tactile quality to them – think of handmade woven baskets, rough carved wooden furniture and smooth marble. Differing textures keep a room visually rich and their natural

Look to incorporate accessories in interesting and unusual fibres. These woven grass baskets would make a decorative centrepiece as a coffee table.

looks are a wonderful foil for colourful paint tones and fabrics. If the idea of bringing the world into your home appeals, then global style is the look for you.

Key colours

Colours from around the world vary from country to country and from region to region. For example, deep reds are symbolic in China, you'll find vibrant pinks in India and vivid blues and whites are commonplace in the Mediterranean. So, pick a few colours that you like and try to stick to these throughout the scheme to allow colour and pattern to flow. Most global furnishings, however, are colour-led by the pigments and natural dyes available from their native surroundings, which is why natural tones of rich reds, browns and earthy shades are fairly widespread.

The best starting point is to choose an object that is to be a main part of the scheme – a bold patterned rug, colourful wall hanging or work of art, for example – and pick out a colour from the piece to use as a basis for the decorating scheme. For a more classic approach, which combines traditional western pieces with exotic touches, opt for a more neutral colour such as off-white, cream or beige, which will bring a sense of calm to a riot of colour and also provide a soft background to highlight the global features.

Decorative details add the unique and interesting features that make all the difference to a scheme, however small they are. Have fun searching out an eclectic mix of styles and patterns.

Key characteristics

• Exotic style and atmosphere

Whatever mix of furniture, furnishings and accessories you choose, the combination of exciting objects and global artefacts will add unique features to your home.

• **Textiles** Textiles can be used to cover walls, furniture, windows, floors and beds. They can add warmth to a scheme and, with their wonderful array of pattern, colours and textures, will have instant impact. Use them simply for a more streamlined approach or fill a room with a medley of layers.

• **Wooden objects** Wood lends itself to a variety of furniture and accessories, from the roughest-hewn timbers carved into naive bowls and sculptures to the mellow aged patina of an Indian cupboard.

• **Texture** Texture plays a vital part in a global interior and can include rattan, cane, wicker, bamboo or palm leaves made up into furniture, screens, window dressings or floorcoverings and accessories.

A wall painted in a soft colour provides a simple contrast to the vibrant patterns and colours of global style. Dilute the paint 50:50 with water and apply it with a large brush for a weather-worn look.

Walls

Paint is the most obvious material for decorating walls in a global-style scheme. Instead of a perfect painted finish, go for a much more informal approach with a soft wash of flat matt colour in earthy shades. This provides an ideal simple contrast to the riot of pattern and eclectic design, yet also makes a defining statement and sets the mood in a room. Textured stucco plaster is also a consideration and again painted in a wash of soft pastel colour works wonderfully well with rustic-styled furniture to bring a sun-faded mellow look to a room.

You could also consider wallpaper. There is a plethora of unusual and effective materials to choose from (see page 40). Look at grasses, bamboo and handmade papers for a natural textured approach, or vibrant large-scale designs with rich colour and gold or silver leaf – ideal for a feature wall teamed with elaborate dark wood Indian furniture or Moroccan accessories.

Window dressings

Avoid fussy traditional curtain styles or frills and flounces, and instead opt for a simple approach using the diverse range of textiles and materials available.

Although you could make plain floor-length curtains from a colourful patterned fabric or textured weave, be inventive and use traditional textures in clever ways. A silk sari, for example, makes a wonderful and dramatic curtain by stitching a casing through which to slot a curtain pole. Lightweight throws, rugs, scarves and linens can also be adapted into curtains or blinds. You could also use natural blinds to keep window styles simple and streamlined – wood, bamboo or paper are a good choice. Alternatively, look at wooden shutters and decorative carved panels. Be inventive with antiques, too, as there are many unusual and decorative carved panels that can be adapted and used to frame or add a decorative feature to a window.

Lighting

Although practical lighting is essential in kitchens, bathrooms and work areas, global style is all about capturing an exotic mood and creating a cosy and inviting atmosphere. For a more classic take on global style, introduce dramatic and unique pieces that enhance the furniture and furnishings you already have. For example, a pair of chinoiserie lamps in a living room or a decorative silver Moroccan lantern in a hallway can add impact and interest to a scheme. For a more dramatic approach, choose chandeliers and table lamps, candles, lanterns and sconces in eye-

Pretty coloured lanterns with a hint of Morocco are ideal for adding a colourful touch to an interior or exterior scheme and can be moved between the two depending on the season.

Natural textured flooring provides the perfect link for the basic ingredients of global style and is a neutral base on which to add layers of colour.

Soft furnishings and fabrics

Fabrics from exotic countries have long been a source of inspiration and a welcome treasure in interiors over the last few centuries – just think of the silks from China or paisley shawls from Kashmir, which are as popular today as ever. The charm of soft furnishings lies in their diversity and in the age-old techniques used to produce the batiks, appliqués, block prints or weaves that look surprisingly contemporary, yet are often traditional handed-down designs.

Soft furnishings from around the globe can be used to transform every room in the home, from wall hangings, cushions and upholstery to curtains and window dressings. Styles can be diverse, too, from a kelim-covered sofa in the living room and Japanese kimono in the bathroom to a silk sari in the bedroom and batik-printed linens in the dining room.

Ensure that the fabrics you choose are practical for your needs – many highly decorative, delicate or embroidered fabrics require careful laundering and are fragile, so in a busy family household, opt for more durable woven cottons and washable materials.

catching shapes, and let light flicker and dance around a space, accentuating the bold colours with shadows and highlights.

Floors

Rugs are an essential part of any global-style look and will instantly transform a room, reviving a plain decorating scheme by introducing fresh colour and pattern. Many of the designs such as kelims, dhurries and gabbehs have been around for thousands of years, and often the rugs are still produced using traditional methods and colours that vary from region to region. Rugs are one of the most versatile furnishings for your home and, since they come in every colour, pattern, shape, size and price imaginable, there will always be one to suit any size and style of home. As well as for the floor, consider using a rug on the wall – they make wonderful works of art.

For a neutral base beneath a rug and to provide a wall-to-wall flooring solution as an effective contrast for a bold colour scheme, opt for natural floorcoverings (see page 86) such as coir, sisal, seagrass or bamboo, or, for a softer approach, a natural textured carpet made from wool.

A mix and match of exotic textures and materials brings luxury and opulence to a global-style interior. Remember that flowers can be used to add an instant splash of colour, too.

Romantic style

A comfortingly familiar and accessible look to achieve in any home, romantic style is all about following your instincts and creating an interior in which to retreat and relax, surrounding yourself with things you love – be it faded florals, mismatched glass and crockery, handed-down treasures or an eclectic mix of antique and junk shop finds.

The look

Romantic style is never about the 'worth' of the objects. Instead, it is a style that is all about surrounding yourself with favourite things to create an environment that evokes memories of nostalgia and an embodiment of comfort and charm.

Romantic style doesn't have to look overcluttered and traditional. A pared-down approach with elegant white painted furniture or utilitarian enamelware, for example, has a simplicity of style that looks modern and would work in a more streamlined romantic scheme, yet has enduring appeal. Indeed, the renewed trend for vintage-style and retro homes has resulted in many manufacturers reintroducing contemporary fabrics and furnishings printed with vintage-style designs, reproduction furniture aged with vintage characteristics or updated traditional-style enamelware and kitchenware.

Classic romantic style has a used, faded charm and lived-in look. Fabrics are soft and natural textures – linens, cottons, muslins and chintz in faded and tea-stained patterns or scraps of antique linens, silks, velvets or tapestry. Vintage finds are key to the look – a wrought-iron bed in creamy white distressed paint, an overstuffed sofa with a faded linen cover or an antique glass chandelier hidden under decades of grime – left as they are or restored to their former glory.

Why it appeals

Comfortingly familiar to all of us yet uniquely personal, the appeal of romantic style is its embodiment of our nostalgia for days gone by. As well as being cosy and relaxing with its eclectic displays of mismatched objects, it can also provide a form of escapism by creating an environment that is far removed from everyday life yet remains practical and durable and suits almost any home.

You don't need to spend a fortune on creating a vintage-style interior. On the contrary, the style is achieved by instinct rather than fashion. Second-hand shop finds, visible patching and even chipped and slightly damaged items have their place in the interior, providing they have a use. This informal look is ideal for a family, as items need to be practical and not too pristine or precious. Although romantic style can be cluttered, it does not need to be untidy or inefficient – in a well-organized kitchen, every item should have its place and at least one purpose.

An old painted wrought-iron bedstead teamed with an eclectic mix of patterned linens gives a homely lived-in feel to a small bedroom. The soft colours and sheer drapes give it a feminine feel.

Sweet-scented fresh-cut flowers are an essential addition to a romantic-style decorating scheme, as they add impact with their bright splashes of colour as well as make a room smell delightful.

Decorating your home in romantic style and discovering new and exciting pieces from antique market or junk shop expeditions is an ongoing gradual process that develops over time and is as rewarding and enjoyable as living in the finished rooms. The key to success is to not take the style too seriously so that your home becomes a museum – instead, follow your individuality and instinct to create a home full of atmosphere, cosiness and warmth.

Key colours

Romantic style is a blend of past treasures, so even the colour palette has the faded, lived-in charm of a bygone era. No furniture or furnishing colours are bold, bright or jarring in the scheme; instead, everything should have the patina and aged looks of vintage finds. Accents of bright colour can be introduced to the scheme via a vase of pretty garden flowers, a tapestry cushion or a handpainted china bowl to add a little impact to the romantic scheme without being overpowering.

Painted furniture is key to the look, but tends to be creamy white or pastel shades in soft blues, greys and pinks painted with a distressed, worn appearance – paint finishes should not be perfect, as any imperfections only add to the character of the piece. Since fabric and pattern are vital to the look, walls tend to be soft blends of matt paint or rough plaster with a soft wash of colour that echoes the furniture tones.

Key characteristics

• **Treasures** A rich and varied mix of treasures, even with a little quirkiness and eccentricity, is key to the look – a kitchen dresser (hutch) full of mismatched china collected over the years, a comfortable battered sofa covered with a pretty floral throw or layers of mix-and-match rugs over a mellowed wood floor.

• **Countryside inspiration** The inspiration for a romantic-style scheme is drawn from the gardens and countryside with its old-fashioned roses, cottage garden floral prints and organic textures and surfaces provided by soft woven linens and antique cottons and muslins.

• **Flowers** These are a must. Forget styled arrangements or over-the-top displays – pick flowers fresh from the garden and arrange in glass jam jars, simple pieces of enamelware or pretty china.

• **Cosy and relaxing** The style requires comfortable upholstery, rustic wood or painted furniture in mismatched styles. A traditional fireplace can make all the difference, too – choose a cosy log fire or wood burner for living rooms and a large stove in the kitchen.

• **Aromatic fragrances** These are key to creating the ambience of a romantic-style interior. Whether it's the wood smoke of a roaring log fire, fresh flowers from the garden or scented night lights and candles, always inject finishing touches into a room scheme that tantalize the senses.

Pattern is an eclectic mix – never coordinated, but an inspirational collection of faded florals, vintage ticking, country-style ginghams and traditional plaids. Antique linens are also central to the scheme – for example, antique cotton or monogrammed linen sheets, sheer voile and lace panels at windows and crisp white table linens.

Walls

Textured chalky paint in soft natural colours seems to work best in a romantic-style interior, as these colours provide a subtle background for the mix of pattern and texture in the scheme. White or off-white walls or soft pastel creams, yellows and pinks are a versatile choice and bring a cohesive look to the eclectic mix of treasures – from painted to mirrored and gilt surfaces, china and coloured glassware. Bright colours are often avoided, as they would seem out of place and harsh with the vintage look. However, the resurgence in fashion for vintage-style interiors has led to a slightly brighter colour palette being introduced – clean minty greens, soft baby blues and pinks – although these bring a much more contemporary look to the end result.

Panelling, painted in a soft colour, can also be a key feature in a romantic-style interior and is decorative as well as being a practical surface. Wallpaper is a worthwhile consideration, too, as there are plenty of pretty floral sprig and tea-stained designs as well as faded stripes available, which are ideal for adding a romantic touch to a room. Teamed with vintage-style pickings, wallpaper can add instant character and charm. If the patterned paper could be too overwhelming, use it on just one wall as a feature (see page 126) and paint the other walls to coordinate.

Printed voile fabric in soft pretty colours allows sunlight to flood into the room, while providing a degree of privacy. This type of window treatment is more suited to a living area than a bedroom.

Window dressings

Window furnishings should be in unfussy styles, but not streamlined or clinical. Opt for flowing floor-length styles in faded florals or checked linens, cottons or muslins. Although simply styled, the curtains can still have attention to detail – pretty tied or tab headings, or button or ribbon trims – but incorporated in a subtle and clever way instead of being dressy and showy so that the curtains blend into the scheme in the room. Roman, roller or roll-up blinds are also a good choice and can be made from cottons and linens or from recycled materials, such as a simple blind made from a vintage tablecloth or tea towel.

Lighting

While the addition of soft candlelight, lanterns and mood lighting is the most obvious choice for creating a romantic atmosphere in your home, incorporating as much natural daylight into a scheme is a wonderful way of adding a soft haze to rooms. It also adds to the faded look of furnishings and décor, softening any harsh colours and fabrics with its natural bleaching qualities. Instead of using pendant fittings or harsh spotlights, introduce a variety of different size and style

Neutral walls in a soft white or off-white paint provide a plain canvas for treasured possessions in a mix of styles, and bring calm and cohesion to the scheme.

A chandelier is a must for romantic style. Scour junk shops and flea markets for wonderful vintage finds or opt for a modern reproduction and distress it with a coat of mottled paint.

of table lamps around room schemes to create scattered pools of soft light. In keeping with romantic style, choose complementary lampbases made from painted wood, brass, glass or ceramic, topped with pretty fabric shades.

Floors

Highlight the rustic charm of a romantic-style interior by using a mix of mellowed surfaces for flooring. Wood is the obvious first choice, but should be aged and distressed planks, or painted boards in soft pastel shades. These don't need to have a perfect finish either – imperfections in the wood such as knots or cracks are all part of adding the character and charm to the look.

Wall-to-wall carpet contributes a more contemporary and luxurious approach, but does add a warm, soft touch underfoot and can be introduced into a scheme, then topped with soft rugs to add layers of pattern and texture. Rugs are key to the romantic style and tapestry, woven or homespun designs with faded vintage looks can be used in every room in the house – incorporate two or three into a room scheme by positioning them around the room or by making a patchwork effect with them.

Soft furnishings and fabrics

Fabrics and soft furnishings are a highly recognizable element of romantic style and give the look its enduring appeal. As with wallpaper, light pretty florals and faded stripes are the patterns of choice. Original vintage fabrics are now hard to find, but luckily there are many modern yet authentic-looking alternatives available – from beautiful faded linens and eiderdowns to well-worn aged ticking upholstery and quilted silk cushions. Pretty voiles, organzas and sheer fabrics in plain muted colours or printed florals also suit the romantic style.

Layering is an important part of achieving the romantic look. In the bedroom, team pretty embroidered linens with plump pillows, feather-filled duvets (comforters) or eiderdowns and a stack of cushions. In the living room, cover a linen sofa with a pretty silk throw and plump cushions made from scraps of vintage fabric teamed with velvets, wool, linen and tapestry. Fading and patching are all part of the appeal and give the style its unique look.

Bed or table linens made from a mix of vintage floral remnants and pretty trims instantly add a romantic and personal touch to a furnishing scheme.

Natural style

Using nature as its starting point and inspiration to make the most of natural organic materials, their soft colours and timelessly classic shapes, the natural-style home is unfussy, tactile, unique and one that simply cannot go out of fashion.

The look

Mellowed or rough-hewn wood, cool stone, fresh cotton, natural wicker and heavy textured fabrics are some of the key elements essential to the natural look and, with its soft neutral colour palette and wonderfully eclectic mix of texture, there is an enduring appeal to the natural look that works equally well in both urban and country homes. Using natural colours and tones allows plenty of freedom of choice in the look and style of your home. In its purely natural form with a mix of rough textures, chunky shapes and heavy textiles, it can take on a simple rustic

With a sophisticated neutral palette and classic enduring finishes, this natural bathroom combines tactile textures such as smooth and rough with glossy and matt surfaces.

appearance; while teaming natural materials with sharper, more modern and streamlined forms and finishes sees a contemporary take on the natural look.

Whichever style you like, the fundamental rules are the same when it comes to creating the basis of the style. Start with a simple canvas for walls, floors and surfaces and use a few dominant textures from nature, such as smooth stone or reclaimed wood flooring, mellow timber cladding or exposed beams for these surfaces, keeping the canvas tonal and avoiding hard contrasts to create a harmonious and cohesive look. By incorporating your chosen furniture and accessories within a neutral shell, the end result will be a calm and restful environment.

Why it appeals

With its soft colours drawn from nature and tactile organic elements, natural style cannot fail to inspire and appeal, as it is simple, understated and creates a relaxed and comfortable look. As well as being a good choice of style for those who like the easy-on-the-eye

Soft white walls teamed with furniture and furnishings in an interesting mixture of textures and tones creates a restful living room with a sense of space and light.

Key characteristics

• **Natural materials** Wood is the recurring element of natural style and indispensable for adding warmth. It can be untreated timber with its rough-hewn rustic looks, smooth and bleached driftwood, antique and mellowed or sleek contemporary veneer. Use this versatile material on floors, walls, ceilings, panelling, furniture and accessories. Stone is also a practical surface material – use rough flagstones, sandstone and limestone or rustic bricks and terracotta.

• **Texture** Aim for interesting surfaces around the home and create a mix and match of texture on fittings, furniture, furnishings and accessories. Juxtapose soft with hard and rough with smooth – a basin or bath made from stone or wood will create a spectacular and streamlined look for a bathroom, while a dining table made from simple blocks of rustic wood adds individuality and character to a scheme, and a linen-covered sofa adds a cosy yet informal touch to a room.

• **Focal fireplace** A fireplace is a bold focal point and practical addition to the look – choose a rustic log burner for a more traditional look or a sleek, contemporary hole-in-the-wall-type fireplace in smooth limestone for a more modern approach.

• **Simple window dressings** Window dressings should provide an unstructured simple outline and be made from natural materials. Floor-length flowing curtains in calico, linen or wool, or simple streamlined wood or hessian (burlap) blinds are ideal for an unfussy scheme.

• **Natural light** Forget atmospheric lighting – the key to creating a natural look is to use as much daylight as possible. Pale colours, simple window styles and uncluttered rooms all help achieve a light, airy feel in a home.

colour palette and informality, the natural look gives plenty of scope for those who want to explore and utilize the increasing range of natural materials on offer. With the rising trend for more ecofriendly interiors, the natural look continues to gain popularity, with the widespread availability of specialist paints, furniture and furnishings that don't compromise on style, comfort, efficiency or functionality.

The natural look with all its variations of style – from country to restrained modern – is extremely versatile for all types of lifestyles. Even the mix of pale colours can be practical, as natural fibres and textures tend to be extremely durable and hardwearing – ideal for a busy family home.

Key colours

The natural colour palette is made up of colours derived from natural objects in their purest form. Think of surfaces from the landscape for key colours, then work up a palette of tone-on-tone colourings for a harmonious scheme or contrasting shades for a more dramatic look. Take inspiration from soft white chalk, mottled stone in greys and taupes, mellow wood tones, sand and earth – colour combinations that will work in almost any interior. Although the palette extends to deep nut browns and dark slate greys, unless these are introduced into a scheme cleverly and with balance, they can look overpowering. For example, a dark slate floor used with pale wood may make a room appear smaller and rather cold, while a softer-coloured stone floor would blend harmoniously.

Choose elegant accessories in pared-down shapes and with interesting surface textures to coordinate with the natural look – these rattan coasters perfectly complement the neutral table.

There is a huge range of white tinted paints available – from soft blue/whites to grey/whites or yellow/white. Here, a soft creamy white works well with the mellow golden tones of wood.

Walls

Walls should be in tones of soft colour, although they don't have to be limited only to large areas of flat paint. Texture is key, too, so wall options include a whole variety of materials, from paint with special finishes like suede or plaster to wallcoverings, wood, weaves, tiles and stone. Paint, however, is probably the most obvious and inexpensive solution, as it comes in an infinite variety of colours with subtle variations of tone that can make all the difference to a decorating scheme. It is important that you make the most of the natural light in your home so that it works in conjunction with the colour you choose. Bright white is not always the antidote to a naturally dark room. It may be too harsh and uncomfortably dazzling on the eye, so softer off-whites, creams, putty, taupe or tones of grey may be a better choice.

Textured wallcoverings (see page 40) are a practical alternative for covering less-than-perfect walls and come in a huge selection of styles from natural grasses, woven fabric or faux fabric finishes to leather, bamboo

and natural papers. They are a good way of introducing interesting texture to a scheme to enhance the character of the room.

Wood is also a popular choice and, depending on the type of timber you choose and the way in which you use it, can make all the difference to the look and style of a scheme. It can be sleek and modern with contemporary veneer wall-to-wall panelling or organic looking with rough-hewn timbered oak beams.

Window dressings

Window dressings should be predominantly plain with a mix of wonderful textures to add interest. Look at utility materials such as lightweight calico, muslin, cotton or linen for soft flowing curtains or blinds with fluid shapes, or add warmth and privacy to a scheme with heavyweight hessian (burlap), cotton drill or more luxurious wool and weaves. Opt for full-length floor-to-ceiling flowing curtains in unfussy styles to make rooms look larger and lighter, and top with tie, tab or simple gathered headings.

Blinds or shutters are ideal for keeping window styles simple – plain rollers or romans are streamlined and unpretentious, or pretty roll-up blinds can add a decorative touch to a window. Wooden shutters look wonderful on large-proportioned windows and make an elegant feature of the window.

Lighting

Lighting should be understated and look natural, and should simply be used to accentuate the relaxed mood so characteristic of natural-style décor. The play of

For a contemporary approach in a natural scheme, choose lighting details that will be a feature in the room as well as providing a practical light source.

Limestone flooring is hardwearing and durable. It comes in a range of wonderful soft tones, from natural beige to creamy white, and adds a contemporary look to a neutral scheme.

sunlight and shadow is key to the look, so make the most of this in the room by using pale colours and reflective surfaces to bounce any natural light around the room.

Supplement the natural light with understated spotlights on a dimmer switch so that you can vary the ambience in the room. You could also add table or floor lamps to make a practical and decorative feature. For a more contemporary natural look, opt for eye-catching streamlined lighting with boxy shaped lampbases in wood or glass teamed with natural woven or linen shades. For a more traditional or organic approach, choose lamps made from unusual and interesting materials that will add a unique feature to the room, such as a driftwood sculpture or a rough-hewn piece of oak combined with a plain textured fabric shade.

Floors

Flooring should be natural-textured and pale-toned to emphasize the feeling of light and space in the rooms. Solid floors such as stone, slate, marble and limestone are hardwearing and practical and look wonderful, but they are heavy and can be cold underfoot. Consider underfloor heating to take away the chill, as it makes all the difference between a clinical and a warm, cosy ambience in a room.

Carpet and matting is a softer option and there are plenty of pale tones and interesting textures to choose from. Wood is another practical solution and, if you opt for a good-quality wood, will last and mellow with age. Avoid shiny laminates and instead go for solid wood, which comes in a wonderful range of materials with unique characteristics and colour tones.

Soft furnishings and fabrics

Unbleached cottons, billowing muslin, textured linen and soft wools in neutral colours are all fabrics essential for creating natural style and adding texture and character to a tonal scheme. The simpler the style, the more important it is to get the balance right to create a room that has comfort, appeal and practicality. For an easy-living neutral room, choose washable furnishings that are simple to clean and maintain as well as look good.

Floor-length flowing curtains, comfortable loose-covered upholstery and luxuriously tactile wool rugs are ideal for a cosy, relaxed style. For a more streamlined contemporary approach, well-made fitted upholstery is more suitable and is a look that is dressed up with visual emphasis on every detail in the scheme.

Furnishings can have detailing, but it should be unfussy and work with the natural scheme – a row of pretty wooden buttons on a cushion, for example, or a throw fringed with a suede trim.

A mixture of different natural textures in neutral colours, with subtle detailing, will provide wonderfully soothing and tactile soft furnishings for a room scheme.

Kitchens

Planning the use

Traditionally regarded as the heart of the home, the kitchen is certainly the most practical space, so before you start thinking about decorating and the designs and colours you would like, you need to work out exactly what you want from your kitchen. If you are able to start from scratch with a newly rebuilt or extended kitchen, so much the better.

Wear and tear

Consider how much time you will spend in your kitchen, whether it's a room just for cooking or whether it needs to provide an eating space, too, and what appliances and storage are essential to the way

A breakfast bar with stools provides a compact eating area in the kitchen and encourages social interaction while the cook is hard at work.

Laundry location

Count yourself lucky if you already have a separate utility room for washing, drying and ironing clothes, and for storing recycling bins, outside coats and muddy shoes and other unsightly sundries. If you don't have a utility room but you have enough space in a large kitchen to consider partitioning it off to create a utility area, it is well worth doing so.

For those without utility space, consider whether you need to do your laundry in the kitchen, or whether it is feasible to install your washing machine in a separate room, such as the bathroom. If space is limited and you are also reliant on a tumble dryer for getting washing dry, especially in winter, consider getting a single washer/drier model rather than having two separate appliances each taking up valuable room.

you like to cook. The classic image of a spacious kitchen with a huge range and a table large enough to seat the extended family for Sunday lunch does not accurately portray many people's homes today. In fact, in a small home, the chances are that the kitchen is more of a pitstop than a centre of operations, with traditional 'family kitchen' activities like meals and homework redistributed to living areas and bedrooms. Whatever its size, the kitchen still needs to function efficiently. And some will have to put up with more knocks than others, so also take into account how many people will regularly be using the room.

Be honest about your cooking capabilities. Don't plan for a mass of appliances you will never use, and think about what your cupboards really need to hold. Will you want a permanently stocked larder (pantry) of essential ingredients and exotic extras ready to produce meals at a moment's notice, or do you buy just what you need for one meal at a time?

Then there is the issue of worksurface capacity to consider – do you need enough space to prepare three courses at once and still have room to roll out the pastry, or are you realistically more likely to cook one-pot meals that can be chopped and assembled in very little space?

Besides preparing and cooking food and perhaps dining in the kitchen, you may also want to use the room as a utility area in which to carry out household chores such as washing, drying and ironing clothes (see box, opposite).

Rethinking and redesigning

If you have the opportunity to make some structural alterations, decide whether you want to keep your kitchen as an entirely separate entity or if it might actually work better as part of a larger open-plan room. The great advantage about open-plan living is that you can choose where you want your boundaries to fall. This means that if your current kitchen is somewhat on the small side, it's a brilliant way to steal back a bit of space and make your kitchen bigger if you feel you need it.

If you are planning to redesign the entire kitchen layout, this is the ideal opportunity to think about making any lighting and plumbing alterations that

A table and chairs in the middle of an open-plan kitchen/living room create a dining area, while folding seats and light-transmitting perspex chairs enhance the small space.

would improve its working effectiveness and, if necessary, reposition or add extra power points for your kitchen appliances.

Creating a dining area

Some large kitchens give you the option of using them as full-scale dining rooms, too. Even in small kitchens, you can often still carve out an eating area big enough for breakfast or coffee. A breakfast bar is useful in a fitted kitchen, but you may be able to accommodate a small table. Circular tables take up less space than square designs – little garden tables are ideal – and a couple of folding chairs will help keep floor space free.

If the kitchen adjoins an open-plan living room, you can extend into the latter and create a more spacious dining area in the border territory between the two. A kitchen unit or storage cabinet can act as a boundary if you want a clear divide between the two areas (curved-end island units would soften the divide and avoid jutting corners), or rely on a shift in decorating style to define the territory. Changing the floorcovering – from linoleum or aluminium to warm wood, for example – will make the dining area feel more 'furnished', or simply paint the walls a different colour.

An island unit is useful in a large kitchen, providing extra worksurface and storage space, and possibly marking the boundary of the kitchen in an open-plan area.

Planning the layout

Take your time deciding on the design of your kitchen, thinking through how it will function rather than concentrating purely on the visual effect. It is worth talking to kitchen planning experts to get their advice – many companies offer this as a no-obligation service.

The work triangle

The key thing to remember when planning a kitchen is what kitchen designers usually refer to as the 'work triangle' of cooker, sink and fridge. These need to be positioned so that moving between them is easy and unobstructed. Site the sink area first because, once you include the draining boards, it is probably going to be the longest unit. (If you want a dishwasher and washing machine, position them near the sink to keep plumbing costs down.) Now plan your food preparation and cooking areas close by. Make sure that the hob and oven are only a few steps from the sink so

that you do not need to wander around with hot pans. Position the fridge near the food-preparation area, but keep it away from the busy traffic around the sink. Try to have worksurfaces between all key areas, but keep the main food preparation area between hob and sink.

Tailor-made treatment

For small kitchens that will be used by only one person, a U-shape or horseshoe layout is ideal. If there is going to be more than one of you in the kitchen, a run of cupboards and fittings creating an open L-shape provides a better layout, so that you have room to get past each other. Long, thin rooms suit a galley-style kitchen with appliances and worktops running the length of the long sides of the room. Larger kitchens obviously allow more flexibility and you may be able to incorporate an island unit, breakfast bar or dining table into the scheme.

Unit size

Modern units come in a range of widths so that you can make the best of the space that you have. As a general guide, however, standard kitchen base units are 60 cm (24 in) wide and around 60 cm (24 in) deep (and therefore accommodate most standard kitchen appliances within them), although there are specialist slimline ones available, which are 50 cm (20 in) deep. Wall cabinets at eye level are usually about 32–35 cm (12½–13¾ in) deep.

A small kitchen can easily be swamped by furniture and fittings. To keep it feeling open and light, find out whether you can have the depth of units reduced (it is easy to cut a slice off the back of cabinets without affecting the look of the front) or have only floor-standing cabinets and leave the upper walls clear.

A practical work triangle of cooker, sink and fridge is the basis for most kitchen layouts, allowing you to access all three points equally and work efficiently in your kitchen.

Circular walls in a kitchen present a challenge and require precision fitting of units and worktops, so you would do well to consult a bespoke fitted kitchens company.

Think, too, about individual preferences for height and reach. Decide whether you find drawers or cupboards easier to access. Plan for ovens, fridges and freezers to be at a convenient height – it is usually best to have the oven and fridge at eye level, with the freezer lower down, as it is used less often. Make sure that worktop and sink levels can be adjusted to suit your height – it is very uncomfortable standing and working in the kitchen if they are the wrong level for you; well-made units will have legs that can be individually adjusted to suit.

Measuring up for cabinets

Before you start visiting kitchen showrooms and choosing the units you would like to install, you need to know exactly how much room you have available for them. Even if you have decided that your kitchen will be planned by a professional, taking your own measurements and creating an accurate floor plan on graph paper will give you and the expert planner a much better feel for the project and for what is practically possible:

- Measure the overall dimensions of the room, including the height of the ceiling – many manufacturers produce wall cabinets in a range of different heights.

- Mark fixed features such as radiators or other heaters, doors, windows, alcoves and skirting boards (baseboards), including their dimensions, and note the positions of gas, water and electricity supplies.
- Measure any awkward projections such as pipes that will need to be avoided. Additionally, you might find it useful to take a photograph for reference, so that you can use this as guide if and when you visit a kitchen planning company.
- Measure any existing appliances you want to keep, so that you can work them into your plan.

Worktop lighting

Plan for good lighting to illuminate your worktops. Choose well-positioned ceiling lights if there are no wall-hung units above your worktops. If you do have eye-level wall cabinets, lights can be fixed beneath them so that the fittings do not show, or you can position individual halogen spotlights in corners for a more sparkling effect. Lights fitted inside glass wall cupboards will provide a gentle background glow, and you can also fit lighting panels to the wall behind a worktop, creating a sort of illuminated splashback.

A narrow galley-style kitchen demands streamlined furniture and surfaces to complement the room's shape. The absence of eye-level units means ceiling spotlights can directly light the worktops.

Kitchen furniture

The style of your kitchen furniture tends to dictate the look of the whole room. Take time to get it right, because you will probably spend more money on your kitchen than on any other room. Free-standing furniture is usually associated with larger, traditional-style kitchens, whereas fitted cabinets can make better use of a small space.

Fitted furniture

Fitted cabinets are likely to cover most of the wall space in a fitted kitchen. This means that the style and colour of the units will in effect be your background for all other furnishings and accessories. Most people choose the same colour and finish for all the units in the kitchen, but you might like to opt for a slightly contrasting look between the base units and those at eye level. Bear in mind that units with smooth, flat fronts will attract less dirt than panelled ones and be easier to keep clean, while units with reflective surfaces and handles (gloss paint, metal or glass) reflect as much light as possible and give the kitchen a sleek, functional modernity.

Colour and finish

Plain white Always neat, understated and space making, plain white is a good choice if you are not sure about your colour-scheming plans or need a neutral colour to blend with the rest of the room. White fittings will go with anything and are easy to redecorate around if you want to update to a new look in a few years' time.

Natural wood The warm tones of natural wood suit a country- or farmhouse-style kitchen, but can also look cool and urban if the styling is kept clean and simple. In a small space, opt for pale woods such as maple,

Natural wood units are normally associated with country-style kitchens, but flat-fronted with metal handles and combined with stainless steel worktops, they have a contemporary urban look.

Fitted cabinets in pale yellow with frosted glass fronts help reflect light and add to the illusion of space in an already large kitchen with a horseshoe layout.

beech and light oak (as dark finishes will appear oppressive), and choose flat door fronts or square-cut Shaker-style panels, without any decorative moulding or other ornamentation.

Painted or lacquered This gives you the chance to indulge in a little colour in the kitchen, with bold primaries adding a dash of cosmopolitan drama and paler pastels doing their bit towards light reflection and space creation. Bubblegum pink, banana yellow and powder blue all have a retro feel, reminiscent of American milk bars, and can add a touch of fun to functional fittings and appliances. Choose a colour that matches or schemes with adjoining rooms, or, if the space is a self-contained room, have fun designing a one-off colour scheme by painting individual drawers and cupboards in contrasting harlequin shades.

Glass Natural wood, white and painted cabinets can all be fitted with glass fronts as an alternative to solid panels, creating a lighter, more open effect as well as display space. Look for industrial-style frosted, textured or steel-reinforced glass. Alternatively, go for glass as your core material for a really contemporary look. Cool frosted cupboard fronts in pale blue or green glass with steel handles are among the most dramatic of contemporary cabinet designs, and can be fitted with interior lighting for even more impact.

Stainless steel Formerly used only in a professional chef's kitchen, this is the other material you might want to consider in a contemporary-style kitchen. Already established as the smart option for kitchen appliances and increasingly popular for worktops, wall tiles and splashback panels, stainless steel is now being used for units and cabinet fronts, too, letting you create a whole run of sleek steel for a really professional look.

Easy to keep clean, stainless steel-fronted cabinets and drawers reflect light into the room and provide a sleek look for a contemporary-style kitchen.

Replace drawer and cupboard handles to completely transform the look of an outdated fitted kitchen. These full-width metal bar grips are particularly easy to keep clean.

Instant updates

If the existing kitchen units are in good condition and you are happy with the layout, you can save time and effort by updating them rather than ripping them out and starting again.

- Shabby cabinets can be transformed with a coat of clean colour – use gloss or eggshell for a really smooth surface with a washable finish, or look for specialist melamine paint if your units are made of melamine (see pages 12–15). Add a couple of coats of good-quality clear varnish for extra protection if the room is a busy family area or subject to lots of wear and tear.

- New door and drawer handles will complete the look – go for unobtrusive metal drawer pulls, long D-shaped handles or full-width metal bar grips for the neatest finish and handles that are easy to clean, or have fun with coloured glass knobs or pewter-finish designs in distinctive geometric shapes.

- For a total transformation, keep the basic units but remove the original doors and simply attach new ones. Ready-made replacements are available from many manufacturers and simply need attaching to existing fittings, giving you an instant new-look kitchen without the expense of total refitting.

These fitted kitchen units have a light-coloured metallic plinth (kick board), which gives the illusion of space and light below the units, more typical of free-standing furniture with legs.

Practical issues

The practical design of the cabinets is an important consideration, too – including the mechanics of how they open and close – especially in small kitchens. Normal hinged doors can take up masses of space when fully open, which is a big issue in narrow galleys or U-shaped layouts where an open door can block the whole kitchen. If you need space-saving solutions, look for doors that fold or slide, either sideways on runners, or upwards on a sash-window principle. Half-height or split wall cupboards are useful, with doors that swing upwards or fold back into the cupboard recess rather than swinging out into the room. Bear in mind that normal hinged doors on narrow units will not swing too far out into the room when open.

Off-the-peg or made-to-measure?

Off-the-peg units come flat-packed for home assembly with all the necessary hardware (like wall fixings, screws and hinges) or as ready-assembled carcasses. You will be restricted to standard unit sizes, which may mean some wasted space in corners. If precision fit and use of space is a priority for you, or you have a particularly unusual-shaped room, you might prefer to seek out a bespoke or custom-build company, who will design exactly what you want, made to measure. Weigh up the costs carefully. Flat-pack units are much cheaper, but you will have to pay for fitting on top, and you might decide it is worth spending more on a bespoke design with fitting included.

Free-standing furniture

Free-standing kitchen furniture allows you to be flexible with your kitchen layout and has the advantage that you can take it with you if you move house. It is not as dominant as fitted cabinets, it can be used throughout a large kitchen or it can be interesting to include the occasional free-standing piece to give a fitted kitchen a more individual look and added character, particularly if the kitchen adjoins a living or dining room that naturally has a more 'furnished' feel.

A big plus point for choosing free-standing units over fully fitted modular units is that the time and cost of installation is much reduced – just put the pieces of furniture in place and connect services (gas, electricity or water) where appropriate. In addition, you can buy a single piece at a time when convenient rather than footing the bill for an entire fitted kitchen in one go.

Ideas to consider

A wooden dresser (hutch) or a tall cupboard in the traditional French armoire style – like a sort of wardrobe (closet) for the kitchen, but fitted with shelves – is ideal for storing tableware and linens, and

A wooden dresser (hutch) is a popular choice of free-standing furniture, especially in a country- or farmhouse-style kitchen, and offers both hidden and display storage options.

An island unit in a fitted kitchen has the appearance of free-standing furniture, but cannot be moved and may even house the cooker or be plumbed in for a sink.

Space-saving tips

In a kitchen with limited space, you need to keep the shapes clean and streamlined, avoiding unnecessary decoration.

• Consider installing half-height wall cupboards where ceilings are low, or to help prevent units from appearing to dominate the whole room.

• Fit a run of cabinets with an end piece of curved shelves in order to cut off the corner and give a more streamlined look.

• Fit doors and drawers with hidden handgrips so that the sleek run of the unit fronts is not interrupted by knobs or handles.

• Hide appliances behind fascia doors to keep the cabinet lines clean.

• Have the cupboard depth reduced by cutting a bit off the back so that they do not protrude so far into the room.

• Look for doors that slide or fold up and swing back into the cupboard cavity instead of opening outwards.

makes an intriguing contrast with modern fitted units. Other wooden free-standing items worth considering for your kitchen include a sideboard (buffet), butcher's block, pastry table with a stone insert (see page 188) and a traditional-style settle bench. All of these offer possibilities for storage and are available from specialist kitchen cabinet-makers or may even be found as individual pieces in second-hand and antique shops.

For a more industrial feel, an alternative to a wooden dresser (hutch) is a steel shelf rack or mesh-front metal cupboard – rather like an updated version of the traditional meat safe. For up-to-the-minute free-standing pieces specifically designed to help make limited space work harder, look out for steel laboratory-style units incorporating a sink and worktop – and sometimes even a hob, too – which can take the place of a run of units, or provide an island workstation dividing the kitchen from the adjoining space. Some of these units are fitted with cupboards underneath. Other types are constructed on legs, which creates a more open, spacious effect at the same time as providing room for individual storage crates, trolleys or spare folding seating underneath.

Kitchen storage

Because kitchens are called upon to accommodate such diverse things as electrical appliances and gadgets, cookware, utensils, crockery, groceries, table linen, laundry and utility sundries, recipe books and items for recycling, they need clever storage ideas, more than any other room in the house, and contemporary furniture designers are falling over themselves to provide maximum storage in minimum space.

Fitted solutions

Most storage spaces are built into fitted units, which – for anyone who has more than the barest of essentials to store – are the best way of keeping the kitchen tidy, and will also make the most of 'dead' space that does not normally get used. For example, you can take advantage of plinth (kick board) drawers fitted into the base of units at floor level, carousel fittings that revolve to give you access to items stored in awkward corners, plus built-in extras like wine racks, vegetable trays and rubbish (garbage) bins that would otherwise take up precious worktop or floor space.

Cupboards, drawers and shelves

Some people find drawers easier to access than cupboards and they do tend to help you organize your storage more efficiently. Interior trays and dividers will 'file' contents neatly, and different sizes of drawer are available to take specific items, for example extra-deep drawers for pots and pans, and miniature spice drawers for small jars and packets.

For the upper wall, cupboards create a streamlined background, but can sometimes feel oppressive in a small space. Open shelves create a lighter effect as long as you can keep them tidy – and clean, as they will collect kitchen dirt and grease more easily than

'Floating' shelves have concealed supports rather than visible brackets and become part of the décor itself. As open shelving, they attract dirt and grease and must be kept tidy.

cupboards. They are great for displaying china and glass, and for anyone who positively enjoys colour-coding their spice jars and lining up rows of matching containers. Chunky 'floating' wooden shelves, fixed with long screws or bolts so that there is no visible support and painted to match the background wall, will look as though they are part of the fittings. Metal or toughened glass shelves give a cooler, slightly industrial effect.

Designer drawers

A standard base unit will fit four drawers in the same space occupied by two shelves, and allow you to see what is in them with a clear overhead view instead of forcing you to rummage around below-waist cupboards to retrieve items buried at the back. Most efficient of all are narrow pull-out units designed like one deep drawer, but divided by individual trays or racks inside so that you can see and reach everything from either side. These are available as base units or as full-height cabinets that will fit all your larder (pantry) supplies behind one slim door front.

Extra-deep drawers are an alternative to cupboards for providing easily accessible storage for pans that you want kept out of sight instead of on display.

Kitchen clutter control

• Reclaim your surfaces. Unless you deliberately want the everything-on-show farmhouse look, lift spice jars and food containers on to shelves or into cupboards to clear your worktops.

• Don't let out-of-date food cans and packets take up unnecessary space. Check your cupboards regularly and throw out anything beyond its best-by date.

• Don't let unwashed dishes accumulate. As soon as possible, load them into the dishwasher or wash up and put them away.

• Find an out-of-sight yet easily accessible space for containers for recyclable items like newspapers, glass and cans, and empty them often.

Trolleys, trays and crates

You can supplement fixed drawers with individual containers that can be pushed into spaces beneath tables and worktops or stacked on top of wall cupboards to make the most of high ceilings. Woven baskets or wire-mesh trays become free-range drawers that can be slotted in where needed to store cutlery or other essentials. Larger steel crates will hold pans, colanders and drainers. And practical trolleys can be pushed into position where needed. The most useful of these is the butcher's block trolley, which provides an extra worktop and chopping block on top with storage shelves underneath.

Rails, racks and hooks

Hanging storage always helps save space. A steel rail fixed on the wall behind the worktop, or running along the front of the worktop, can be used to store utensils, and ceiling-hung racks will store pans in overhead space. Wall-fixed hooks and pegs will take individual items from mugs and cheese graters to measuring jugs, and a wall-mounted plate rack fixed over a draining board combines storage and draining in one.

Rail-hung storage solutions help keep worktops clear for more important items – in this case, an attractive tiered wine rack that can be extended as necessary, row by row.

Walls, worktops and floors

You cannot choose fitted cabinets in isolation from worktops, splashbacks and other surfaces, so include these in your plans when thinking about colours and materials. There is plenty of choice, so do your research thoroughly for materials that suit your budget and lifestyle.

Hard-working backdrops

Painted walls will provide a backdrop for whatever kitchen furniture you choose, but you will need to add some sort of protective covering behind worktops and sinks. Ceramic tiles are the traditional splashback material – tough, washable and decoratively versatile. Painted tongue-and-groove wood panelling is a slightly mellower option – a good way of covering up a less-than-perfect wall surface and still washable as long as you use an oil-based paint such as gloss or eggshell. Slate and granite will look smart and dramatic; and newer, more unusual materials include stainless steel, aluminium and heat-resistant glass (available in sheet or tile form) for an urban, industrial look.

Choosing worktops

Worktops can make all the difference to the look of a kitchen – cheap surfaces can downgrade a smart kitchen, while smart choices can make basic kitchen furniture look like an expensive designer fit. But you need to think of practicality as well as style – different materials have different merits.

Laminates Cheapest – and probably the most common choice – are easy-to-clean laminates, available in a huge choice of colours and patterns, including imitation marble, slate and granite. However, laminates are not very tough, and cutting directly on to the surface can cause lasting damage.

Stone Genuine granite or marble are much more expensive, but practical for hob areas as they are hardwearing, resistant to heat and low on maintenance. In a small kitchen, where you are looking at fairly short runs of worktop, it is more feasible to pay for exactly what you want. Granite, slate and marble are also good for pastry making, so you might want to consider insetting a slab as part of a longer surface.

Wood When it comes to choosing appropriate surfaces for chopping, you are better off with softer, cushioned wood. Look for end-grain blocks, where wood has been turned on its end and glued together, then sliced through into cross sections. These surfaces are more resistant to knife damage and are easy to restore if marked, although they can be susceptible to heat and must be regularly oiled to keep them conditioned. Again, wood can be inset as a cutting slab if you don't want a full worktop.

Water-resistant oiled hardwood is useful as a soft landing for glass and china around the sink.

Modern alternatives Expensive but increasingly popular options, stainless steel creates a seamless effect where it adjoins a steel sink, and manmade composites such as Corian or Surell can be moulded to provide a single-piece sink and worktop.

Ceramic tiles are the traditional choice for kitchen walls and splashbacks, providing a durable and easily wiped surface as well as plenty of design and colour options.

Mix and match different surfaces for a successful modern kitchen – here, laminate worktops work with brightly coloured base units, white and chrome accessories and a cushioned vinyl floor.

Forgiving flooring

Kitchen flooring (see pages 70–85) needs to be easy to clean, anti-slip and preferably soft enough for dropped crockery to survive the impact. Wood fulfils these criteria and always looks good. Existing boards that are in good condition can be sealed with varnish, or new wood can be laid on top. Vinyl or linoleum (sometimes referred to as Marmoleum) will be softer and (in the case of vinyl) cheaper. Linoleum is harder-wearing and more resilient because it is made from a blend of natural ingredients including cork and linseed oil, which actually gets tougher with age. It also offers you more design choices, including customized patterns cut to match your room.

Surface detail

Use your kitchen appliances (see page 190) to add another element of style and colour. There is now a much wider choice of finish than ever before. As well as the traditional plain whites, you will find lacquered finishes in bright colours making much more of a statement. Steel, aluminium and chrome, in brushed or polished finishes, give a professional look, and heat-resistant glass can be used for surprising items like extractor hoods, to match glass splashbacks and worktops.

Material effects

For a contemporary style, try mixing different surfaces – for instance, industrial steel with mellow wood, or smooth glass with slate.

• Wood – for worktops, chopping blocks and floors. Make sure the surface is sealed and/or oiled to protect the finish.

• Tiles – for floors, walls and worktops. They are colourful, but unforgiving if you drop something, and the grouting may get dirty.

• Glass – for shelves, splashbacks, worktops and even extractor hoods.

• Metal – for appliances, flooring, cupboard fronts, splashbacks and worktops, plus power points, handles and hanging rails, or try it along the front of a wooden worktop to give it an industrial edge.

• Granite – for sinks, splashbacks, worktops.

• Slate – for worktops, splashbacks, floors.

• Marble – for floors, worktops and pastry boards. Dark marble will be marked by acidic substances such as lemon juice.

• Rubber – for floors. Available in sheet or tile form and polyurethane, it combines a modern, functional look with a warmer texture underfoot.

Kitchen accessories and appliances in brushed or polished metallic finishes are very popular. They provide a light-reflective surface and often come in stunning contemporary designs.

Kitchen appliances

It's easy to go for extra features when fitting out your kitchen – everything seems so useful that you want to include as many options as possible. But first concentrate on the essentials like a fridge and cooker, then work out your priorities, depending on space and budget.

Size and scale

Standard appliances are 60 cm (24 in) wide (the same width as standard base units), but if your kitchen doesn't need to service a whole family, you could probably manage with less than full-sized models. Dishwashers and washing machines, for example, are available in 45 cm (18 in) widths and other sizes, to suit cramped spaces and smaller households. Fridges in 55 cm (22 in) widths and mini fridges are also an

Gadget sense

• Avoid buying gadgets and appliances that you don't really need, and get rid of any that you are unlikely to use.

• Check for duplicates among kettles, blenders and toasters – choose the smartest and most efficient and dispense with spares.

• Don't keep gadgets like a food processor or breadmaker out on the worktop unless you use them regularly – they will sit in the way collecting dust and require unnecessary cleaning. Store them out of sight.

option where room is exceptionally tight. At the other end of the scale are super-sized appliances like the American-style larder (pantry) fridge-freezers.

The standard cooking hob comes in the four-ring square format, but many manufacturers now make hobs with rings in different configurations. You could opt for just two rings if that is all you need or, if you have a stretch of worktop that is too narrow for a full-sized hob, you could fit a slimline one with four burners in a single row. Another option is a hob with a lid that will fold down to cover the burners. It looks neater and gives you extra worktop space.

If space is no problem, you might want to consider the one or two extra hob rings available in some styles of cooker, a double oven or even a range cooker.

Smart sinks

Sinks, the most basic but essential of kitchen fittings, come in all shapes and sizes, including corner sinks to make the most of space that would otherwise go to waste. You can even find miniature butler's sinks, giving you the smart square shape and roomy depth, but without taking up valuable worktop space. If you have a dishwasher, or wash up only small amounts, you will not need so much draining space.

Retro-style fridges with their contoured design and various colours are very much in vogue and a far cry from the white squared-off models we have become accustomed to.

Hidden assets

Where space is really tight – for instance, if you are trying to fit a working kitchen into one corner of a living area in a studio apartment – you can get a miniature kitchen, which provides all the basic appliances in a single unit or enclosed cupboard. Some are stylish and sleek stainless steel designs. Sink, fridge, draining board with built-in hotplates, grill, microwave and even a dishwasher can be supplied as one dresser (hutch)-sized unit, complete with eye-level cupboards above. Some include built-in ovens and tall fridge-freezer cabinets, and others are designed as triangular modules that will fit into a corner behind neat folding doors.

No longer restricted to the standard four-ring square shape, cooking hobs are now available in a variety of configurations to suit the layout and style of your kitchen.

A double (or one-and-a-half) sink is always useful if you have the room to accommodate it, but if you are short of space, look for a design with a chopping board that fits over one bowl to act as an extra worksurface. A mixer tap (faucet) with a spout that can be pushed to one side is an equally useful space saver.

Clever combinations

If your kitchen is on the small side, make use of appliances that combine several functions in one. Washer-dryers will keep laundry space to a minimum and fridge-freezers give you a decent-sized freezing compartment along with your fridge. Combination ovens provide microwave and conventional heating in a single cooker. Among the more recent advances in appliance development are microwave ovens that feature handy toaster slots on the side, together with multi-skilled food processors that not only cook and steam, but even include electronic weighing scales.

One important additional accessory for your cooker is an extractor hood to help reduce condensation and cooking smells. This is really essential if the kitchen is part of or adjoins another room. Most cooker hoods incorporate a useful light, too, and one of the latest designs combines a cooker hood and microwave oven.

A round counter-sunk sink is a useful space saver in a small kitchen, as is a mixer tap (faucet) that can be pushed out of the way when not in use.

Soft furnishings

Whether your kitchen is a compact workspace for a single cook or a larger room in which to spend time as a group, it needs to be cheerful and welcoming. Kitchen textiles of all kinds are useful for introducing comfort and pulling together a colour scheme.

In an unfitted kitchen, you can use simple gathered curtains on rods or wires to conceal unsightly shelves or open cupboards of pots and pans. Choose a washable fabric, prewashing it before making up, so that further shrinkage is kept to a minimum.

Make the most of an odd set of dining chairs by adding tie-on cushions (see page 141) all in the same fabric. The chairs can also be painted in a colour taken from the fabric, while an off-white or similar pale colour will make old chairs look more contemporary.

Textiles in the kitchen

There are plenty of opportunities to use fabric in the kitchen to soften the look – at windows, on tables and seating, among others. An instant solution is to replace tired and shabby tea towels, hand towels and oven gloves (pot gloves) with new ones in coordinating colours. Consider other accessories, too – for example, you can bring life to a plain kitchen by using fabric that ties in with a collection of china displayed on shelves.

Kitchen windows

Flapping fabrics can be a danger near hobs, and as the sink is often found under the window, curtains here may get splashed and stained easily. For these reasons, kitchens are generally kept free of curtains, although this may leave them feeling cold and bare.

Roller blinds are a good option in that they avoid cluttering the window sill and you can customize them to suit (see page 148), but even these can seem a little clinical. Roman or london blinds are a good alternative – in a traditional fabric for a country-style kitchen, or in a smart striped or checked fabric to go with modern metals and laminates.

If there is a good view from the window, you might want to dispense with any kind of window dressing at all. However, privacy may be an issue, particularly at night in urban kitchens, in which case opt for some form of simple screening at the window.

If you prefer curtains to blinds, they don't necessarily have to be full curtains – a simple pole carrying a short, gathered pelmet or a band of trimmed linen hung on rings is often all that you will need. Alternatively, install café rods to hang a simple curtain halfway up a window. This way you can have privacy in a ground-floor kitchen, but still let in plenty of daylight.

In basement kitchens, which need all the light they can get, pale colours and an uncluttered window area are essential. You can keep the window area free and maximize light by extending the curtain track or pole well outside the frame.

Attractive tea towels and oven gloves (pot gloves) designed to coordinate with other accessories in the room bring colour and texture to this plainly decorated kitchen.

The addition of a simple tablecloth instantly transforms an ugly table and makes a stark-looking, plain contemporary-style kitchen appear welcoming.

Handy hints

• Don't use delicate or expensive fabrics in the kitchen that cannot be cleaned, as they will probably be spoiled very quickly.

• Choose fabrics that are not likely to attract smells or grease – heavy wools and textured fabrics should be saved for rooms where they will not need to be cleaned too often.

• If you are lucky enough to have a dedicated room for evening dinner parties, rich colours like crimson and raspberry for your walls and soft furnishings are wonderful, giving a dramatic enclosed feel.

• If the dining area has to double as a breakfast room and work area, keep the colours lighter, to appear less oppressive during the day.

Dining area solutions

The dining room – or more accurately, the eating area in your home – should be based on your own mealtime routines, be it informal suppers, sit-down meals or weekly dinner parties. Few of us have a dedicated dining room nowadays. Instead, we eat in a room that needs to suit a range of activities. A cloth kept permanently on a table will help protect a tabletop or disguise an ugly surface. Classic white is not always the best choice of colour – apart from the obvious need for frequent laundering, white and other pale colours reflect light back into your face, which could become tiring if you are trying to work or write at the table. Opt for some colour and bring seasonal changes with spare tablecloths.

An oilcloth (see page 139) is a useful permanent covering if you have small children, as it helps protect the tabletop from spilt food, crayons and play dough, and is easily wiped clean.

For entertaining and special occasions, replace the everyday cloth with homemade sets of table linen (see page 138) in completely contrasting colours and styles to introduce a sense of occasion or atmosphere.

If you use your dining area for additional activities, keep the décor light and introduce rich colours in the table linen for an atmosphere conducive to evening dining.

Living
rooms

Planning the space

However tempting it is to launch straight into designing the ultimate comfort zone in your living room, your first move is to think about what other roles the room may need to play. How many people are going to use it, what for and at what times of day?

Multi-purpose living

Few homes today can afford to have a room that is kept for visitors only – most living rooms have to work hard all day and every day. It may well have to act as dining room, study and playroom as well as sitting room, so it needs to adapt easily from practical to comfortable, day to night, casual to formal. If your living space is destined to be a multi-purpose room, it needs careful planning to get the best out of it. Flexibility is everything. There are two ways to approach this:

In this very large open-plan room, rugs on the wooden floor help zone the space by marking the boundaries of the distinct seating areas in the room.

- To allocate different parts of the room for different activities.
- To keep the whole area as a unified space, but furnish it with dual-purpose furniture.

Zoning your space

Décor To some extent, the furniture itself will define the purpose of the area – seating, dining table or computer desk, for example. But the distinction between each one can be reinforced by a shift in decorating mood, so that it feels right for the purpose as well as being practically equipped. Painting a couple of walls at one end of the room a richer colour will create a dining area with a sense of drama for evening use, while a corner or alcove could be allocated a different shade for use as a study space.

Flooring Flooring can signal a change, too, with carpet or natural matting in the sitting area, for example, giving way to wooden boards in the dining space.

If your living room also has to function as a dining room, careful positioning of the furniture can help visually separate the two areas – a sofa often provides the perfect division.

Handy hints

• Plan for the different uses to which the room will be put before you start to decorate and furnish it.

• Think about who is going to use the room and when, and make sure that your furnishings will be robust enough to withstand the wear.

• Make sure that the lighting is flexible enough to adjust from day to night and between different areas of the space. Fit dimmer switches to vary the level of light and add plenty of free-standing lamps so that you can move the focus of light.

Textures Furnishing textures have their own subliminal effect, with fabrics and other soft surfaces automatically denoting comfort, and hard surfaces spelling practicality. But fabrics themselves can divide into simple, robust linens and cottons for daytime and working areas, with more luxurious materials restricted to the comfort zone.

Lighting Lighting is crucial in establishing and altering atmosphere – make sure that you can adjust your lighting levels to create different effects in different areas and at different times of day.

Furniture as boundaries Some rooms lend themselves to being divided up more obviously, with furniture used to form the boundaries of different areas. For example, a sofa positioned at right angles halfway across a long living room will effectively divide the room into sitting and dining areas, while two small sofas at right angles to each other will create a corner with a protected, enclosed feel. A tall shelving or storage unit standing against the wall at right angles can also create the beginning of a partition – just enough to mark the start of a separate area without actually cutting the room in half. For a more emphatic division, you can extend this further, or use folding screens and Japanese-style sliding partitions – these are a neat solution for providing instant privacy for a study area.

Adapting your furniture

If you can, choose your furniture to match the different roles that your living room needs to play. A decent-sized table can act as a desk and turn into a dining table when needed. A sofa bed is slightly more expensive than a sofa, but will give you the option of turning the living room into a temporary guest room if necessary. Futons are a good alternative if you are on a budget. The mattress spreads out on the floor or on a low-level wooden slatted base, but is rolled up into useful seating at other times.

Footstools are useful surfaces for trays and magazines as well as providing extra seating, and ottomans and blanket boxes go one better by supplying handy storage inside for toys, papers and other items. For more organized storage, use the multiple small drawers of classic pharmacy chests, perfect for filing paperwork and stationery, and providing an extra display surface, too.

Remember that the furniture can be rearranged to demarcate different areas at different times of day or year. A work table can stand under a window during the day, then be moved into the centre of the room for a dinner party. Sofas and chairs arranged round a fireplace during winter months can be regrouped to face the room in the summer. Furniture on wheels is always helpful in a multi-purpose room, as it makes rearranging the layout an easier option.

If you don't have a dedicated guest room, invest in a good-quality, comfortable sofa bed for the living room so that you can accommodate overnight visitors.

Comfort and colour

Comfort means different things to different people. Some need a living space that feels calm and restful; others need it to be lively and stimulating. The important thing is that the effect can be felt as well as seen – furnishings need to establish the right mood as well as style.

Choosing your colours

Calm and elegant, neutral colours (see page 102) are a classic option for a living room that has to please everyone. Add plenty of warm honeys and browns if the room is dark and receives little daylight, or introduce more grey and stone shades if you want to cool it down.

If you fancy some colour without being overwhelmed by it, pastel shades are restful and understated. Their effect is cool but not cold, providing a good sense of space without the starkness of plain white. Soft pastel shades mix effectively together because of their similarity of tone, so try

mixing a pastel palette of accents and contrasts – pale blues, greens and mauves, with touches of pink and creamy yellow to add warmth.

Avoid anything too deep or dark, as it will feel gloomy and oppressive during the daytime. Instead, if you want stronger colour, go for bright, clean shades that feel fresh and stimulating, or for muted colours with a 'natural' character, for example denim blue, earthy ochre and soft moss or leaf green.

Layering texture

Where the colour scheme is restrained, you need plenty of texture to provide warmth, contrast, variety and a degree of pattern. In living rooms, build up layers of texture with soft furnishings – rugs, cushions, throws and upholstery all contributing their own element of comfort. Try a streamlined square-cut sofa covered in heavy slubby linen and piled with cushions in different textures – suede, flannel and chunky cord – then complete the look with neat textural detail such as buttoned cushions and blanket-stitch throws.

All-day rooms need to provide a relaxing background, so opt for a classic colour scheme like neutrals and warm browns rather than hard-to-live-with strong colours and busy patterns.

Muted tones of violet, blue and green are easy on the eye and, combined with light-coloured walls and floor, help create a calm and restful living space.

Look for plain-coloured fabrics that provide their own self-patterning – like herringbone woollens, jacquard weaves and corduroy – and adjust the quality and quantity of texture to suit different times of day and year. Add extra layers of warmth and richness in winter, or to boost comfort for evening use, and use fewer layers, in cooler, crisper fabrics during summer.

Carefree furnishings

Since comfort is largely to do with peace of mind, think about practicality as well as aesthetics. If your living space has to suit a busy working or family life, there is no point in going for cream sofas. You need to keep the furnishing fabrics tough and washable – an upholstery fabric with some texture or a small repeating pattern is the best choice, as plain, light colours show marks easily and can become shabby on furniture that is used daily. Try traditional denim or drill, or thick linen in mid-tone colours – these will create an understated, contemporary look without showing every mark, and will also be easy to clean when necessary.

Window dressings

Curtains are expensive, but a living room can look bare without some sort of window dressing (see page 142). Even a small amount of fabric used in a roman blind is a great improvement. If you live on your own or on the ground floor, some form of window dressing is essential for giving a sense of security.

Curtains are often the focal point of a room, so they need to harmonize with the rest of the furnishings. Choose neutral colours for curtains (and sofas) to make them last, then bring colour to the scheme with accessories such as cushions, rugs, lamps and flowers.

Wide picture windows are harder to dress successfully than tall windows. Try to divide them into separate sections using two or three roman blinds side by side, for example, rather than one large one across the whole window. If you have an ugly radiator or heater below a window, floor-length sheer fabrics are useful for covering it without trapping the heat.

Flooring solutions

Flooring contributes its own layer of colour and texture (see pages 70–89). Natural wood – the original boards or new-laid wood (solid planking, parquet or laminate veneers) – always looks smart and creates a feeling of space, while white-painted boards have a modern simplicity. But these may not provide enough comfort, especially if you have children to consider.

Neutral carpet is the soft option, with natural floorcoverings (see page 86) falling somewhere between the two – although quieter than wood, the hardwearing, rough naturals like coir can be even less comfortable, while some of the softer jute and cotton weaves are not tough enough for an all-day area. If you want comfort, look for a weave with a high proportion of wool, which will also provide medium resilience.

A room with a restrained colour scheme needs plenty of texture – like deep-pile rugs and throws and cushions in assorted fabrics – to keep the scheme lively.

Planning your seating

Instead of the traditional layout of the three-piece suite arranged in a semi-circle around the fireplace or television, today's living areas are more likely to be fitted out with individual pieces of furniture in a mixture of sizes and designs, letting you tailor your seating plan to the shape of the room and establish a more personal sense of style.

Flexible options

The furnishings need to be flexible – a small sofa, several armchairs and some spare folding chairs with cushions are more useful than a single row of seating. Some people like to sit down, and some like to sit up, so you should have both options available, if possible.

Arrange corner sofas to suit your room. Use them against two walls to save space or in the middle of the room to create a cosy seating area.

This modern version of a traditional antique couch is right up to date with its simple clean lines and use of contemporary natural materials.

Sofa shapes

Sofas are still the most luxurious idea, and you will probably want to include one if you have room for it, but measure up carefully. Look at different sizes, and don't just go for the biggest one you can fit in the room. You might find that two small sofas, creating an L-shape or arranged opposite one another, suit the proportions of the room better than a single large one. Supplement sofas with footstools, pouffes or outsized floor cushions if there is not enough space for individual chairs.

Particularly compatible with open-plan living, corner sofas are widely available. Low backed and square cut, they squeeze extra comfort out of wasted corners and, best of all, come as modular units, which can build up to whatever shape and size you want.

Look out for variations on the basic sofa shape, too. Antique couches, many of them with decorative wooden frames and neat, slightly padded arms, are often smaller and more graceful in design, and create interesting contrasts in modern settings. The classic

Handy hints

• Don't try to cram too much furniture into your living space – if it doesn't look right, it won't feel comfortable. Keep to a minimal seating layout and supplement it when necessary with chairs from other rooms.

• Don't keep adding new pieces just for the sake of change. If you are bored with the furniture you have, introduce variety by creatively adapting what is there – rearrange the layout or change covers and cushions to suit different seasons or occasions.

• Don't let the television dominate your seating plan. Consider the positions of windows, doorway and fireplace, if there is one, then put the television in the space that's left.

• In a small living room, choose low-level seating that will make the ceiling feel higher and the room generally more spacious, but bear in mind that low seating may not be convenient for elderly or disabled visitors.

• Large pieces of upholstered furniture are expensive. Budget sofas and chairs are available, but you get what you pay for and they will not last for ever. Quality second-hand upholstered furniture can be an excellent investment.

Keep your seating options flexible by incorporating some individual pieces of furniture that can be moved around the living room as necessary.

chaise-longue, with a head-rest at one end and only a rudimentary back support, looks trimmer and lighter than a full-scale sofa (although its position will be limited by which end has the head-rest, so think carefully when you are buying). And elegant daybeds, with frames that sweep up into a curved arm at either end, can stand flat against the wall and be piled with cushions to create a comfortable back.

Chairs

Don't feel obliged to have a sofa if your living room is simply not the right shape. Individual chairs, chosen for their own style and outline, will look more comfortable and have more impact than a sofa that has

been forced into a space that is too small for it. Leather chairs are particularly good at holding their own, with a smart, classic look that works well in neutral modern settings. Don't let the effect get too functional and office-like, however, and avoid the Regency study look at the other extreme. The most comfortable and attractive style is squashy and slightly worn – suggesting a practical, hardwearing quality without actually looking antique.

Measuring up

After the kitchen, the living room is the room that benefits most from careful measuring and planning. Don't be tempted to buy major pieces of furniture without double-checking the measurements first. Tape together some large pieces of old wallpaper or newspaper to the size of the piece of furniture you are considering, and try it out at home. You may be surprised at how much space it will eat up. Can you walk around it comfortably if necessary? Is there room for people to get past with drinks, or loaded plates? Will it block the source of heat, or perhaps be too visually overpowering? Most rooms end up with some gentle compromises, and it may be impossible to make your own living room absolutely perfect, but good interior design is about understanding and working with all the options.

Eating and entertaining

Some homes have a dedicated dining room; others have a dining area within the kitchen. Alternatively, if the main dining area in your home is within your living room, you need to think carefully about the style of furniture you choose.

Adaptable dining furniture

If the dining area gets constant use for family meals or entertaining, you can make a clear shift in style to distinguish it from the sitting area (see page 196), but there is no point in maintaining a dining area if it is needed only occasionally. You would do better to incorporate it into the main space and create a streamlined link between the areas, then use lighting and furnishing tricks to turn it into a dining room when you need one.

Dining tables

Where space is short, dining tables either need to be compact and unobtrusive or must earn their keep by serving another purpose when not being used for meals. Circular and oval designs often make more efficient use of space than square or rectangular, because they can seat the same number of people without wasting space with jutting-out corners. Tables that can be enlarged when necessary are always useful. A drop-leaf design can be folded to half its size and placed against a wall to act as a desk, then opened out for meals. Some tables have an 'envelope' design that works the opposite way, with flaps that reduce the size by folding up instead of down, so that the tabletop folds inwards on itself and the corners meet in the middle. Others have extra panels that can simply be slotted in to extend the tabletop when the need arises.

Alternatively, you could replace a single oblong table with a pair of smaller square ones, using just the one for everyday eating, with the second acting as a

A folding table and chairs set, ideally with castors, that can be pushed to one side when not in use is ideal in a living room/diner where space is limited.

side table in the living room, then pushing the two together to accommodate more people as necessary. This is also a useful option if you have a narrow or awkward doorway that makes access hard for larger pieces of furniture.

Temporary tables

A basic worksurface such as the classic trestle table is incredibly useful, as it can switch from worktop during the day to dining table at night, and will also fold away for quick storage if you want to reclaim the space. Another option is to keep a separate tabletop that can be laid on top of an existing smaller table to enlarge it for when you are entertaining. For this purpose, you could use a sheet of 2 cm (³/₄ in) MDF (medium-density fibreboard) or plywood, appropriately painted or covered with a cloth.

Folding bistro-style chairs are stylish options for occasional seating and can be stored flat when not required. The Mediterranean blue of these chairs is perfectly suited to alfresco dining.

Seating

For chairs, you need to decide between upright dining chairs and softer tub or basket shapes. Some of the uprights are a little less straight-up-and-down than they used to be, with streamlined curves, providing a modern functional look in wood or moulded plastic. However, the overall effect is still hard rather than soft. If you want more comfort, add some cushions or opt for the tub shapes with arms and sprung or padded seats, which are more conducive to leisurely meals and relaxed entertaining.

If you need extra seating, use folding chairs that can be stored out of sight – slatted garden or metal bistro designs are stylish and handy, while canvas-slung director's chairs contribute a rather more relaxed feel.

Mood lighting

Atmospheric lighting is essential for entertaining, as a badly lit table can have a profound effect on enjoyment of the meal. A low-hanging chandelier or candelabra will shed diffused light over the table and create extra shine. Other ceiling-hung lights can be fixed on rise-and-fall mechanisms, and wall sconces will provide gentle background illumination. This combination provides a good level of ambient light and enhances the decorative style of the room. Don't underestimate the importance of candlelight, which adds a sense of life and movement as well as a beautifully intimate soft glow. Keep your china plain and pale, and set the table with plenty of glassware (including coloured glass) to reflect the light and increase sparkle.

Painted wooden furniture

Be aware that too much wood can have a deadening effect on a room. To relieve this, you can include other surfaces in a dining area such as metal-framed furniture, glass-topped tables and perspex chairs. Alternatively, choose painted wood, which has a slightly fresher, lighter feel.

White-painted wood gives a clean, Shaker-simple look, or you could opt for mixed shades for a more casual effect. This is a good way of recycling second-hand chairs, which can be turned into a dining set with paint in toning shades. Try ice-cream pastels or bright schoolroom colours.

Carefully prepare the chairs before painting. If they are already painted, sand them down thoroughly to create a key to help the new paint bond to the old. If they are varnished or waxed, use a proprietary stripper to remove the coating (see page 18), then scrub with wire wool dipped in white spirit. When the chairs have been prepared, apply a primer and undercoat, then add a topcoat in gloss or eggshell (see page 12) for easy cleaning – gloss gives a shinier, more reflective finish; eggshell a subtler semi-matt sheen.

Candlelight is ideal for entertaining. In addition, the candles can be scented and there are hundreds of styles and colours of holders to add interest to the room.

Creating a work space

Like a dining area within a living room, a work space within the same room will probably not need to be in use all the time, so you will want to make the most of dual-purpose ideas that let you adapt the room as necessary.

Ergonomic seating

When creating a space to work, the one thing that should really be purpose-built is the seating. If you are going to be sitting at a desk for any length of time, you need a proper office chair, ergonomically designed for comfort and support, rather than something borrowed from the kitchen or dining room.

Practical pointers

• Make sure that you have enough power and telephone points to fulfil all your needs within easy reach of your work area.

• Look for compact desktop equipment when it comes to equipping your home workstation – choose laptops instead of full-sized computers and combined systems offering, for example, printer/fax/photocopier/scanner all in one, to save on desk space and eliminate trailing wires.

• Never lose sight of the fact that this is still part of the living space – don't let your work clutter spill over and spoil the relaxed atmosphere of the room.

Well-designed cupboards that neatly store everything out of sight help create a home office that doesn't overdominate the rest of this open-plan living area.

Working surfaces

After the chair, the most important items are a desktop that is a comfortable height and good lighting to see what you are doing. You will need a good directional lamp that can focus on your work, and ideally some natural light from a window, too. For a fixed desk, you could consider building a worktop into a corner of the room as part of a run of fitted cupboards. This is a good way of making use of low or sloping ceilings and awkward corners – spaces that are too cramped for most other purposes, but fine for one person sitting down. To give yourself the deepest desk space while taking up the least room, fit a worktop right into the corner with a curved front edge to sit at, making it less obtrusive.

Dining tables and trestles are another option, especially folding designs. A neat alternative is to fit a tailor-made desktop that folds back against the wall, hinged to a wall-fixed batten so that it can be pulled up (or down) when needed and supported by fold-away legs or by brackets that swing out from the wall. If you don't want to improvise like this, there are various free-standing purpose-built furniture designs that provide organized workspace. Like an updated version of the traditional bureau, these incorporate pull-out shelves to take paperwork or a computer keyboard, and the most impressive of them include filing racks and have fabric-backed pinboard space on the inside of the doors, so that in effect you open up a complete miniature office when you open the cabinet doors. And, of course, when it is not in use, you can neatly close the doors on it as well.

If you have a handy alcove or recess, you can build a series of chunky shelves into it and make the lowest one deeper to create a desktop. This will keep your work space confined in a neat area, and when not needed for work, it can be used as an extra shelf or a display surface.

Filing systems

To keep paperwork and other office clutter in order, the neatest solutions are all 'closed' storage. Filing cabinets and trolleys can be slotted under your desk, and there is no shortage of handy-sized boxes and files, readily available in wood, cardboard, plastic, metal and other materials, that can be neatly shelved to present a smart face to the world, while hiding all sorts of horrors. Label or colour-code them so that you don't need to ransack the whole lot to find your latest bank statement. Domestic, work and personal papers should be kept separately, and make sure that you have easy-access places for essentials like passports, licences and emergency-repair contact numbers.

As well as ready-made storage systems, you can improvise your own 'files' from everyday containers such as baskets, bins and buckets. Wicker picnic hampers are a useful size for document files and stationery; kitchen cutlery trays and bottle carriers will create neat pen holders; and gleaming galvanized buckets can be used either as smart wastepaper bins or to hold rolled-up plans, sheets of wrapping paper and other larger papers that you do not want to fold.

Make use of wall space, too, with hanging storage on hooks and pegs. A row of square-cut aluminium cans – the sort sold as kitchen containers – fixed to the wall above your desk will hold pens, paperclips and other bits and pieces. Maps do double duty as decoration and information, and a pinboard fitted into an alcove will provide practical memory prompts for invitations and messages to be answered.

If your work space is incorporated within the living room, take care to keep the area tidy so as not to detract from the rest of the room.

You'll find a huge range of filing boxes available in all sizes, colours and materials, designed to provide inconspicuous storage or to coordinate with your colour scheme.

Storage and home entertainment

Since most living rooms are multi-purpose spaces, you need enough storage for all the different items associated with each activity – books, files, toys, tableware and entertainment equipment. It's easy for things to accumulate, so be strict about clutter control and don't allow the room to become a general dumping ground.

Conceal or display?

There are two options for finding room for your possessions in your living space: hiding things away or putting them on display. There is no simple rule that dictates which is best, or which of the many forms of storage suits which type of object. Some people enjoy keeping books, CDs and tableware out on show, while others prefer everything behind a slick, streamlined

Since you can never have too much storage space, do consider useful dual-purpose furniture like this carousel-style revolving coffee table that also offers storage for books and CDs.

Warehouse-style shelves

If you don't mind a few rough edges, you can create your own flexible storage system by stacking up wooden crates. Make sure that they are sturdy and clean, and 'anchor' each one by giving it something heavy to hold (books are ideal). The effect is functional and slightly industrial, with the printed contents or freight details on the timber adding an individual touch. More shallow storage along the same lines can be achieved with planks stacked on bricks, giving a basic, warehouse look that suits simple modern furnishings.

façade of closed doors. The only general guideline is that the less tidy you are by nature, the more hidden storage you will need.

Behind closed doors

Closed storage is the neatest option. Cupboards, cabinets and drawer units provide storage slots of different shapes and dimensions, so work out what you need them to hold before you commit yourself to any particular design. You may find individual free-standing pieces that fit the bill, but built-in furniture will make the best use of your space, by taking advantage of the wall height so that it can afford to stay slim-fitting and use up less of the floor area.

Remember that things like books, CDs, DVDs and videos don't need deep storage. The average paperback is only 11 cm ($4\frac{1}{2}$ in) wide, so you can store masses of

Drawer units allow you to store possessions out of sight. Seagrass storage solutions are particularly popular, being part of the current vogue for natural materials in the home.

Selective display

Be disciplined. Use photographs to establish a personal feel, but don't let them cover every surface. Instead, select your favourite pictures and turn them into a wall display rather than scattering them over shelves and tables.

lot of space unnecessarily. Do not assume, for instance, that books all need the same amount of space. Create shelves for different book heights and you will find you can fit two shelves of paperbacks in the same space needed for a single row of illustrated hardbacks.

Cube units provide very effective open storage, with the neat, fitted benefits of built-in furniture yet the flexibility of free-standing pieces, letting you move them where and when you want. They make excellent room dividers and you can also arrange your cubes to suit the shape and height of the room – particularly useful under sloping ceilings. Perfect for hi-fi equipment, they will also effectively house photographs, display items, tableware and glasses.

these items against a single wall without shaving more than 15 cm (6 in) off the size of the room. Where you do need deeper storage – for things like vinyl record collections or stacks of tableware – make use of existing recesses by fitting them with shelves and then fronting them with doors to sit level with the adjacent wall or with other built-in cupboards.

If the idea of a whole wall of doors feels too oppressive, but you are not tidy enough to trust yourself with open storage, consider partly glazed or frosted glass doors instead, or line the panels with wire mesh to screen off the contents without obscuring them completely.

Supplement your wall cupboards with floor-level furniture containing hidden storage space. Look for chests and coffee tables that have lift-up lids or integral drawers, or buy individual under-sofa drawers – huge shallow trays on wheels that cleverly slot underneath the sofa, so all that is visible is a wooden panel that appears to be part of the sofa base.

On display

The same principle can be applied to open shelving, with deep shelves built into alcoves (useful for things like televisions and video recorders) and shallow ones fitted against walls. Plan the shelf heights carefully, or use a flexible system that allows you to shift them up and down to different levels, otherwise you will waste a

With no visible fixings, so-called 'floating' shelves are a neat, streamlined, open storage solution – the perfect place for a mini sound system, pictures and ornaments.

Alcoves either side of a chimney breast are ideal recesses in which to build permanent deep shelves or cupboards for either hiding things away or putting them on display.

Mixing the two

You don't need to stick rigidly to one approach or the other. Both built-in storage and cube systems can combine open shelving with hidden cupboards to vary the look and give you the best of both worlds. And you can customize your cube system by incorporating smart boxes, baskets and trays. Leave some sections open for display or 'tidy' storage, and then slot in extra containers that can pull out like drawers and store your clutter to keep it organized.

Cleverest of all are systems that hide closed storage behind your open shelves. This needs an expert cabinet-maker, but you can create a deep layer of spacious storage slots for televisions, hi-fi equipment and files to which you don't need regular access. Then add a set of slim, open bookshelves in front that will pull open like a door to reveal the hidden storage behind.

Compact hi-tech

Home entertainment gadgetry gets a frequent design update simply because it has to keep up with technology. Most developments involve condensing more technology into less space, so the systems are becoming increasingly compact – good news if you have a small living room.

Television cabinets and music centres used to be additional furniture needing a lot of floor space, but the newest designs take up far less room.

If you don't want the television to dominate your room, go for a small screen that will fit neatly on a shelf or can be hidden inside a cabinet. The size quoted is the diagonal width. If you are a film buff and want an image that does justice to wide-screen technology, look for flat screens that don't take up much depth – the latest LCD and plasma screens are very thin.

Sound systems have been combining radios, cassette decks and CD players in a single unit for years, with the packages getting progressively smaller and neater, and their speakers, once large cumbersome boxes, now dainty and shelf-fitting or wall-mountable as wafer-thin panels. The same principle has been applied to televisions, videos and DVDs, with combined units eliminating the need for several different boxes accumulating masses of trailing cables. Some televisions come with integral video recorders or DVD players; others incorporate DVD player, CD player and radio.

Most larger gadgets come with their own housing, stand or frame, many with a shelf or other integral storage for essentials like discs, tapes and remote controls. Smaller items can be accommodated on shelves or in cupboards, or mounted on adjustable brackets that will swing out of the way when the equipment is not in use.

A redundant fireplace or alcove is the perfect recess for housing items like wine racks or this home entertainment system on a portable trolley.

A mixture of open and closed storage units prevents the living room from looking either too cluttered or too streamlined and austere.

A free-standing open shelving system allows light through, but is substantial enough to make an effective room divider, while offering plenty of display space.

Techno style

The other difference today is that the machinery itself is designed to be put on show rather than encased in cabinet furniture. Brushed steel, aluminium and titanium reflect the up-to-the-minute technology and suit sleek modern furnishing styles. Matt black is discreet yet contemporary, and wood veneers and leather-effect finishes add a touch of luxury beyond the purely functional. For a little more fun, you can find systems in bright colours or even with clip-on frames that can be changed to suit your scheme. As a contrast to all that technological wizardry, you can add a dash of classic styling with fashionably retro designs from the 1950s and 1960s, recalling the days when the portable wireless was the height of sophistication.

Hide and seek

Televisions are the bulkiest of the entertainment gadgets, so hide the television if you can. It saves space, gets rid of an unwanted focal point and frees you up to arrange the room as you want – there may even be space for an extra chair.

Bathrooms

Bathroom priorities

A priority for many, while a mere practicality for others, the bathroom is one of those rooms where decorating is daunting. Usually small, sometimes windowless and with plumbing and pipework to work around, bathrooms often get left at a compromise simply because the idea of ripping everything out and starting again is too intimidating.

Modern requirements

The modern bathroom is frequently regarded as a sanctuary, and the rise of single-person households gives many of us an opportunity to spend more time in the bathroom rather than fighting for a ten-minute slot with other family members.

A large bathroom offers the possibility of installing a free-standing roll top bath in a modern or traditional style – either is a luxury in most people's eyes.

Newly built homes reflect these changes in our lifestyle and society, and pay far more attention to the size and layout of the bathroom, incorporating second bath or shower rooms and en-suite washing facilities where possible, and creating better access from other bedrooms. You may not have quite so much flexibility if you are redesigning an existing dwelling, but it is worth using the same principles to devise a room that suits the way you live.

Assessing your options

Start by working out what you need from your bathroom – and what you can quite happily live without. There is, for instance, no law dictating the gold-standard installation of a full-sized bath, separate shower cubicle, basin, lavatory and bidet in every bathroom. It may be a dream layout in the sort of hotel suite where the bathroom is as big as the average living room, but it simply is not necessary if you prefer showering to bathing anyway, have a separate lavatory down the corridor and never use the bidet.

You could be much better off by fitting a full-strength power shower in a luxury cubicle, doing without a bath and bidet and using the extra space for a built-in airing cupboard, a linen cabinet for spare towels and bedding or even a washing machine and tumble dryer. On the other hand, if the bath is an indulgence you cannot do without, make it a priority to choose the most comfortable size (see page 216) and be prepared to sacrifice something else to make room.

Of course, your options will also depend on the size of your bathroom. If, after the essential basics, you still have plenty of space, you may want to make it a real chill-out zone by incorporating comfortable seating, some form of music and scented candles for those indulgent evenings spent relaxing in the bath. On the other hand, if you have a large and growing family, storage solutions may be at the top of your list.

How much privacy?

Privacy is another important issue to consider when it comes to bathrooms. A single person or a couple may be happy with an open-plan layout where the bathroom is simply a walk-in area adjoining the main bedroom. Or for the ultimate indulgence (and if you

A 'wet room' is an increasingly popular style of bathroom in which the shower is unenclosed, so the whole room and its contents are likely to get wet quite regularly.

Bathroom clutter control

Bathrooms are often on the small side, so you need to be especially strict about keeping clutter under control. Whether you are aiming for streamlined practicality or a luxury retreat, unwanted items will interfere with the purpose and spoil the effect.

• Plan plenty of storage, either built-in or with a range of attractive free-standing containers (see page 224).

• Be ruthless about throwing out non-essential equipment or accessories.

• Pack away any spare toiletries until they are needed.

• Throw away old or unused cosmetics. If you have not used them before now, you are never going to. They gradually deteriorate anyway, so impose a six-month shelf life and get rid of anything that is out of date.

have the space), you could install a free-standing bath in the bedroom and turn the whole room into a luxurious retreat. Family homes, though, will probably require proper doors and enclosed shower cubicles, and you will need to think about the best position for sanitary ware as well as appropriate access points. If the room has enough free wall space, it might be feasible to plan for access from two separate bedrooms on either side of it.

In all bathrooms, even open-plan designs, it is worth creating private areas with partitions so that the main washbasin area can be used while the shower and lavatory are screened from view, making the room more practical for use by more than one person at a time. These can be built as tiled or glass-brick partitions, or created with panels of frosted or sandblasted glass, providing a ready-made shower screen without the need for a separate enclosure. Part walls like this can also house plumbing, letting you position a lavatory or basin against it and free up existing wall space for other fittings. Alternatively, you could simply fix ceiling-hung bamboo blinds that can be lowered when you want to divide up the room, oriental style.

Glass-brick walls make ideal partitions and can be used to separate the shower from the washbasin, allowing the bathroom to be used by more than one family member at once.

Bathroom layouts

Unlike living and sleeping areas equipped with free-standing furniture, bathrooms do not let you rearrange the layout when you feel like a change, so you need to try to get it right first time. You can always introduce new accessories if you want to update the look.

Planning on paper

Using graph paper and a scale of 2.5 cm (1 in) to represent 1 m (3 ft), draw up a floor plan of your bathroom. Mark all the fixed features such as doors, windows and alcoves, and try out the fittings you want to include in different positions until you are happy with the effect. Take a look at the bathroom furniture designs on the following pages to get an idea of the different shapes and sizes available, including pieces specifically and often ingeniously designed to fit into corners or other small spaces.

A partition wall provides extra wall space against which to install this washbasin. The bath is ideally placed below the sloping ceiling where head room is not essential.

Don't automatically position the bath along the longest wall. A slightly shorter design may well fit across a shorter wall instead and leave you with more free floor space. Other useful positions for baths are against walls with windows (the bath will fit beneath the window, whereas a basin or lavatory cistern here might be a problem) and beneath sloping ceilings (where there is insufficient space to stand at full height, but plenty of room to lie down).

Bear in mind that doors and windows can be moved if necessary to improve the layout. A doorway repositioned across the corner of a bathroom will leave you with more usable wall space for essential fittings. And if the bathroom is under the roof, you might consider installing skylight windows and blocking up an existing window to provide extra wall space.

If you are short of wall space on which to hang heating fixtures such as radiators, consider installing plinth (kick board) heaters instead in the base panels of fitted furniture. Keep the floor and other surfaces clear wherever possible. Look for wall-hung furniture and fittings, and take advantage of any space-saving accessories such as wall-mounted soap dispensers.

Fitting in furniture

Bathrooms can be fitted with cabinet furniture on the same basis as kitchens, with streamlined units housing the sanitary ware and offering useful storage in the spaces between them. Tailor-made floor-to-ceiling units, incorporating just one or two panels of open shelving, provide a particularly sleek and stylish solution, although at a relatively high cost. Alternatively, you could build cabinets around individual items. Washbasins in particular benefit from cupboard housings that readily turn them into vanity units, providing a handy surface for toiletries around the basin as well as additional storage space below, behind closed doors.

If the room has any useful alcoves or recesses, make the most of these, too. A lavatory or basin can be positioned in a recess and the space above it fitted with a series of shelves to hold towels or toiletries.

Louvre doors and partition walls give the bath its own little room – a luxurious retreat from the rest of the family, who can still access the lavatory and washbasin.

Using screens

If you are planning to divide the room with screens for privacy, their positions need to be taken into account at the planning stage. A shower or lavatory, for instance, could be sited at the far end of the bathroom, with a partition built out at right angles to screen it.

If there is enough space in your bathroom, you could install both fittings like this, on opposite walls, each of them screened off from the rest of the room. This also has the advantage of giving the main room additional wall space, against which you can site the bath or washbasin.

Handy hints

• Check how much space is taken up by the door when it opens into the room – you might be able to free up space by rehanging it so that it opens outwards instead, or by replacing it with a sliding design.

• Positioning your bathroom suite around the edges of the room or against internal partition walls is generally the most sensible option for making the most of the floor space and for best dealing with all the necessary pipework.

Plumbing and pipework

Installing a new bathroom suite is a relatively uncomplicated and inexpensive process if you are happy to stick with the position of the existing fittings. The pipework is already in place, so all you need to do is plumb in a new bath, basin and lavatory.

To improve a badly designed room, though, especially if it is small, you may well find the best solution is to rearrange things, and this is when extra pipework becomes necessary, so be prepared for extra expense and upheaval:

• Moving a lavatory involves running an internal pipe to the external position of the waste pipe or repositioning the waste pipe, which is very costly. Consider simply rotating the lavatory by 90 degrees instead, which may be a good enough compromise for your requirements.

• Adding a shower, either over the bath or in a cubicle, means new pipework, plus connection to the electricity supply if the shower is a powered model.

• To save on running costs, keep the pipes for hot water as short as possible.

• Bear in mind that if you are going to end up with ugly internal pipework, it could be a good idea to install fitted furniture that will hide it all away behind neat panels and inside cupboard units, or to employ a good carpenter to box in the pipes for you.

An alcove makes a useful recess in which to site a washbasin or lavatory, while recessed shelves within a wall provide handy storage space for towels and toiletries.

Furniture and fittings

Bathroom fittings are increasingly designed with limited space in mind, with ingenious ideas to save inches and make use of wasted corners. Furniture that leaves floor space free always gives the impression of a larger and less cluttered room. Of course, if you have the luxury of a large bathroom, you are far less restricted in your choice of fittings.

Bespoke baths

A free-standing bath is a good choice for a large bathroom, always creating a focal point and adding a real touch of luxury. If your bathroom is on the small side, you don't necessarily need to give up on the idea of a classic bath that is long enough to stretch out in.

A free-standing bath is always a focal point in a bathroom, be it the classic antique roll top with traditional claw feet or a contemporary one like that pictured below.

Both fitted and free-standing baths are available in slightly shorter lengths – unless you are very tall, you will actually find shorter baths more comfortable because they provide a foothold, letting you relax totally without fear of drowning. Or look for tapered designs that narrow at one end to save space. A corner bath is a practical option, but for a modern style, go for plain white rather than a colour, and install it in a smart tiled or neat wood-panelled unit rather than a moulded plastic shell.

Half-length baths fit into very tight spaces. They are usually extra deep and incorporate a ledge seat, so that you can still submerge yourself without having to

An ultra-modern look for the bold minimalist – a square bath and steel-mesh baskets for towels and toiletries in a startling white and red bathroom.

Handy hints

- To save space in a small bathroom, replace a moulded plastic bath panel, which tends to be bulky and obtrusive, with a flat surface – tiled or painted MDF (medium-density fibreboard), sandblasted glass, plain wood or neat tongue-and-groove panelling.

- If you box in the bath behind any sort of fixed panelling, check that you can still access pipework when necessary for dealing with repairs and emergencies.

- Consider the space you need around a washbasin before positioning a new one – enough room in front to bend over comfortably to wash, and plenty of elbow room on both sides.

- If you're considering buying an original cast-iron bath, check that your bathroom floor can bear the weight and inspect the condition of the bath carefully. Hairline cracks in the enamel can be repaired, but avoid a bath with deep cracks or chipped enamel.

- If you have the space and the room is well ventilated, a comfortable chair or padded bench in the bathroom will make it an appealing place to relax.

- Make sure that the lighting is specifically designed for bathroom use. The potential for electric shock means that there are regulations governing the type of lights to be used and their position.

Perched on a countertop to take up the least space possible, this circular washbasin with its space-saving wall-mounted tap (faucet) provides plenty of space around it for toiletries.

Innovative basins

Washbasins have completely reinvented themselves in the last few years, so take inspiration from the innovative ones you see in designer restaurant cloakrooms, and explore showrooms and catalogues for a full range of styles. The classic rounded ceramic pedestal basin resting on a floor-standing column is still available – in all sizes and styles – but if you have a small bathroom, the pedestal does waste unnecessary floor space.

It is worth looking at basins that come as an integral vanity unit instead. They take the same amount of floor space, but give you a lot of storage with it. Alternatively, a basin fitted into a built-in countertop – like those in train and boat cabins – gives you a storage surface for toiletries as well as hiding away ugly pipework.

Even more efficient in their use of space are wall-hung designs, where the basin is suspended on brackets and pipework diverted into the wall to keep the floor below clear. In fact, if the floor space is freed up, you can get away with a larger basin because the overall effect is less cluttered and more spacious.

stretch right out. The latest take on these are square bath tubs, often with wooden surrounds, which conjure up a minimal Japanese or Scandinavian effect, resulting in a cool blend of utilitarian function and designer style.

Bear in mind that if you scale down other fittings in your bathroom, you can afford to be more indulgent in your choice of bath. For example, if you leave out the bidet and sacrifice the shower cubicle, you could find that you have room for that free-standing roll top after all. Additional bath features like a whirlpool option add to the luxurious experience.

Surface interest

It is the materials, though, that have made the biggest difference to modern basin design, and opened the way for sleek new shapes. Glass (chunky and textured like ice, or frosted and opaque) and stainless steel both create shallow, elegant 'dishes' that can be wall-mounted on brackets or can sit on countertops. These are the best for saving space, as the curves are streamlined, with no intrusive corners. If you have more room, robust materials like stone and marble create a more down-to-earth look, but still conjure up imaginative effects such as circular 'tub' basins or deep butler's-style troughs, like a smaller version of the traditional kitchen scullery sink.

Lavatories

Like basins, these are neatest when they are wall-hung, so that there is no pedestal cluttering up the floor, and the cistern is concealed behind the wall. Some are designed to fit right into corners; others to protrude as little as 50 cm (20 in) into the room. If you fit a floor-standing lavatory, it might be a good idea to look for a two-piece circular pan (originally a Victorian design, but still made by some specialist companies), so that the waste pipe link can be swivelled to the best position

By freeing up the floor space beneath them, wall-hung lavatories and basins give the impression of space and are an ideal solution in small bathrooms.

before the two parts are cemented together – really useful if you are trying to fit the lavatory into an awkward space. Another space-saving option, but in complete contrast to the sleek modern look, is to fit a high-level cistern with a pull chain if you fancy an Edwardian-style bathroom.

Buying and fitting a new lavatory seat – there are plenty of modern designs to choose from – is the easiest way to improve the look of an existing lavatory that you don't want to have to replace.

Shower spaces

Now that the technology is so advanced, showers are increasingly desirable as the most refreshing, water-efficient and space-saving way of washing. Powerful pump-driven showers can be fitted over a bath (so as not to take up any extra room), in very restricted spaces such as under the stairs, in the corner of a

Tap talk

There are dozens of different tap (faucet) styles and finishes – you need to make appropriate choices for your style of bathroom and decide whether you want individual hot and cold pillar taps or mixer taps (faucets). For example, a streamlined contemporary suite needs minimalist lever-style taps (faucets) with similarly clean lines, whereas traditional cross-head taps (faucets) suit a classic-style bathroom suite. Use the same design for your bath, basin and shower fittings for consistency.

Taps (faucets) can be fitted directly to the basin or bath, to the horizontal surface around it or wall mounted for a really neat look. Wall-mounted taps (faucets) help save space and keeps the surround free for toiletries. The mechanism will take up about 8 cm (3¼ in) of concealed depth behind the wall. Wall-mounted taps (faucets) are easier to keep clean, as there are fewer visible fittings to trap dirt. They are particularly recommended in the shower.

You can install a shower above an ordinary bath, but a specially designed shower bath is slightly wider at the taps (faucets) end and gives you more room in which to stand.

Open options

In many ways, it is better not to enclose the shower at all. If the bathroom is already small, why build an even smaller room inside it? Instead, leave the cubicle open, so that it has sides to contain the water jet (best tiled floor to ceiling for maximum water resistance), but no door boxing it off. If you do want to create a screen for privacy, the best curtains to use are double-sided, with a waterproof liner on the inside and a fabric outer layer in towelling or smart textured waffle, to soften the clinical edge.

Most luxurious of all is the 'wet room', where the whole space is tiled, and water simply flows away through a drain in the floor. This is costly to install because of the expanse of tiles required and the need to devise safe water drainage, especially in timber-framed houses. However, designers are already coming up with ways to solve the problem, for instance by setting an aluminium tray into the floor beneath the tiling, so it is worth thinking about. If you do opt for an open shower, remember to install effective storage for towels and bathroom tissue, otherwise these will get drenched along with the rest of the room!

The semi-enclosed shower in this completely tiled 'wet room' has no door and no shower tray – the water simply runs away via a drain in the room's tiled floor.

bedroom or as part of a small en-suite. They can even, if necessary, take the place of the bath altogether in the main bathroom.

If you don't want to give up your bath, you have the option of fitting it with an overbath shower or installing a specially designed shower bath, which is shaped with an integral shower tray at one end to create a larger area in which to stand. If you can find the space, though, a separate cubicle is more satisfactory – partly because it allows the bath and shower to be used at the same time, and also because the latest cubicles are now being designed with luxury extras such as body and steam jets.

You need to allow a square metre or yard for the average-sized floor tray, and make sure that there is enough space around it to allow you to get in and out of the enclosure easily – if you're short of room, a shower curtain or bi-folding door takes up less room than a normal door. Alternatively, corner cubicles are a neat way of maximizing the floor space.

Colour and surfaces

You need to take care in the bathroom not to break up surfaces with too many patterns or changes of colour and texture. Choose one colour, or similar tones, for the walls and ceiling, and keep your tiles and floor design unfussy.

White rules

White is widely regarded as the *only* colour for sanitary ware. Every now and then bathroom designers try to reintroduce subtle shades of cream or pink (usually referred to as champagne) for baths and basins, but it is not the same. White is clean, classic and – unless you have decided to splash out on a material like marble or stone instead of traditional porcelain and cast iron – it simply feels the most natural choice for bathroom fittings. It will never date (white fittings are sought-after at architectural salvage centres in a way that aqua and burgundy never will be) and when the time comes to sell your home, you will find it far easier with a white bathroom suite.

Colour scheming

In small bathrooms a palette of pale, light shades is a good idea for the rest of the decorating, but you might want to deviate from bright white, which can look a bit clinical, and add a stronger element of colour or character. As well as choosing colours that will open up the space, you can create very different effects and alter the mood of the room. Richer, creamy whites used for walls or tiles will look elegant and throw the white sanitary ware into sparkling relief; deeper contemporary neutrals such as stone and taupe will add a Zen-like natural calm; cool blues, greens and mauves will reflect the room's watery associations; soft plaster pinks will add warmth, and give you the chance to create a more luxurious, boudoir look if you have had enough of all that understated minimalism.

A purely white bathroom could look clinical, but the touch of lilac in the décor and the use of soft furnishings ensure that the look in this bathroom is far from stark.

In larger bathrooms you can consider brighter colours, but don't darken the room too much – a good light is essential for applying make-up or for shaving. Ocean blues and aquas are popular and effective bathroom colours, but take care not to swamp the room with them. Warm, soft colours like peach look good against skin tone and make you look healthy.

These unusual wall tiles are an attractive feature in themselves, while protecting the walls from the potential steam and water damage of a typical bathroom.

Handy hints

• If you have a window in your bathroom, don't swamp it in unnecessary fabric. Instead, obscure the glass with a frosted or sandblasted design for privacy, or add a simple blind that will screen the window without blocking the light.

• Use reflective surfaces like chrome, stainless steel, glass and large mirrors to lighten, open up and magnify a small bathroom space.

• Daily exposure to steam and water can cause damage, so choose your bathroom surfaces well and make sure that everything in the room is fixed or sealed properly.

• Healthy-looking real plants in the bathroom add to the room's aesthetic appeal and bring a fresh, invigorating quality to your bathing experience.

Wall protection

A mixture of paint and tiles is the simplest choice for bathroom walls. If the room is well ventilated, you could opt for a specialist wallcovering, but you will need to apply it with a fungicide-containing paste.

Look for emulsion paint specially formulated for bathrooms so that it will resist mould and damp. If you are interested in authentic architectural materials, it might also be worth considering limewash, which can be mixed with pigments to create different colours. This will need to be applied over lime plaster or brick (you cannot paint it over modern emulsion), but it responds well to damp environments without blistering or developing mould.

Choosing tiles

You need tiles in order to create a protective splashback around the bath, behind the basin and to line shower cubicles, but do think twice before tiling the entire bathroom from floor to ceiling. A vast expanse of tiles can be overpowering; patterns will confuse the eye, and even plain tiles can be surprisingly uncomfortable, creating a rather clinical effect in a restricted environment – more like a hospital than a luxurious sanctuary.

To avoid this, it might be worth looking at the new generation of natural-finish tiles, which present a matt surface, recreating the look of limestone, slate or alabaster rather than the high gloss of traditional glazed tiles. Glazed surfaces are useful for their

A stylish solution for tiled surfaces in the bathroom, mosaic tiles are most effective when used to make intricate patterns against a plain background.

reflective finish, which acts almost like a mirror in bouncing light back into the room and helping to open up a small space, but the effect can be fairly easily overdone, creating too prominent a glare. So matt tiles are an effective compromise, combining practical water resistance and plain colour with a more subtle, comfortable finish.

Mosaic effects, created from hundreds of tiny tile chips, are always intriguing and can sometimes work in small rooms, where their 'miniature' nature seems appropriate for the proportions. But again, be careful not to overdo and in consequence spoil the effect – it will be accentuated by a confined space, and therefore may be better limited to a single wall or shower lining rather than covering the whole room.

Other types of tile worthy of consideration in the bathroom are modern glass and lustred tiles. These are not to be confused with the chunky glass bricks used for partitions and interior walls, but are delicate wall tiles with either a clear, jewel-like glow or an iridescent mother-of-pearl finish. These provide a glorious range of colours and subtly shifting shades, with a gently reflective surface that gives a light-enhancing gleam rather than a bright shine.

Most often used on walls and floors, tiles are in fact useful for sealing any surface exposed to water. Here, they make a very effective bath surround.

Underfoot issues

The bathroom floor needs to balance aesthetics with practicality – you can bend some of the rules if the room will be used by just one or two adults, whereas a busy family bathroom will need a more rigorous approach (see pages 70–89).

Tiles Ceramic tiles, along with stone and marble, look smart and are waterproof and easy to clean, but they may feel cold and hard underfoot, and are inclined to get slippery when wet. If you want a little more comfort, or have children to worry about, you will need to add washable cotton rugs or go for a softer option altogether.

Wood Wood has a practical appeal that looks good and suits many different styles of décor, but floorboards will need to be well sealed (or painted) to make them waterproof, and you need to be careful with laminates, which have a tendency to warp and lift if subjected to constant damp.

Vinyl and rubber You may find sheet vinyl a better option; it is easy to lay (see page 84) and can imitate

Wooden flooring in the bathroom is unusual, but very stylish, as these decking-style tiles demonstrate. The wood must be well sealed to prevent water damage.

almost any look you want, from wood to stone or marble. Alternatively, you could go for something uncompromisingly modern such as rubber, which is warm, waterproof and incredibly hardwearing.

Bear in mind that you can always add wooden slatted duckboards to give a vinyl floor a more utilitarian look, or to provide a safe, non-slip surface on top of marble or ceramic tiles.

Turning up the heat

Bathroom heaters are part of the furniture these days, with sleek designs and contemporary colours contributing as much to the look of the room as the suite and tiles you choose. If you have wall space to spare, fit a ladder design that will double as a towel rail.
Radiators If your home's central heating system relies on radiators and you have limited wall space, extra-narrow radiators can be fitted into narrow strips, or look for floor-level cylindrical designs that run along a skirting board (baseboard) and pump out ample heat from a compact shape. The chunky scale of old school-style pillar radiators would be too big for a small bathroom, but you will find new versions with a reduced number of pillars and sometimes an integral towel rail, too, bringing this classic design right up to date for the modern home.

A chrome ladder-style heater/towel rail is an effective and stylish way to heat the room and to store and dry damp towels all year round.

Adding warmth and texture

Glass, mirror, chrome and ceramics are the key elements of most modern bathrooms – hard, cold, reflective surfaces that are practical, but not terribly inviting or comfortable for a room in which you want to be able to linger and relax. You therefore need to add softer materials that balance the chill and contribute warmth.

The most obvious of these ameliorating elements are bathroom linens – piles of towels in thick fluffy cotton or textured waffle, a deep-pile bath mat for wet bare feet, a bath pillow for relaxing against in the bath and an attractive fabric shower curtain. Classic white linens are always the simplest and soundest, but you can select other shades to coordinate with the room's colour scheme or add contrasting accents.

You might also want to incorporate areas of plain wood, for bath surrounds and fitted furniture. Antique pine or stained tongue-and-groove panelling suits a country-style bathroom, while the mellow finish of beech and cedar adds a smart European-style simplicity to contemporary bathrooms.

Piles of fluffy towels add a sense of comfort to the bathroom, while the texture provides a good contrast to the tiles, glass, mirrors and metallic surfaces typical of bathrooms.

Bathroom storage

There are ever-more inventive ideas for storage solutions on the market, particularly for bathrooms, which are often in need of careful management to prevent the room becoming cluttered with everyday toiletries and cosmetics, spare supplies, cleaning products, laundry, first-aid kit and children's bath toys and towels, among other bathroom essentials.

Fitted versus free-standing

Where space is limited, fitted bathroom furniture provides the best storage, with cupboards built beneath and between the various items of sanitary ware and worktops, providing handy surfaces to hold toiletries. Like kitchen furniture, fitted bathroom units can combine open shelves with closed cabinets, giving you quick access to regularly used items and letting towels and toiletries create their own colourful display.

If you don't want an entirely built-in look, which can sometimes feel cold and functional, you can create a more casual effect with free-standing furniture. Trolleys, shelf units and steel basket stands stack 'layers' of storage on top of each other without taking up valuable floor space, and may come on castors, making it easier for you to shift them into the most practical position. Individual shelves and cabinets can then be fixed to the wall. Among the most practical are peg rails that combine a row of hooks for hanging towels, washbags and laundry bags with an integral shelf above.

By opting for halfway between the fitted and free-standing solutions, you can make use of areas that are crying out for built-in cupboards, while leaving the rest of the room less structured. Building a cabinet around the washbasin, for example, looks neat and makes use of the space wasted by the pedestal, and the same

Mail-order catalogues and high-street stores are full of clever storage solutions for bathrooms, like this ingenious circular chrome shelving unit, designed to fit around the washbasin pedestal.

treatment can be given to the bath, with shallow cupboard storage built into the space behind the side panel. This has the additional benefit of boxing in and concealing ugly pipework.

Bath surrounds

If there is room, it may be worth building the bath surround out slightly – just a little will allow you to accommodate cleaning materials and spare toiletries. It should also provide a wide shelf right around the bath to add a sense of luxury – enough space for a book and a glass of wine as well as practical bath essentials. Remember, too, that the wall space on the far side of the bath, and at the head or foot if these butt up

Open shelves can add to the décor in a bathroom, but by their very nature are for public viewing and so need to be kept clean and tidy with the minimum of toiletries on display.

Finding extra space

• Opt for dual-purpose items like a linen basket that doubles as a seat or bath-side table, and a slim bathroom cabinet with a mirrored door that stores toiletries without protruding too far into the room.

• Fit a heated towel rail beneath the basin or around the pedestal to keep towels handy and to save on precious wall space, or choose a style of washbasin with a built-in towel rail beneath the sink.

• Fit the bathroom with a deep, double-skin door with storage 'pockets' cut into the inner skin so that it can hold small items.

against a wall, can be fitted with shelves or hooks without obstructing the room. In a room with a high ceiling, you might also consider building the bath up on to a platform so that you can fit storage into the space beneath.

Smart shelving

Open shelves are perfect for making good use of otherwise 'dead' space, such as narrow strips of wall behind doors. They can also be employed to create useful partitions between items of sanitary ware. For instance, you can fit a set of bookcase-style shelves at right angles to the wall across the foot of the bath to provide extra storage space at the same time as creating a screen to hide the lavatory.

Shelves like these are perfect for storing spare colour-coordinated towels in attractive neatly folded piles, displaying a group of colourful bath oils in interestingly shaped bottles or holding a row of attractive glass containers or woven cylindrical baskets to store toiletries and cleaning materials.

In contrast with solid wooden shelving, glass or metal shelves have reflective surfaces and help give rooms a feeling of space, but glass shelves do smear easily and require regular cleaning. An alternative to wall-mounted shelves are the large free-standing shelf units, often made of open metal work, specially designed to fit snugly around the washbasin pedestal or to stand against the wall above a lavatory. The downside of having open shelves in general is that they can far too easily become piled high with messy-looking clutter and are readily visible to any visitor using the bathroom.

Bedrooms

Planning your sleeping space

The bedroom is the one place where you can afford to indulge your creative decorating instincts without restraint. This is private space that does not need to keep the rest of the world happy 24 hours a day, so you can choose colours purely to please yourself and design tailor-made storage to suit your clothing.

Creating calm

For bedrooms to provide the restful space you need for sleep, they should be free of clutter. That means clothes put away, the floor clear of books and shoes and not letting the casual layering of bed linen degenerate into a tousled muddle.

Feng shui principles go so far as to dictate that bedrooms should be used for sleep and nothing else, that you shouldn't keep books here or have a study area, or have clothes out on show. In particular, outdoor clothes should not be visible, as these distract you from the inward calm of rest and sleep.

This approach may be a little extreme for some, but you can see the point. Especially in small bedrooms where space is limited, it is all the more important that the 'sleep centre' takes precedence.

To get your sleep centre right, you need to make good storage a priority so that you keep clothes, footwear and accessories out of the way and leave the floor clear for the bed. Do not automatically buy a massive wardrobe (closet) if most of your clothes do not need full-length hanging room – it will be wasted on separates and shirts that take up only half the space. Work out whether your clothes need shelf, drawer or hanging storage, allocate space accordingly (see page 234) and stick to the system – don't let things stray.

If possible, position the bed where you can walk freely all the way round it and don't have to climb over it to reach essential items. If space is really tight, for example in attic bedrooms or beneath awkward

Make your bedroom a calm haven to which to retreat at the end of the day – decorate the room in restful colours and keep it free of clutter.

ceilings, fit the bed where the height is lowest. This space will not be much use for storage, but is fine where you will only be lying down, and can create a cosier place in which to lay your head.

Dual-purpose bedrooms

In reality, contrary to the feng shui ideals above, many people's bedrooms are increasingly used not just for sleeping and dressing, but also function as a work or sitting room, especially if the room is a particularly large one. Indeed, bedrooms can successfully double as work spaces as long as the decoration is kept neat and simple and the space is well organized between the two areas. If the room is multi-functional, you might want to disguise the bed with tailored covers during the day.

Adaptable furniture allows your bedroom to be used for more than just sleeping. Here, an attractive daybed doubles up as a comfortable place to sit during the daytime.

Clutter control

• Always put clothes away when you take them off, or put them in a linen basket or laundry bag ready to wash.

• Throw away clothes that no longer fit you, that you regret having bought, that are marked or damaged beyond practical use or that are no longer in fashion (you can keep the occasional favourite for fancy-dress parties). Don't hold on to them on the basis that you paid for them and want to get your money's worth – better to cut your losses and get rid of the guilty irritation you feel every time you see them.

• Don't allow magazines and books to accumulate beside the bed. Recycle, file or return them to the bookshelves.

Screens and partitions

One way of keeping the bed area separate and free of clutter is to create a floating wall at the head of the bed, which divides the bed from storage. This need not take up much space – it simply gives the bed a sort of extra-high, free-standing headboard, pulling it forwards into the room rather than standing it against a structural wall. The extra space behind the bed can then be used for storage or a dressing room. Although it reduces the floor space that the bed stands in, it makes the area look bigger by freeing it up from other furniture. If you don't want to construct a fixed wall, you could achieve the same effect with a free-standing screen.

Proportion and scale

A large bedroom gives you plenty of scope for some grand-scale furniture like a four-poster and a double wardrobe (closet). If the bedroom is small, you need to create a light and airy impression by making sure that any peripheral furniture is small and neat. Slim console tables – the sort designed to stand against a hall wall – can take the place of full-sized dressing tables, and bedside tables only really need to be big enough to take a lamp, clock and perhaps a separate radio.

The one item that is worth having as big as possible in the bedroom is a mirror. As well as providing that all-important clothing check, it will reflect the available light and make the whole room feel twice the size. You don't even need to fix it in place – a huge mirror leaning casually against the wall can look wonderful.

A large bedroom can provide a quiet and private work space, but keep the décor simple and the desk area tidy so that it doesn't encroach on the room.

Colour and texture

A bedroom should be a haven – comforting, relaxing and in your own taste and style. A good night's sleep is essential, so bedroom furnishings should be as comfortable as possible, and window dressings designed carefully.

Creating atmosphere

The atmosphere in your bedroom is up to you – go for luxury and decadence, with rich fabrics and sumptuous textures; or for calm sophistication, defined by elegant tailored lines and cool, neutral colours; or perhaps the refreshing simplicity of painted floors and furniture and crisp gingham covers. The trick is to devise a bedroom that is a retreat from the rest of the world, where you can switch off and totally relax.

Since you see the fabrics in your bedroom first thing in the morning and last thing at night, it is worth taking time to find something you really like.

Handy hints

• Cream-coloured curtain linings, and cream or off-white sheers and voiles, are often better than pure white ones in urban homes, where the city grime seems to creep in at every window.

• A small stool or armchair in the bedroom that is rarely sat on could be covered in a lightweight silk or a pretty cotton rather than a heavier furnishing fabric.

• A bed that doubles as a seating area during the day needs a hardwearing cover made in a durable upholstery fabric. Light, curtain-weight fabrics are unsuitable for this purpose, as they crease and look worn if sat on regularly.

• A simple cream or white cotton bedspread is an excellent way of brightening a dark bedroom, as it will reflect light back into the room. It can easily be livened up with patterned cushions.

Bedroom colours

Colour is a crucial element here. Choose shades that will be gentle and relaxing at night and look good by artificial light – and if used during the day, refreshing and comfortable in natural light, too.

Soft blues, greens and mauves are cool and restful; pinks and yellows will add more warmth if you want it; creams and whites are unfailingly calming and elegant. However, you might want bright, rich or deep shades that surround you with more definite colour. In a small bedroom that already feels warm and protective, such colours will accentuate the womb-like effect.

Layered linens

Bedrooms automatically provide masses of fabrics with which to build up your colour scheme and add texture. Most people now opt for a duvet (comforter) on the bed, which is practical and comfortable, but does swamp the bed in a layer of single colour or pattern. The contemporary revival of classic sheets and blankets offers more elegant lines. Alternatively, for sheer luxury, indulge in an extravagant collection of contrasting fabrics and varied textures. For instance, combine the elegant drape of heavy woven blankets with silk eiderdowns, then add deep piles of different-sized cushions and pillows on top.

The sparkle factor

With so much light-absorbent texture around, a bedroom can feel slightly muffled by fabric, so try to incorporate a few reflective surfaces to catch the light and bring the space to life. Mixing silks and satins among your bed linens will help, as will using mirrors and metal-framed furniture, lamps and frames, while the glass droplets of chandelier light fittings can add a more decorative sense of sparkle.

Flat wall colour can be enlivened by painting any woodwork in eggshell paint, which has a slight sheen to it. You could even cover one wall or a chimney breast with painted wood panelling to extend this effect over a larger area of the room.

Barefoot comfort

A neutral-coloured carpet, or a natural floorcovering in cotton, linen, wool or jute, will be soft and warming beneath bare feet. Wood – especially white-painted floorboards – looks good in bedrooms, too, and is

White-painted floorboards look good in a bedroom, although you may want a soft rug beside the bed for your bare feet when you first get up in the morning.

useful in small rooms for opening up the space. If you have a hard floor surface, consider using soft rugs or carpet pieces to both soften the room a little and provide more sound insulation.

Low lighting

Lighting needs to be kept subtle and atmospheric; aim for mood rather than practicality – unless, of course, your bedroom is a multi-purpose room. Fit dimmer switches to keep levels soft and adaptable, and use lamps to diffuse the light source and accent individual areas rather than flooding the whole room, providing illumination where required for reading or applying make-up. If you have built-in cupboards, consider fitting interior lights (in heat-resistant casings), which make it easier to find things.

Restful windows

In bedrooms, curtains and blinds need to exclude light, provide privacy and also be heavy enough to help soundproof the room against outside noise.

Keep the colour of your curtains or blinds similar to the walls to avoid jarring blocks of sudden colour or pattern. Curtains will be drawn closed more often here than in daytime rooms, and a dominant fabric that provides an attractive frame for the window when drawn back or rolled up may look overpowering when opened out in larger panels. It is usually more restful to surround yourself with a single sweep of colour.

Instead of heavy curtains, you could use a light-resistant or roller blind, and combine it with a drape in a sheer fabric to soften the look.

A large mirror in this run of cupboards (which slides up to reveal a concealed television) helps reflect light and make the room seem larger.

Bed styles and shapes

The style of the bed makes all the difference to the look of a bedroom. You can choose to dominate the space with a scene-stealing centrepiece or go for something more discreet that blends into the background. Comfort is of course paramount, but the style can create a host of different effects.

Simpler styles

The simpler the style of bed, the less space it will appear to take up. If you want to maximize the space in your bedroom or need to fit in other furniture such as a writing desk or dressing table, look for streamlined beds without head- or footboards. Simple frames, though, can add a sense of style without overwhelming

An eye-catching feature in a feminine bedroom, this white metal-framed bed with its simple barred ends adds an understated touch of style without overdominating the room.

Choosing the right bed

• Always try beds out in the shop to test the mattress for comfort.

• Arm yourself with accurate measurements, including doorway and staircase dimensions, to make sure that you will be able to get the bed into the room.

• Where access space is tight, look for hinged bed designs that fold in half, or that come in two halves and can be bolted together in situ.

• Map out the bed size on the floor of the room to accurately gauge how it will look and to make sure that there is enough space to walk around it. Even if it fits, it may overwhelm the space visually, so you might want to opt for a slightly smaller size to keep the room in proportion.

• If you are short of storage, bed bases with deep drawers built into them are extremely useful for holding spare bed linen or clothes that don't need hanging up. Alternatively, look for a bedframe with plenty of space beneath it and add separate wheeled drawers like shallow trolleys that can be pushed under and pulled out with ease.

the room. Plain metal frames with barred ends, like classic hospital or school dormitory beds, are a neat alternative to the traditional, high-standing brass bedstead. Look for painted metal or brushed steel rather than the bright polished finish, to keep the effect understated and contemporary.

Wood sounds a mellower note, warmer than metal but still keeping the look practical. Simple flat-packed pine beds are widely available and easy to assemble yourself – avoid shiny orange pine (which always looks uncomfortably bright and is especially harsh in bedrooms) in favour of more authentic-looking antique pine. Decorative carving and turning on the end boards and posts will suggest a traditional country-style bedroom, but if you want to give the room a modern edge, aim for light wood and simple, square-cut designs to maintain the streamlined look.

Think about the height of bed you want – a simple low bed will add to the sense of height in a low-ceilinged room, but you may find it more awkward to get in and out of.

Daring decadence

It is sometimes more fun, though, in a room that is your own personal space and where you can decorate to please yourself to splash out on something more dramatic. Wooden sleighbeds, with end pieces carved into gentle curves faintly reminiscent of a traditional sleigh, have a classic elegance that does not fight with

Extra sleeping space

If you have a box (lumber) room, living room or study that you want to turn into an occasional sleeping space for overnight guests, or you live in a studio apartment and want the daytime effect to be of a living room rather than a bedroom, look for clever beds that can be neatly hidden away when not in use.

The most practical of these are the ones that masquerade as something else during the day. Sofa beds turn sitting space into instant bedrooms (look for a design with a properly sprung mattress if it is going to get regular use), and Japanese-style futons provide basic low-level seating on a slatted wooden base that will fold out to a double (full-size) or single bed. You can also find double-layer divan beds that are a neat size to act as a makeshift sofa in a study. The lower mattress slides sideways and upwards to sit level with the upper one and double its size to make a bed. In addition, specialist companies are designing all kinds of 'instant' beds, with mattresses that can unfold from boxes and beanbags.

A dramatic headboard enhances the bed's role as the main visual focus of the room. The simple square-cut design of this bed complements the style and dimensions of the room.

contemporary furnishings. The wood is usually dark, which may look rather heavy and oppressive in a small room, but if you paint it a light colour, it will instantly appear smaller and less obtrusive.

Decorative metal looks elegant and romantic, with a delicate framework that will suit a small space as long as it is painted in a light colour. Alternatively, you could go for leather, one of the smartest new looks – a plain headboard in soft, matt leather combines a streamlined simplicity with an irresistible sense of luxury.

For a real flourish, and to turn the bedroom into a cocoon of comfort, add still more fabric and dress the bed with its own curtains. Gauzy white muslin is a brilliant way of casting a feeling of romance over the setting without swamping the room completely. A ceiling-fixed mosquito net is the simplest way to achieve this effect, but for more drama, and to screen off the bed from distracting storage or work areas, create a contemporary four-poster. Forget any visions of the old style four-poster with overblown flounces and heavy drapes (unless you specifically want a period look) – with a frame in plain unadorned metal or wood, and sheer cotton muslin curtains, this looks wonderfully romantic and restful.

Bedroom storage

Most of your bedroom storage will be for clothes and accessories, but you may also need to house toiletries, make-up, books, personal papers and mementos. As with storage in living rooms (see page 206), you need to decide how many of your possessions can stay out and how much room you need to hide things away.

Bespoke systems

As in living rooms, closed storage will help keep the room free of clutter and, once again, the most efficient system is to build it in to make full use of the area available and to create customized spaces for different kinds of item – in effect, taking the principle of the fitted kitchen and applying it to the bedroom. Fitted-bedroom companies have perfected this as an art form, and it is worth looking at the gadgets and tricks that they employ to find a place for everything, even if you don't want to buy their cabinets. The key is to create several individual compartments behind your closed doors rather than one long hanging space, giving you the flexibility to treat each section independently and devise different storage systems for each one.

First, work out how many of your clothes need to be hung rather than folded, then divide hanging clothes into full length and half length. Dresses, coats and long skirts need full-length space, so one section of your cupboards will need to be fitted with a high rail. Shirts, trousers, skirts and jackets need only half the length, so you can save space in another section either by fixing two rails, one above the other to create double-decker storage, or by fixing one high rail and then fitting cupboards or shelves beneath them.

Built-in storage makes full use of the space available, while glass-fronted rather than solid doors help avoid the potentially austere effect of a run of matching cupboards.

Headboard shelves

By building a slimline cupboard out of MDF (medium-density fibreboard) and securing it firmly to the wall behind a plain divan bed, you can make a custom-made headboard and bedside shelf at the same time, thereby creating space for books, photographs, radio and a reading light, and eliminating the need for bedside tables if floor space is in short supply.

Make the cupboard about 15 cm (6 in) deep, 1 m (3 ft) high and a little wider than your bed. If you design it with end panels that open to let you slot flat items inside, you can create extra storage space for things such as pictures that you have no room to hang, artwork and document portfolios.

The rest of the space can be taken up with shelves and drawers in different sizes and depths. Fit extra-deep drawers for jumpers, with smaller, shallower ones for underwear and socks. Look out for transparent drawers in wire or acrylic, which let you see their contents without too much rummaging. Make use of high-level shelves to store items not needed so often, then take advantage of additional ideas that are designed to be slotted into larger systems to help keep things neat.

Racks fixed to the inside of the door, for example, will hold items like scarves and ties; honeycomb organizers can be fitted inside drawers to 'file' small items individually; shoe racks will stand in the bottom of the cupboard to keep pairs together without scuffing; and shoe hangers comprise a strip of open-sided canvas 'cubes', each one taking a single pair of shoes. Incorporating a few deep shelves will also give you space to stack boxes and baskets commandeered as improvised 'drawers'.

Space-saving doors

If space is tight, you don't want to obstruct it with cupboard doors. Consider fitting sliding doors rather than hinged ones, so that they don't swing out into the room. In a very small space, it helps if the doors are also mirrored, to increase the amount of light and make the room appear twice as large.

Double-depth cupboards

If you have two bedrooms linked by a partition wall, you can 'pool' their storage space by replacing the wall with a deep layer of cupboards, in effect creating a double wall with a storage cavity between them. This lets you give each room a double-depth cupboard, each one using up the full depth of the wall space yet only half its length, so that the two cupboards sit side by side, but face in opposite directions, like the storage equivalent of a loveseat.

To create a 'shared' closet with access from both rooms, leave one end of the wall free of cupboard fittings, but fix a door on both sides so that you can walk from one room to the other. This area can then be equipped with a rail running the full depth of the double wall and will provide ample hanging space.

Creative hanging

Additional hanging storage can be supplied by free-standing clothes rails on wheels. As an alternative to the full-sized wardrobe (closet), canvas-sided designs that close with zips (zippers) or fabric ties are a good temporary measure, as they can be collapsed and folded away when not in use.

Portable clothes rails are useful for temporary storage, for example for overnight visitors, and for odd corners where there is not enough room for a full-sized wardrobe (closet).

Rigid wicker baskets are widely available in all sizes and make attractive storage containers for all manner of items. Baskets lined with fabric are ideal for storing spare bed linen.

seat on top. Similarly, a collection of wicker hampers or old leather suitcases stacked stagecoach-style in descending order can be used to hold out-of-season clothes or other items not used regularly, creating a smart display in an alcove or corner.

Smaller boxes are perfect for storing scarves, gloves, underwear, belts and jewellery. Look for decorative hat boxes that will sit on a chest of drawers (dresser) or in a disused fireplace, and Shaker boxes, traditionally made from thin layers of cherry wood curved round into an oval shape. On a more prosaic level, salvage and cover shoe and boot boxes with fabric or paper, or choose from the numerous designs of ready-decorated storage boxes in assorted shapes and styles. Label them and store under the bed, on top of cupboards and in shelf units.

Under-bed storage Rigid plastic 'under-bed' boxes are another option for storing things away. These large, shallow, lidded boxes on castors are specially designed to fit under beds (even low ones) and can be easily pulled out when required. Alternatives are heavy-duty plastic or canvas zip-up box-shaped 'bags'.

Use an ordinary vacuum hose to suck out all the air from plastic vacuum-storage bags and the bags will then take up less than half the space that they would otherwise occupy. This makes them ideal for storing bulky items like spare duvets (comforters) and pillows.

Hanging storage is particularly useful if it keeps floor space clear, so look for sets of fabric pockets for hanging inside a cupboard or on the back of a door to hold shoes, socks or underwear. A peg rail or row of hooks fixed to the wall in traditional school-cloakroom style will keep belts, scarves and hats neatly lined up, or can be used for drawstring bags to hold dirty laundry and clothing accessories.

Extra storage ideas

There are masses of additional storage devices to help keep bedroom paraphernalia hidden and turn your room into a stress-free space for relaxation and sleep.

Chests, trolleys and cabinets Look for free-standing chests fitted with extra-deep drawers designed to hold jumpers, dressing tables with drawers or deep-drawer trolleys that can be pushed into place wherever you need them. Or improvise the same effect with an office filing cabinet painted in bright enamel paint.

Baskets and boxes Useful for items that don't need everyday access, big laundry baskets – reminiscent of out-size picnic hampers – and wooden blanket boxes can hold spare bed linen and bulky sweaters, and additionally provide a useful table surface or window

These attractive seagrass storage baskets with lids can be filled and then stacked up on one another to create a display feature in themselves.

Indulge in some creative thinking and you may come up with some unusual storage solutions, like this idea of using a wooden stepladder to hold shoes.

Shelving Open shelves keep things more colourful, so you could stack T-shirts and jumpers in colour-coordinated ranks like a shop display, but you will need to be scrupulous about folding them, cleaning them regularly and guarding against moths, which like nothing better than a soft pile of woollens.

Shelves are great, too, for books and ornaments, but are obvious dust traps and need regular cleaning and tidying to prevent accumulation of clutter. If you don't trust yourself to keep them looking neat, consider hanging fabric in front to curtain them off from view.

Lateral thinking

Make use of storage not specifically designed for clothes or bedrooms. Pharmacy chests and kitchen spice chests provide useful little drawers for items that would easily get lost in a larger space. Modern stationery shops stock all sorts of miniature filing cabinets, originally intended for desk essentials, but perfect for things like jewellery and hair accessories. Vegetable racks can slot inside cupboards to hold foldable clothes, and old-fashioned bicycle baskets, with one usefully flat side, can be strapped on to a tie rack on the inside of a cupboard door.

Tailor-made storage

Coats really need to be hung on well-padded hangers to keep their shape. Hanging them by a skimpy collar loop drags the fabric and gradually spoils the line of the tailoring. An even better proposition is a proper dressmaker's dummy, complete with life-sized curves so that it provides coat storage and an innovative sculptural display all in one. Unfortunately, the classic solid wood models are rarely found nowadays, but simpler versions with cotton stretched over a basic frame are more commonly available. Alternatively, you could use a shop-window dummy made from moulded plastic or clear perspex.

Family heirlooms or antique finds like wooden sea chests or old leather trunks are great for storing out-of-season clothes or other items that you don't need to access every day.

Children's rooms

Creating room to grow

Children's rooms are self-contained worlds quite unlike anywhere else – they can easily become 24-hour hideouts, where children live by their own timescale, and where work, rest and play merge seamlessly into one another. Decorating needs to be practical – plan for durable surfaces, effective storage and children's preferences for bright colours and peer-group fads.

Easy as ABC

You could say that the best approach to furnishing children's rooms is to make it as easy as ABC – A being for adaptable, B for bright and C for cleanable:

- **Adaptability** is essential if the room is to cope with growing children (and possibly extra children), multiple uses, all-day activities and sleepovers.
- **Brightness** is stimulating and space making, and steers a neat path between soft baby pastels and teenage grunge.
- **Cleanability** is a must for all ages, however sophisticated the children regard themselves.

In addition there are issues like safety to consider (see box, opposite), and good lighting for bedtime reading and desk work, plus a tabletop for homework and enough floor space to spread out toys, games and puzzles. You also want to create an environment where the child's imagination will flourish and develop.

Work, rest and play

Children's rooms must provide areas for private work and play, as well as a safe space for sleeping. So the room must either have a separate section for each, or be flexible enough to adapt. In most homes it has to be the latter, so think laterally and be inventive.

Allow an older child some input into the decisions regarding the décor of their room. They are more likely to look after it and may even help paint the walls!

Children's tastes and needs change much faster than those of adults. You don't want to have to redecorate at every stage of their development or every time they acquire a new cartoon hero or pop idol. The trick, therefore, is to stick to a background of plain colour that can be updated with accessories when a trend is outgrown or a new look called for.

• Bunk beds are not advisable for children under six years old.

• Avoid trailing flexes and fit unused power points with safety covers.

• Be careful with furniture that can trap fingers – use stoppers on doors and drawers to stop them slamming shut, and replace heavy-lidded wooden blanket boxes with lighter baskets.

• Fit childproof window locks if window access is at all possible.

It is also a good idea to get the children involved in the initial decorating decisions, because if they feel that the room is really theirs, they are more likely to look after it and keep it tidy. That doesn't mean wallpapering in the latest 'brand' pattern that will quickly outgrow its useful life – just let them help choose colours and fabrics.

Defining with colour

Children need colour for stimulation, and although pale, space-making pastels are soothing for nurseries, once children become aware of their surroundings, they tend to be more inspired by bold, bright colours with a sense of fun and contemporary style. If you are letting them choose for themselves, you may need to steer them in the right direction to prevent their choice of colour resulting in an enclosed, oppressive feel, especially if the room is small. Bear in mind that yellows (being naturally lighter) and blues and greens (being receding colours) will feel less oppressive than bright reds and deep purples.

The best way to satisfy the demand for current crazes is to have painted walls as your base and accessorize them with peel-off borders and cut-outs that can be replaced and updated. Look out, too, for luminous stick-on effects such as planets and stars to create a night sky on the ceiling, or metallic or glow-in-the-dark paint. Areas of blackboard paint will encourage creative games and writing, and magnetic paint can be used with letter and number magnets, or with fridge magnets to clip pictures to the wall. You can repaint these as often as necessary.

Give children floor space for their games and areas for creativity like this boarded-up fireplace painted with blackboard paint to encourage drawing.

Decorate children's bedrooms in bold, bright colours – this pink and yellow combination makes a stimulating colour scheme for a little girl's room.

Carpet is always comfortable underfoot in bedrooms, but a neutral-coloured one is probably best kept for older children who are beyond the messiest age.

Ground rules

Children's floors need to be tough, washable and – again – adaptable to different themes and colour schemes. If your children are past the messiest stage and have reached an age where they demand a few luxuries, you could go for a comfortable carpet in a mid-tone neutral colour that will not show too many grubby marks, can be cleaned when necessary and does not restrict your decorating plans.

For younger children, cushioned vinyl or plain wood both fit the bill, and can be covered with washable rugs and playmats for colour and comfort. It is important, however, that you add a non-slip backing so that they don't slide on polished surfaces.

The advantage of wooden floorboards is that you can repaint them as often as you like (see page 76), sticking to a single all-over colour to match the furnishings, or adding fun patterns and games for a more inventive effect. Either use specialist floor paints for a tough, hardwearing finish, or add several coats of clear varnish to seal the colour after you have finished painting.

An alternative – if you like the idea of colour on the floor, but want to keep it adaptable – is to use multi-coloured carpet tiles that can be relaid in different patterns as often as you want, creating stripes or chequers, or a block of central colour contrasting with the outer border, to mimic a rug. Carpet tiles also have the practical advantage of allowing you to move worn or marked areas to a less-obvious position, such as under the bed, if the flooring is past its best.

Flexible furniture

If you are thinking about adaptability, keep the furniture as simple as possible. A few specialist buys are invaluable. Beds need careful thought (see page 246) and it is useful to choose a cot that will 'grow' into a bed. A changing unit is essential for a small baby, but look for one with plenty of practical cupboard space so that it will still have a useful life when the baby develops beyond the nappy (diaper) stage.

Over and above that, think flexibly and plan for furniture that will adapt to different uses. Instead of miniature chairs and tables, opt for squashy beanbags and basket chests that can be used for seating and storage when the child is older, too. Modular furniture that can be rearranged into different layouts is always an advantage, and anything on wheels is useful.

You can easily attach add-on castors to furniture and storage boxes – this gives you plenty of options for keeping room layouts flexible.

A changing unit is useful for a baby, but choose one that has the potential to be adapted into an equally useful piece of furniture for an older child.

This is also the place to make use of unwanted furniture from other rooms, as well as jazzed-up junk shop or flea market finds. Keep a lookout for any useful, adaptable cupboards and chests that can be transformed with a coat of bright, washable paint. Again, you can change the colour as often as you like or select a range of tones or contrasting colours for doors and drawer fronts.

Versatile themes

Avoid blue-for-a-boy and pink-for-a-girl colour schemes that will limit your furnishing ideas and make it much more difficult to arrange for room swaps and sharing at a later stage. The same goes for gender-specific patterns such as flowers and footballers – you are better off with generic designs such as checks, stripes, spots and plain bands or blocks of colour.

Accessory accents

Fabrics and bed linens give children a bit more scope to indulge in their current crazes, although it is still best to avoid strongly branded products that will be out of date or outgrown by next season. Look for bright colours and stimulating patterns – reversible, if possible, to provide extra variety in a single duvet (comforter) cover or pillowcase.

Mixed textures make children's furnishings more fun, and help to stimulate younger children's imagination, so try to incorporate different fabrics such as furs, felt, velvet and wool. Furry cushions and soft rugs are always popular with children.

If your children can't live without their favourite character in their bedroom décor and you are reluctant to introduce it in fabrics, look for lampshades, wastepaper bins, cardboard storage boxes, coat hooks and of course posters which are relatively inexpensive items that can be replaced more often and may be a suitable compromise against a fairly plain background.

For older children, introduce intriguing accessories such as lava lamps to bridge the gap between child and adult – they will enjoy the combination of 'fun' and 'vaguely scientific', and these items also create a very soothing effect to help them sleep.

Children love bold colours, patterns and textures like shiny metallic fabric, animal prints and faux fur – these shocking pink and orange furry cushions will delight most little girls.

Shared rooms

Children need their own territory to help them establish their personality and take responsibility for their possessions. If they have to share a room, find ways to create room divisions so that each child feels they have their own private space.

Division by colour

Colour-coding different areas is one of the simplest solutions with room sharing. Let each child choose their own wall colour – or, if that seems too risky, pick two distinctive colours yourself that will work together yet create a definite contrast. You could then give each child two adjacent walls in their colour, so that the corner formed by each pair becomes their own territory. Alternatively, divide the room down the middle so that the colour changes halfway across two facing walls. You can have decorative fun with this border line by painting a wavy line or jagged zigzags so that the two colours fit together like a jigsaw.

Provide different styles of bed linen to maintain the division – where possible, look for duvet (comforter) designs that contain both colours, so that they

Individual style

To emphasize the idea that each child has their own separate territory in their shared environment, make sure that both sides of the room have plenty of display space to allow them to get creative in their own individual way. Fix pinboards to the walls to display pictures and poems, and include areas of magnetic paint (brilliant for attaching things without the need for drawing pins/thumb tacks or sticky pads) and blackboard paint, so that they can use coloured chalks to scribble on the walls to their heart's content.

You may not be able to literally divide a shared room down the middle, but different-coloured bed linen and accessories help mark 'territory'.

coordinate well, but provide contrasting patterns – and make sure that the floor changes colour from one area to the other, too. Wooden floorboards can be painted – and repainted – as often as the need arises. Loose rugs (with non-slip backing) in contrasting shades will effect a quick change and add a soft surface. Alternatively, you could create two reverse-image patterns with carpet tiles, designing a layout of, for example, blue tiles scattered across a green background on one side of the room, with green tiles against a blue background on the other.

An open shelf unit can divide a room very effectively, either partitioning a shared bedroom or, as here, separating a work area from a play area.

Dividing lines

For a more definite divide, furniture can be used to great effect, forming an actual partition. Open shelf units are the most practical because they provide useful storage for both sides – for books, toys, CDs and school stuff – but their open structure still lets light through, so that the room does not feel blocked off.

Look for wide-based, solid structures to make sure that they can stand securely without support, and children should be made clearly aware that they are not for climbing on. Modular cube systems work particularly well, because you can devise a partition in exactly the design you want. Stack the cubes to different heights to build a battlement-like structure, or arrange them in an ascending slope with full height at one side of the room, reducing to ground level.

Trellis screens

If there is not enough space for a chunky storage system to divide the room, create a trellis screen instead. Again, this will maintain plenty of light in the room, but will also provide useful hanging space and a pinboard background for displaying pictures and posters or sticking reminders in place. You can use standard garden trellis, either fixing it in place as a permanent divide, or joining two or three sections together with hinges so that they form a free-standing zigzag screen that can be moved into different positions or folded away when not needed.

Temporary partitions

Children are very capricious, and the clamouring for a partition could easily change to demands for a return to the open-plan room, so a flexible screen that can be supplied and removed again at short notice is a sensible solution. If you are short of floor-standing space, you could achieve a screen effect simply by fixing a row of ceiling-hung blinds to form a removable fabric divider, which can then be lowered or raised in just a few seconds.

Children's beds

Adults spend about one-third of their lives in bed, while small children with early bedtimes and older children with a reluctance to get up in the mornings spend closer to half. It's therefore important to get the bed right, although for young children it's not just for sleeping – it's also a play area for a thousand imaginary games.

Beds with storage

Children tend to have so many games and toys nowadays that the usual rules of clutter control have to be relaxed a little when it comes to planning a child's domain. It is therefore worth looking for a bed that incorporates or allows for some form of storage. At its most basic, this could simply be a bed with a frame that stands clear of the floor so that there is plenty of space to push large robust boxes and crates underneath (see page 236). Alternatively, choose a wooden divan-style bed with storage built into the base. This can take the form of full-length storage drawers or a mixture of drawers and cupboards.

More imaginative options are the mid-height play beds or 'cabin' storage beds designed along bunk bed principles, with the mattress on a platform reached by a ladder, and the lower level providing cupboards, drawers, shelves and pull-out desks. Some styles even incorporate a full-scale playhouse underneath, with doors and windows cut into the side of the raised bed; others have fabric to create a tent. Alternatively, you could always make a play area or private den in the space under a simple platform bed yourself by hanging colourful curtains that can simply be drawn across and placing a low level table and chair inside.

A recess with a sloping ceiling is the ideal location for a snug built-in child's bed like this one, which has handy storage space incorporated within the base.

Fantasy beds

Young children will devise their own games around any structure in the home – hence the enduring popularity of the cupboard under the stairs, and the tent improvised from blankets and a clothes airer – and this includes their bed, however basic it is. If you want to give their imagination a prompt, however, you can find children's beds designed as racing cars, fire engines, boats, buses, cottages, castles and spaceships. It may seem indulgent, but it may be worthwhile if it provides a complete play centre in one piece of furniture and keeps the rest of the house clear of toys and chaos.

Bunk beds

Full-scale bunk beds with double-decker sleeping spaces are always a favourite with children, so exploit their enthusiasm – bunks are a godsend if you have two children sharing a single room or if their friends need to be accommodated overnight.

The frames can be made of traditional wood (which can be painted if you want to introduce extra colour in the room) or contemporary steel, and both types come flat-packed for home assembly. Some bunk bed designs

Handy hints

• Instead of a cot that becomes redundant once the child has outgrown it, opt for one with removable sides that converts into a proper bed, so that he or she can carry on sleeping in the same place. The most elegant ones are designed like French lits-bateaux, and can even be used with cushions along the back as a sofa or daybed when the child reaches teenage years.

• Bunk beds make good use of vertical space, but standard sizes are often wider and longer than they need to be. For very small rooms, consider commissioning a reliable carpenter to build tailor-made bunks.

• Headboards provide extra colour and stimulation for children, and you can always create your own by painting a headboard-sized panel on to the wall. Or fix a piece of corkboard to the wall and cover it with fabric, creating a few deep pockets for books, soft toys, torches (flashlights) and various other bedtime essentials.

can be detached into two single beds – a useful feature if your sleeping requirements are likely to change, for example if you intend to move house or as the children get older and require separate bedrooms. Some of the most convenient designs are made with a lower-level sofa bed with a deep padded cushion along the back, so that it provides cosy seating during the daytime or when not needed as a conventional bed.

Make sure, if you do end up with a high-level bed of some sort, that you make the most of the room's height by fitting high-level shelving alongside it to match. A set of slimline shelves next to the upper mattress will provide a useful bedside bookcase as well as a surface for an alarm clock or radio, although some bunk beds come with their own clip-on tables, which is useful.

Lamps should be clipped on to the bedframe for increased stability rather than free-standing on a high shelf, so that there is no risk of either trailing flexes or hot bulbs being knocked over on to the bedclothes.

This high-level bed has a sofa bed beneath, providing comfortable daytime seating and extra sleeping space for an overnight guest, as well as space for a desk.

This standard child's bunkbed has been given a creative makeover with a fairytale theme. It comes complete with a turret and slide and would capture the imagination of any little girl.

Work and play

Work and play are starting to overlap as computers have become central both to children's education and to their entertainment. But traditional play areas and accessories are still needed to encourage creative thinking and to keep homework organized.

Desk space

This needs to be comfortable and well lit. Look for a worktop that can be adjusted for height so that it will 'grow' with the child and adapt from a painting table to a computer desk as he or she gets older. An alternative to having a permanent desk in position is to fit a hinged wooden flap that will lie flat against the wall when not required. This can be supported either by an arm or bracket that swings out from the wall or, for a

An alcove beside a chimney breast is an ideal space in which to install shelves for a desktop and to hold files, creating a little study area for a child.

Colourful desk accessories and a fun noticeboard (this one is a magnetic panel) for important reminders helps keep a study area fun and tidy.

more industrial look, by sturdy ropes or chains attached to the wall above and through hooks or holes in the outer corners of the desk.

Make sure that there is a good directional lamp in place so that the child does not attempt to work by a gloomy overhead bulb and so that glare from the computer screen is minimized. If there is not enough room for the lamp to stand on the desk, look for a jointed lamp that can be clipped to the side or on to a nearby shelf or mantelpiece.

Provide plenty of containers to hold desk essentials – kitchen cutlery trays are perfect for pencils, crayons, paperclips and other stationery. And devise some sort of noticeboard so that they have a designated place to stick messages, reminders, school timetables and invitations. This could be an area of magnetic paint – for notes to be held in place with fridge magnets – or you could create a pinboard from a panel of cork, available in a range of colours to suit your child's bedroom scheme. Either leave it plain and use with drawing pins (thumb tacks), or cover it with fabric and front with a latticework of ribbon behind which cards and notes can be slotted.

If you are building a bespoke flap-down tabletop, the memo board can be fitted on the wall behind it so that it creates a back for the desk when folded down. Alternatively, fix it to the underside of the flap so that it is flat against the wall while the desk is not in use.

Play areas

Children are irresistibly tempted by small spaces that they can make their own, which is why beds with built-in play space beneath are such a brilliant idea. Even most standard-sized bedrooms will not offer sufficient space for a full-sized playhouse, but you may be able to box off an area – like a large cupboard – if, for instance, you have an attic room with sloping ceilings. This will make good use of a low corner that is too cramped to house furniture. Cut a window in the side as well as the door, and you have created an instant camp.

If there is not enough space to spare for a permanent structure like this, make use of the ideas suggested for shared rooms (see page 245) by employing screens and blinds to create temporary playhouses. Hinged screens made from garden trellis, painted panels of wood or fabric stretched over a wooden frame can be neatly folded flat against the wall and out of the way when not in use, while blinds can be hung from the ceiling to form fabric walls. Position two or three of these against an existing wall or corner and you have an instant tent. Look for brightly coloured blinds, or opt for plain cotton and paint them with your own design to represent a castle, shop or whatever theme is currently in favour.

Floor fun

Use the floor to provide imaginative play ideas, too. Paint giant chequers or spots on the floorboards for instant games of hopscotch and Twister, and add washable playmats designed as farmyards, railways or street layouts so that the children are inspired to create their own games.

Find slots under beds and chests for things like toy forts and farmyards to avoid them having to be folded up and boxed away every time they are used. Add plenty of labelled crates and drawstring bags for sets of bricks, construction kits and similar toys (see page 250 for more storage ideas).

Create a themed bedroom for your child that takes care of his sleeping, playing and working needs – you'll enjoy coming up with ideas and he'll love it!

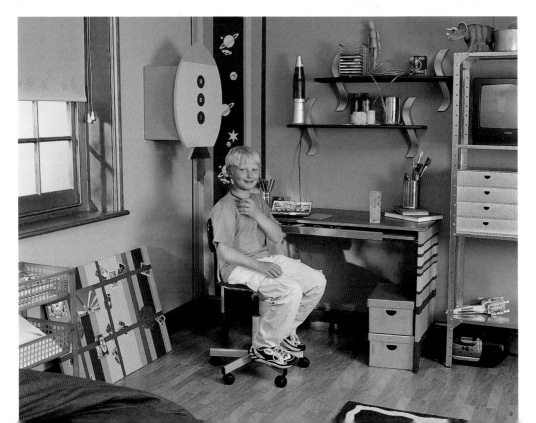

Clever storage

The key to kids' storage is to make it fun, so that they will actually deign to use it. Exploit every possible corner and encourage your children to organize their possessions by keeping clothes, school things and play things separate.

Low-level storage

Low-level storage is the most practical for young children, as they can easily reach and put things away for themselves. Baskets and crates that slide under a bed can also be stacked against a wall so that they don't take up so much floor space. Picnic hampers and laundry baskets make good toy boxes, as the lids are light and will not trap small fingers. Plastic crates that fit together for neat stacking create a colourful display rather like a tower of building blocks, or you can buy or make frames to hold them. The most useful of these

come on wheels to form a sort of movable trolley; if you choose semi-transparent boxes, you'll be able see what is inside.

Cube systems

Cube storage is ideal, as the arrangement can be changed as children grow, starting with a single row of units along the wall to provide low-level cupboards or open slots with a deep shelf or seat on top, and then building them up to higher levels as the child gets older and wants space for books, CDs and a music system. You can also slot individual containers such as shoe boxes and filing crates into the cubes to hold smaller items. Cubes are particularly useful in attic rooms, as you can create triangular systems under sloping ceilings and fit a run just one or two cubes high where the walls are lowest.

Choose storage options suitable for the age and height of the child – you cannot expect a toddler to put his own toys away if the boxes are beyond his reach.

Unfinished wooden cubes can be painted to suit and provide plenty of options for storage, which can be moved around and adapted as your child's needs change.

Hanging storage

Anything that keeps the floor clear is useful, so fix plenty of hooks and pegs for hanging storage. Drawstring bags hung from these can be used to store toys, clothes, shoes and dirty laundry, with plastic beach buckets holding smaller items like farm animals, crayons and magnetic numbers and letters.

It is worth painting the cubes to make them more interesting, as colour is important if you want the idea of storage to appeal to messy children. Similarly, basic wardrobes (closets) and chests of drawers (dressers) can be painted in harlequin shades to brighten them up, each drawer a different colour, or doors and handles contrasting with the main structure.

Fabric covers

If you despair of children being able to keep open shelves tidy, you can easily turn them into cupboards by fitting curtains or blinds to cover them. Fabric covers are simple to make and an economical and space-saving alternative to solid woodwork. You could also opt for canvas or plastic clothes rails rather than full-scale wooden wardrobes (closets); these are much less bulky and provide plenty of adaptable storage to keep children organized. Bear in mind that children do not in general need as much hanging clothes space as adults (most clothes can be folded and laid flat), and what hanging space they do need will be shorter.

Fix storage tubes (open cylinders of cardboard or perspex) to the walls to hold school artwork and posters without crushing or folding them. Neatest of all, fix up a length of wall-mounted trellis to which you can attach as many hooks as you want without damaging the wall behind.

Don't forget overhead space either. Lengths of webbing (like fishing net) and trellis panels can be suspended from the ceiling to provide extra storage, especially for soft toys that won't hurt themselves or anyone else if they fall.

Creative cupboards

Use your creative talents to devise colours, effects and trompe l'oeil façades that incorporate storage into the overall style of the room, so that the cupboards become part of the decoration and open up imaginative new worlds rather than seeming a waste of good play space.

- Paint a lighthouse on a tall cupboard to create the background for a seaside-style room. Do the same with a helter-skelter design to conjure up a fairground setting.
- Turn a little girl's cupboard into a doll's house façade. You could even divide up the shelves inside so that they make different 'rooms'.
- Fit tongue-and-groove panelled doors across alcoves to turn them into cupboards, with rope pull handles for a nautical, beach-house effect.
- Paint a narrow cupboard door in bright stripes reminiscent of a Punch and Judy theatre, or hang a panel of striped fabric across the front for an even more authentic effect.
- Create a jousting-tent cupboard, with a painted pelmet fixed over an alcove to form the turret top, and a length of striped fabric that can be rolled up like a blind for access to the shelves behind.
- Paint a cupboard in alternating blocks of colour for a harlequin pattern. Mark out your design in pencil first, and use masking tape to give each square a neat edge, peeling the tape off after the paint is dry and the pattern complete.

With some creative thinking, pots of paint and novelty cupboard or drawer handles, you can easily transform plain or ugly items of furniture into child-attractive pieces.

Index

Acknowledgements

Executive Editor Katy Denny
Editor Charlotte Wilson
Executive Art Editor Joanna MacGregor
Designer Colin Goody
Senior Production Controller Manjit Sihra
Picture Library Manager Jennifer Veall

Picture acknowledgements

Graeme Ainscough 8, 14 top left, 29 top left, 70, 77, 82, 86, 88, 89, 90, 93 bottom right, 97 top left, 99 top left, 102 top right, 104, 105 bottom right, 116, 117 bottom right, 124, 126 bottom left, 130, 131 bottom right, 134, 136, 138, 140, 150, 152, 153, 154 top right, 154 bottom left, 155 bottom left, 157 bottom, 158 top right, 159 top left, 161, 162, 163 top left, 163 bottom right, 164, 165 top left, 165 bottom right, 166 top left, 166 bottom right, 167 top left, 168, 169, 170 top right, 171 top left, 172 top right, 172 bottom left, 173, 174 top left, 174 bottom right, 175 top left, 175 bottom right, 176, 178, 179 top right, 182 bottom left, 183 top left, 186, 187 top left, 189 bottom right, 191 bottom left, 192, 193 top left, 197, 198 left, 198 right, 200 top right, 200 bottom left, 201, 203 bottom right, 205 top right, 205 bottom right, 207 top left, 208 top left, 212, 213 top left, 216 top right, 216 bottom left, 217, 220, 221 top left, 222 bottom left, 223 top right, 225 bottom right, 226, 230, 231 top right, 232, 242 top left. **Alamy/Nick Baylis** 72 bottom right; /Nick Hufton/VIEW Pictures Ltd. 210; /Tim Street-Porter/Beateworkls Inc. 245. **Alma Home** (12-14 Greatorex Street, London, E1 5NF; Tel: +44 (0)20 7377 0762; Fax: +44 (0) 20 7375 2171.) Black leather embossed crocodile 81 bottom left. **The Alternative Flooring Company** (Tel +44 (0)1264 335111; www.alternativeflooring.com) 87 bottom right, 87 bottom left, 87 centre left top, 125 centre left top. **Amtico** (www.amtico.com; Tel: +44 (0)800 667766) 125 centre left bottom; /AH838/Colour-Flash Blue to Purple 81 centre left bottom; /GL014/Champagne Glass 81 top right; /W685R/Drift Wood 81 centre right. **Anaglypta**/Wallwhite by Anaglypta 111 bottom right. **Armitage Shanks**/Sandringham 215 bottom right. **Armstrong** (www.armstrong.com) Timberwork dark silver vinyl flooring 83. **Laura Ashley** (Enquiries/stockists +44 (0)870 5622116; www.lauraashley.com) Small Pink Roses/Pink 42 bottom left; /Candy Stripe/Sapphire-White 43 top right; /Harlescott/Pale Gold 125 bottom right. **B&Q plc** (www.diy.com) Lemon Shaker style kitchen 182 bottom right; /Mondo Carousel185 bottom right. **Brintons** (www.brintons.net) 125 top left. **Ceramic Dolomite** 219 top left. **Jane Churchill** (Tel: +44 (0)20 8877 6400) 118 bottom right. **Clarence House** (3/10 Chelsea Harbour Design Centre, London, SW10 0XE; Tel: +44 (0)20 7351 1200; Fax: +44 (0)20 7351 6300; www.clarencehouse.com) 119 centre left top. **Cole & Son** (Wallpapers) Ltd. (Tel: +44 (0)20 8442 8844; www.cole-and-son.com) 61-3039/Buckingham Stripe/Green 43 centre left; /62-1003/Humming Birds/Lavender 42 centre left. **Neisha Crosland**/Hawthorn/Gold Leaf 43 bottom left; /Speckle Dot/Pretty Blue 43 bottom right. **Crown Paint** (www.crownpaint.co.uk) 17 bottom, 73 bottom right, 95 top left, 111 top left, 113 bottom right. **Crown Wallcoverings**/Aquino Wallpaper by Crown 40; /Palazzo by Shand Kydd 103. **Crowson Fabrics** (www.crowsonfabrics.com) 14 bottom right; 127 top left, 143 top left. **Crucial Trading Ltd** (Tel: +44 (0)1675 433505; www.crucial-trading.com) 87 centre left bottom. **Dalsouple** (Tel: +44 (0)1278 727733; www.dalsouple.com) Hortensia 81 centre left top. **DIY Photo Library** 16, 50, 72 bottom left, 79, 95 bottom right, 108, 109 top left, 112, 209 top. **Fired Earth Interiors** (Tel: +44 (0)1295 814300; www.firedearth.com) 87 top left; /Moustier 54, 60 top left; /Early English Delft 125 bottom left; /Planet metallic tiles 59; /Antique reclaimed terracotta 75 bottom left; /Flagstones Slate 75 centre right; /Jerusalem Stone/Jericho 75 centre left bottom; /Kobe Mosaic 60 centre right; /Marble Mosaic/Crema 75 bottom right; /Retro Metro 60 bottom left; /Roman Mosaic 60 centre left/Space 60 bottom right; /Turin Stone/Garda Blue 60 top right; /Red Terracotta 75 centre left top; /White Oak 75 top left. **Focus** (www.focusdiy.co.uk) Juniper bathroom 214. **Forbo** (Marmoleum by Forbo; Tel: +44 (0)800 731 2367; www.marmoleum.co.uk) 621 Dove Grey 81 top left. **Furniture 123** (www.furniture123.co.uk) 247 bottom left. **Getty Images** 119 bottom right; /Bob Elsdale 6

Oliver Gordon 7 top right, 13 bottom left, 15, 63, 71 top left, 76, 78, 81 bottom right, 93 top left, 94 top left, 98, 99 top right, 101 bottom right, 102 top left, 105 top left, 109 bottom right, 114, 117 top left, 131 top left, 133, 139, 156, 157 top, 158 bottom left, 159 bottom right, 160 left, 160 right, 167 bottom right, 170 bottom left, 171 bottom right, 179 bottom left, 180, 181 top left, 187 bottom right, 189 top left, 190, 193 bottom right, 194, 196 top right, 199, 202, 203 top left, 206, 207 bottom right, 223 bottom right, 224, 225 top left, 228, 229 top left, 236 bottom right, 238, 248 bottom left. **Graham & Brown Limited** (Tel: +44(0)800 3288 452; www.grahambrown.com) Arc wallpaper by Hemmingway design 48; /Cuba Super Fresco Texture 41. **H&R Johnson Tiles** (Tel: +44 (0)1782 575575; www.johnson-tiles.com) Vetoro Pearl Smoke 188 bottom left. **Harlequin Fabrics & Wallcoverings Ltd** (Tel: +44 (0)8708 300032; www.harlequin.uk.com) Coast 96; /Decadence 36; /Takara 122, 125 centre right top, 126 top right. **Heritage Bathrooms plc** (www.heritagebathrooms.com) Unity wetroom 219 bottom right. **The Holding Company** (Tel: +44 (0)20 8445 2888; www.theholdingcompany.co.uk) 235, 237 bottom right. **Homebase** (www.homebase.co.uk) 222 top right, 240, 241 bottom right, 241 bottom left, 242 bottom right, 243 top left, 244, 248 top right, 249 bottom, 250 bottom right, 251. **Ideal Standard Ltd** (www.ideal-standard.co.uk) Revue 215 top left; /Sophie 7 bottom left. **International Paints** (Tel: +44 (0)1480 484284; www.international-paints.co.uk) Applying anti-damp paint 17 top right; /Applying primer paint 23 bottom left. **KA International** (www.ka-international.com) 42 top right, 42 bottom right, 43 centre right, 143 bottom left. **Cath Kidston Ltd** (Information and order line: +44 (0)20 229 8000) 118 centre right, 119 top right, 119 centre right bottom. **Magnet** (www.magnet.co.uk) Harvard Maple bedroom 229 bottom right; /Minimalist bedroom 234; /Seville Kitchen 184 top left; /Stainless steel kitchen 183 bottom left. **Ray Main/Mainstream** 39 bottom right, 247 bottom right. **Marimekko** (www.marimekko.com) 119 top left. **MFI** (www.mfi.co.uk) 185 top left, 204. **Octopus Publishing Group Limited** 10 bottom right, 11 centre right top, 11 centre right bottom, 12, 18, 30 top right, 30 bottom right, 31 centre left, 31 centre right, 33 top left, 33 centre left, 33 centre right, 33 bottom right, 107, 121 bottom left, 125 centre right bottom, 208 bottom right, 209 bottom left; /Graham Atkins-Hughes 135 top left, 137, 141; /Dominic Blackmore 97 bottom right; /Paul Forrester 11 left, 32, 35 top left, 35 bottom right, 35 centre right top, 35 centre right bottom, 58 bottom left; /Sebastian Hedgecoe 181 bottom right, 231 bottom left; /Tom Mannion 67, 71 bottom right, 237; /David Parmitter 142; /Paul Ryan 123 bottom left; /Russell Sadur 128; /Debi Treloar 144, 155 top right; /Shona Wood 10 bottom left, 10 bottom centre left, 10 bottom centre right, 29 top right, 29 centre right, 29 bottom right, 30 top left, 30 bottom left, 38, 39 bottom right, 56, 57; /Polly Wreford 73 top left, 94 bottom right, 221 bottom right, 236 top left. **Morris & Co. by Sanderson** (Tel: +44 (0)1895 830 044; www.sanderson-uk.com) 119 centre right top. **Mulberry Home** 119 bottom left. **Narratives Jan Baldwin** 100; /Kate Gadsby 246. **New House Textiles** (Tel: 01989 740684; www.newhousetextiles.co.uk) Carousel 149. **Roger Oates Design** (www.rogeroates.com) 87 centre right. **David Oliver** (Distributor: Paint and Paper Library, 5 Elystan Street, London, SE3 3NT) Basketweave/Olive 43 top left. **Original Style Ltd** (www.originalstyle.com) 58 top right, 65. **Osborne & Little** (Tel: +44 (0)20 7352 1456; www.osborneandlittle.com) F5052-03/Modello/Piolo 125 top right. **Red Cover**/Johnny Bouchier 243 bottom right; /Jake Fitzjones 191 top right; /Huntley Hedworth 113 top left; /Paul Massey 53; /Niall McDiarmid 213 bottom right; /Chris Tubbs 233. **Reed Harris** (www.reedharris.co.uk) Atlantic Glass Mosaic tile 62. **Romo** (www.romofabrics.com) Leoni 101 top left; /Arianne 121 top right; /Lorenzo 145; /Mazara 123 top right; /Paros 132, 135 bottom right; /Simonii 120 top right, 120 bottom left. **Sanderson** (Tel: +44 (0)1895 830 044; www.sanderson-uk.com) Reminiscence 118 centre left; /Joie de Vivre 127 bottom right; /Willow Leaf/Terracotta 42 centre right. **Sottini** (Tel: +44 (0)1482 449513, www.sottini.co.uk) 218. **Titley & Marr** (Tel: +44 (0)20 351 2913) 119 centre left bottom. **Wickes Building Supplies Ltd** (www.wickes.co.uk) Evesham dresser 184 bottom right. **Wilman Interiors** (www.wilman.co.uk) Elysees Collection Limoges Opal 110. **Zimmer & Rohde** (15 Chelsea Harbour Design Centre, London,SW10 0XE; Tel: +44 (0)20 7351 7115; www.zimmer-rohde.com) 118 bottom left.